Praise for *All About Index Funds*

Ferri's book is an engaging one-stop storehouse of knowledge on index funds. It is a vital road map for those seeking higher returns and lower risk. Worth its weight in gold!

—William Bernstein
Investment adviser,
author of *The Four Pillars of Investing*

It is said that there is no one more religious than a convert. So when a former stockbroker comes to believe that owning the entire stock market through an index fund is the key to investment success, he presents his case with passion. And Ferri is right! This book tells you why, and how to get started.

—John C. Bogle
Founder and former chairman,
The Vanguard Group

All About Index Funds clearly explains why investing in index mutual funds is the only reliable winning strategy. Ferri compares and contrasts active mutual funds with index funds in a way that even a novice will have no trouble navigating. Once you read this book, you will no longer listen to the hype from Wall Street stockbrokers and their analysts who are paid to make money from you, not for you.

—Larry Swedroe
Investment adviser,
author of *The Only Investment Strategy You'll Ever Need*

ALL ABOUT
INDEX FUNDS

SECOND EDITION

OTHER TITLES IN THE "ALL ABOUT..." SERIES

ALL ABOUT INDEX FUNDS

The Easy Way to Get Started

SECOND EDITION

RICHARD A. FERRI, CFA

McGraw-Hill

New York   Chicago   San Francisco   Lisbon   London
Madrid   Mexico City   Milan   New Delhi   San Juan
Seoul   Singapore   Sydney   Toronto

1 2 3 4 5 6 7 8 9 0   FGR/FGR   0 9 8 7 6

ISBN 0-07-148492-2

This publication is designed to provide accurate and authoritative information in regard to the subject matter covered. It is sold with the understanding that the publisher is not engaged in rendering legal, accounting, or other professional service. If legal advice or other expert assistance is required, the services of a competent professional person should be sought.

—From a Declaration of Principles jointly adopted by a Committee of the American Bar Association and a Committee of Publishers and Associations

McGraw-Hill books are available at special quantity discounts to use as premiums and sales promotions, or for use in corporate training programs. For more information, please write to the Director of Special Sales, Professional Publishing, McGraw-Hill, Two Penn Plaza, New York, N 10121-2298. Or contact your local bookstore.

This book is printed on recycled, acid-free paper containing a minimum of 50% recycled, de-inked fiber.

Library of Congress Cataloging-in-Publication Data

Ferri, Richard A.
  All about index funds : the easy way to get started / by Richard A Ferri.—2nd ed.
     p.   cm.
  Includes index.
  ISBN 0-07-148492-2 (pbk. : alk. paper)
  1. Index mutual funds.   2. Index mutual funds—United States.   I. Title.
HG4530.F427 2007
332.63'27—dc22   2006030958

To my children
Thomas, Nicholas, and Ashley
Be happy, be kind, grow rich and prosper.

CONTENTS

PART THREE

MANAGING YOUR INDEX FUND PORTFOLIO

APPENDIXES

Welcome to the second edition of *All About Index Funds*. Much has changed since the first edition was published in 2002. There are more than twice the number of index funds on the market today, and much of the growth has been in exchange-traded funds (ETFs). Fund providers have greatly expanded their offerings of ETFs to include a wide range of equity sector funds, style funds, and international funds. Commodity funds have exploded over the past few years. As such, a new chapter was added in this edition on commodity index funds and currency funds.

The world of index fund investing is certainly evolving. By the time you finish reading this book, you will be well versed on the many types of index funds available in the marketplace and how to use them in your investment accounts. *All About Index Funds* is a cornucopia of knowledge and advice that you can use to manage your investment portfolio. The strategies are simple, easy to implement, and will lead to greater wealth and personal satisfaction.

Index mutual funds are a *passive* investment methodology. The funds simply hold the same stocks or bonds as one of the popular market indexes, such as the S&P 500 index or the Lehman Aggregate Bond Index. There are several types of stock and bond index funds available, and this book will help you select the right mix of funds for your needs.

A portfolio manager is responsible for the actual mechanics of running an index fund, but computers do much of the work. The efficiency of index fund management means the cost of these funds are much less than traditional *actively managed* mutual funds, where large research staffs are employed to pick and choose individual stocks and bonds.

Besides saving money on fees, a portfolio of index funds saves time and reduces personal stress. No longer will you waste away the hours sifting through thousands of stocks, bonds, and *active* mutual funds trying to find meaning in it all. No longer will you make hasty investment decisions based on incomplete or incomprehensible marketing material pitched to you by a less than competent investment adviser. Indexing is a simple, clean, and cost-effective solution to your investment needs. By investing a little of your time today to learn about this marketplace, you will save weeks of time and torment in your life and thousands of dollars in fees.

Make no mistake about it, embracing the concept of using index mutual funds can be a life-altering event. It is somewhat like switching religions. When you were young you may have been exposed to only one set of religious beliefs and one set of investment beliefs. As you got older, however, you became more experienced and realized that those old beliefs were not working for you. So, you searched for deeper meaning and discovered a better alternative, a better religion.

Now you have discovering indexing. All your life you read the popular financial press, listened to market experts on TV, and went with a few of your stockbroker's recommendations. But the more experience you gained, the less that method of investing made sense. This book introduces you to an alternative style of investing that is based on sound logic and is easy to comprehend. Once you understand the philosophy behind an index fund strategy, your beliefs about investing will change forever.

MY PERSONAL JOURNEY

As a young, impressionable man in my early twenties, I held the belief that stockbrokers (now called financial consultants) were skilled professionals. I assumed they had superior knowledge and training in the areas of accounting and economics and knew things about the markets that common folk did not know. Because of their deep understanding, these people made a lot of money for their clients as well as themselves. So, when I was hired as a stockbroker in 1988, I followed the advice and recommendations of experienced brokers in my office and of the analysts at my firm. I knew by doing this I was going to do very well for my clients and for myself.

Well, it didn't take long to realize that the investment ideas turned out by my firm were no better than those pulled out of the air, and many times much worse. Soon I understood why our recommendations were mediocre at best. The fact is many analysts and brokers have an ulterior motive for recommending certain investments. Specifically, they were doing so to generate commissions and fees for themselves and the firm. To make matters worse, these people apparently had little personal belief in the ideas they were selling. The bottom line of their paycheck was the top priority in their thinking. This revelation created a dilemma in my life. Whereas I had hoped to build a successful business by following the guiding light of expert recommendations, it wasn't going to happen. It was all a façade, an image, a sales gimmick.

Luckily, our brokerage firm had an "investment consulting" division, which included access to top *independent* investment adviser firms and proprietary mutual fund research. Private investment advisers and mutual fund managers do not get paid a commission for managing portfolios. Instead, they are compensated based on a percentage of the money that they manage. The incentive here was to grow the accounts using their superior investment skill so they could collect a higher management fee. This seemed like a win, win, win situation. My clients made money through growth, the managers made money through fees, and I got paid a cut of the fee, or a commission to the mutual fund. Surely it was a recipe for success.

Alas, investment consulting, too, was an illusion. As a group, professional money managers were no more capable of achieving high returns than a bunch of monkeys throwing darts at the stock pages of the *Wall Street Journal.* A small number of managers did achieve respectable returns, but they were far and few between and it was impossible to pick the winners in advance. In addition, I found out that the *independent* investment advisers were not that independent after all. Most of those firms paid large sums of money annually to be placed on our firm's recommended adviser list. Overall, the investment consulting idea was a disappointment, so it was time to move on.

My next brainstorm was in a totally different direction. If success could not be found in the stock market, perhaps commodities would prove more fruitful. Trying to make sense of the oil, grain, and currency markets was like rocket science, and, therefore, the commodities futures industry attracted an extraordinary group of people. Scientists, mathematicians, and physicists that designed Star Wars weaponry during the Cold War were now working for Wall Street firms designing money machines. They sat in large trading rooms staring at computer screens, measuring every wiggle in the financial markets, looking for profitable trading opportunities. These smart people could be hired through a "pooled" commodities account to manage money for my clients. This strategy was certain to lead us all to wealth.

Well, there were certainly a lot of wiggles generated in those commodity pools, and some people actually made money. My firm made money, the rocket scientists made money, I made money, but my clients didn't make much money. The high fees and expenses of commodity pools wiped out most of the gains. It became obvious that alternative investments were not the wisest investment for my clients' money.

Frustrated, I decided to take matters into my own hands. If the analysts, mutual fund mangers, and rocket scientists could not beat the markets, surely there was someone who could, and that someone might as well be me. I realized I needed more education, which took me back to academia. Over a seven-year period I achieved a Chartered Financial Analyst (CFA) designation and a master of science in finance degree. In addition, I read dozens of books, scanned hundreds of research reports, and did a significant amount of personal research, all with the goal of finding the secret to superior returns. During this period, I continued to work full-time as a stockbroker and started writing my first book on investment principles, *Serious Money; Straight Talk about Investing for Retirement.*

The educational barrage began to pay off when I realized I was searching for a false prophet. The old religion was to find a strategy that "beat the market," but that was a flawed idea. The more I studied, the clearer it became that no such strategy exists, at least not with enough consistency for the average investor to benefit. Almost all the academic studies I read came to that same conclusion. The more investors moved their money around searching for superior returns, the further behind they fell. I realized what John Bogle said years ago, "Don't try to beat the market, *be* the market."

It is clear that a vast majority of investors would be far better off if they simply bought the entire stock market and held on rather than trying to find some superior method to beat the market. The best way to buy the market is through index mutual funds. Index funds are designed to track the performance of a stock or bond market rather than to try to beat it. These funds operate the same way as any other mutual fund you may have invested in. The difference is that index funds perform better than average over the long-term because they are lower cost and follow a consistent strategy.

To finish the story, I ultimately resigned from the brokerage industry and opened a low-cost independent investment firm for other believers in the strategy. Our company is dedicated to managing portfolios using many of the same index funds and exchange-traded funds mentioned in this book.

THE GENERAL OUTLINE OF THE BOOK

All About Index Funds is divided into three parts. All three sections are written to help investors at all levels of experience. The sections can be read independent of each other or from one to the next.

Part I explains what a market index is and how index mutual funds work. There is a short history of the index fund industry, including a chapter devoted to new exchange-traded funds. Part I also highlights the performance advantages that index funds have over other types of investments.

Part II categorizes the broad spectrum of index funds based on type and style. Many people are aware of the big index funds, such as S&P 500 index funds, but don't know that there are hundreds of index funds covering a variety of markets. There are funds tracking the bond market, international stock, industry sector markets, bond markets, commodities market, and currency market. New funds are formed every month, and as the number of funds continues to grow, the cost of investing in those funds continues to fall.

Part III of the book is all about using index funds in your portfolio. To help with this decision, there are chapters on forecasting market returns, asset allocation, risk control, and retirement planning. Several model portfolios are introduced.

A GUIDE FOR ALL

All About Index Funds is a guidebook for new index investors and a reference for more experienced investors. The book was written to provide more than enough information to build and manage a quality index fund portfolio. There are a few words of caution before we proceed. Converting to an index fund portfolio does not guarantee positive returns every year. No viable investment strategy can do that. You must be patient. In the long-term, a well-diversified index fund portfolio will make you more money with less risk than any other popular investment method. This is a guarantee. Index funds cost far less than other types of mutual funds, so eventually the laws of economics will take over and index funds will deliver higher returns.

There is one other important point to remember. For any indexing strategy to be truly effective, you must build the right mix of index funds for your needs and wait patiently for the markets to do their magic. If you stick with a well-managed strategy for several years, the fruits of the marketplace will come to you. It is in the long run that index funds truly shine.

All About Index Funds is all about a simple and effective lifelong investment strategy that just plain works.

ACKNOWLEDGMENTS

Special thanks goes to Bill Bernstein of Efficient Frontier Advisors and Larry Swedroe of Buckingham Asset Management for their cover endorsements, and a big thank you to John Bogle, founder and former chairman of The Vanguard Group, for his special endorsement. A must mention is Jim Wiandt, the editor of Indexuniverse.com and other fine publications on index funds and ETFs that made my research easier. Thanks to Dr. Howard Green for being a great friend and mentor and to my business partner, Scott Salaske, for managing our firm so efficiently. Also, thanks to my many Boglehead friends that hang out on the Vanguard Diehards discussion board. Keep up the good work! Finally, this book was only possible with the patience and support of my wonderful wife, Daria.

PART ONE

Index Fund Basics

CHAPTER 1

Index Funds Explained

Key Concepts

- There is a difference between an index and a market.
- Indexes are used as benchmarks for index funds.
- There are differences between open-end funds and exchange-traded funds.
- Not all indexes are created equal.

Common sense, simplicity, and perseverance are ideals we strive for in life. Yet, when we tackle the subject of investing, the guiding principles are often overshadowed by ambiguity, complexity, and irrationality. *All About Index Funds* focuses on getting back to investment basics. It is an instruction guide that will help you invest for the rest of your life.

Many books, magazines, Web sites, and television shows want you to believe that there are undiscovered riches in the financial markets waiting for you to exploit. Those soothsayers attempt to gain your attention and ultimately your dollars by appealing to your desire for riches. This book avoids such deceit.

All About Index Funds is all about accepting the markets for what they can reasonably achieve and using that information plus common sense to build an appropriate investment portfolio. Whether you are a novice investor or have been at it for a while, this book will help you bring your portfolio in line with the laws of economics.

After a careful reading, you will be able to develop a sound port-folio of index mutual funds that is simple, practical, and tailored to your personal financial goal.

Investing is a part of life, like eating, working, and paying taxes. If your habits are poor, then there will be serious consequences. *All About Index Funds* is an etiquette book for good investing behavior.

This chapter provides definitions and general background information on the concept of index mutual funds. It explains what market indexes are and what they are used for. We will also review the idea behind mutual funds in general and how they are managed. Finally, we will look at how mutual fund companies have linked market indexes and mutual funds together, creating index funds.

UNDERSTANDING INDEXES

"How's the market?" This simple question is asked millions of times a day by millions of people around the globe. In the United States, the market that people typically quote is the Dow Jones Industrial Average (DJIA),[1] better known as the Dow. For better or worse, the Dow is the most widely quoted market average in the United States, if not the world. Why is the Dow so popular? More than 100 years ago, people on Wall Street found it difficult to discern whether the general stock prices were rising or falling. There was no published index to measure a composite of stock prices against. So when Charles Dow first unveiled his industrial stock average in 1896, it was considered the bellwether benchmark, more so because it was published every day in a tip sheet called the *Wall Street Journal* (a Dow Jones & Company publication). Although at the time the Dow only covered 12 stocks, people began to view it as an index of stock prices by which to measure stock prices against.

The computation of the DJIA was quite simple 100 years ago, and it remains that way today. Starting in the late 1800s, at the end of each trading day, Charles Dow added up the prices of 12 large industrial stocks listed on the New York Stock Exchange. That was the average, pure and simple.

As time marched on, Charles Dow found that making changes to the average was not an easy task. A whole range of calculation problems developed. Companies merged or went out of business, others split their stock thereby reducing the price, and still others paid cash dividends, stock dividends, or no dividends at all. Though an arduous process, Dow figured out how to manually adjust the index for all its nuances, thereby ensuring the data had continuity.

Over the years, continuous adjustments were made to the Dow including the number of stocks. The DJIA gradually increased to 20 in 1916 and again to 30 in 1928, where it remains today.

Although Dow methodology is simple, it has some major setbacks. A movement in the DJIA average is based on point movements in individual stocks in that benchmark rather than on percentage movements of those stocks. That means a $1 gain in a $5 stock has the same effect in the DJIA as a $1 gain in a $100 stock. Intuitively, that leads to distortion between the index price and market values. For example, assume there are only two companies in the Dow average, Company A and Company B. Assume Company A has a total market value of $100 billion, and its stock is trading at $10 per share. Company B has a total market value of $100 billion, and its stock is trading at $100 per share. According to the Dow pricing methodology, the price level of our two-stock average is 110 (calculated as $100 plus $10). Recall that the total value of both companies is $200 billion ($100 billion plus $100 billion). Let's say that over a one-year period the price of Company A stock doubles from $10 to $20, which means the total value of the company doubled from $100 billion to $200 billion. During the same period, the price of Company B stock stayed at $100, so the total value of the company stayed at $100 billion. Here is the Dow methodology flaw: Although the combined total value of both companies increased from $200 billion to $300 billion (a 50 percent increase), the value of the Dow increased from $110 to $120 (a 9 percent gain).

The methodology on which the DJIA is based does not capture the value movements of companies, only their price movements. That results in poor index methodology if the intent of the index is to measure the overall value of the stock market. In addition to its methodology flaw, the DJIA consists of only 30 stocks and cannot reflect the movement of the entire stock market, which consists of more than 5,000 liquid stocks.

Despite its outdated pricing methodology and other flaws, tradition is tradition, and the DJIA still plays a key role in the minds of investors. It is the main barometer of the stock market activity used by the media. Because Dow Jones & Company owns the *Wall Street Journal*, the country's leading financial newspaper, it practically ensures that Dow averages will continue to have prominence in the media for years to come.

From a practical standpoint, the Dow is of limited use. It is narrow in scope and archaic in structure. It does not accurately measure the direction or level of the 5,000-plus stocks listed on all U.S. exchanges.

A broader measure of stock market performance was developed during the mid-twentieth century. The Standard & Poor's 500 index is a market-weighted index of 500 leading U.S. companies from a broad range of industries. Although 500 stocks are not a complete list of the largest companies on the market, the S&P 500 is a market-weighted index and thus reflects the general market value gain or loss in real dollars. Market weighting means that larger companies have a greater bearing on an index value than small companies. If the stock price of a very large company such as General Electric increased in a market-weighting index, it will increase the value of the S&P 500 index by a greater amount than if the price of a much smaller company such as Tiffany's increased. Measures market weight is simple. Just take the number of shares issued by the company and multiply by the price of the stock. Market weighting measures the true dollar value of the index.

Most major indexes used today on Wall Street are *free-float* market weighted, and as of 2004 that now includes Standard & Poor's indexes. *Free-float* means the index provider weights stocks based on the value of company stock available for trading on the exchange. In other words, it is the stock that you and I can actually buy. It does not include restricted stock or large personal holdings by insiders. For example, a free-float index does not include the value of Microsoft stock personally held by Bill Gates.

There are many market-weighted indexes to choose from. In the United States alone there are hundreds of U.S. stock indexes covering all corners of the market. There are very large indexes that track nearly all U.S. companies, such as the Dow Jones Wilshire 5000 Index, the Russell 3000 Index, and the MSCI US Broad Market Index. There are indexes that track a certain market sector such as large companies, small companies, value companies, and growth companies. There are indexes that track industrial sectors, including new-economy technology industries and old-economy brick-and-mortar industries. There are even indexes that track socially responsible companies. Each of these indexes can include hundreds, if not thousands, of stocks. Major indexes and funds that are benchmarked to them are discussed in Part II of this book.

The United States is not the only country that has multiple stock indexes. Around the globe, exchanges and finance companies have developed their own sets of indexes that track foreign stock markets. A few of the major providers of foreign index data include Morgan Stanley Capital International (MSCI), S&P/Citigroup, Dow Jones, Merrill Lynch, and Bloomberg.

Foreign markets are commonly divided into two types: developed markets and emerging markets. A developed market has a higher per capita income (more than $10,000 U.S.), and an emerging market has a lower per capita income. An example of a developed market is Japan. It is a highly developed country with an extremely active stock market. The most widely quoted index on Japanese stocks is the Nikkei Stock Average. It is an index of 225 leading stocks that trade on the Tokyo Stock Exchange. There is also a Nikkei small company index that tracks smaller Japanese companies. The Nikkei is one of several index providers covering that nation. An example of an emerging market is Mexico. The Bolsa Mexicana de Valores (BMV) is the largest stock exchange in Mexico, and Indice de Precios y Cotizaciones (Bolsa Index) represents the major index covering that market.

Grouping countries together creates another opportunity for a composite index of developed markets and a composite index of emerging markets. There are indexes based on geographic regions such as Europe or the Pacific Rim, indexes covering Latin America and Euro Zone countries, and indexes covering Nordic countries. It seems the only limiting factor in index creation is the imagination of the index providers.

Thus so far, we have only discussed stock indexes and have neglected the largest market in the world: the bond market. Bond markets are also referred to as credit markets and fixed-income markets. Popular bond indexes include the U.S. Treasury bonds, corporate bonds, high-yield bonds, convertible bonds, mortgages, tax-exempt bonds, and foreign bonds. Some leading providers of bond indexes

FIGURE 1–1

The Number of Index Funds in the United States

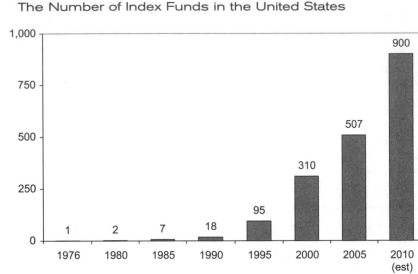

Source: Morningstar Principia.

are Lehman Brothers, JP Morgan, Dow Jones, Salomon Smith Barney, and Merrill Lynch.

There are major differences between bond indexes. One is the quality of the bonds in the index. High yield "junk" bonds have a higher risk than Treasury bonds, so they pay a higher interest rate. The difference between the interest rate on junk bonds and the interest rate on Treasury bonds is called the credit spread. You can track credit spreads between various bond indexes to view the perceived risk between market segments. A larger spread means higher risk is perceived between one bond market segment and another, and a smaller spread means less risk is perceived. More information on index spreads is available in Chapter 9.

As you may have guessed, an index can be created for any group of stocks or bonds, and as Figure 1-1 illustrates, there are over 900 index funds benchmarked to them. I think it is safe to say that if you cannot find an index that covers a particular type of investment, wait a month or so and one will likely be created.

THE DIFFERENCE BETWEEN INDEXES
AND MARKETS

There is a vast difference between a stock market and a stock index. One is a place where stocks trade hands and the other is a measure of value. The DJIA is a measure of market performance, (albeit, not a very good one). It measures the value of 30 stocks. The New York Stock Exchange (NYSE) is a market. It is where approximately 2,700 stocks change hands each day. The S&P 500 is an index. It is a measure of the value of 500 stocks selected by the S&P Index Committee. The NASDAQ is a market. It is a place where stocks and bonds trade even though it is in cyberspace.

The NYSE is physically located on Wall Street in New York City. It is a classic looking building with white columns at the front. Inside the building are several dozen trading stations where the actual stock transactions take place. The NYSE is a stock market, although the exchange has created its own quasi-indexes that cover only stocks that trade on that exchange. A few of these proprietary indexes include the NYSE Financials index, the NYSE Transportation index, and the New York Composite index.

Indexes created by markets are generally considered secondary to broader based indexes that cover all markets. Exchange-created indexes hold only those stocks that trade on that particular exchange. The NYSE Composite index holds General Electric (GE) because it trades on the NYSE; however, it does not hold Microsoft (MSFT) because that stock trades on the NASDAQ, which is a competing exchange. As a result, MSFT stock will not be found in any NYSE or American Stock Exchange (AMEX) indexes even though it is one of the largest companies in the country. GE will not be part of any NASDAQ index because it does not trade on the NASDAQ.

NASDAQ is an acronym for the National Association of Securities Dealers Automated Quote System, which is owned by the National Association of Securities Dealers. The NASDAQ is a computerized market system that links brokers and dealers together who trade stocks over the counter. Although the NASDAQ is not at a physical location like the NYSE, it is a major competitor to the NYSE.

The NASDAQ has created a number of indexes that only cover stocks that trade on that market. Some say that the NASDAQ indexes best represent new-economy stocks such as technology

companies. This is not true. Some of the largest new-economy companies are listed on the NYSE and therefore are not represented in
NASDAQ indexes. For example, International Business Machines
(IBM), Hewlett-Packard (HPQ), and Texas Instruments (TXN) all
trade on the NYSE, not the NASDAQ.

One popular NASDAQ index fund that is greatly misunderstood is the NASDAQ 100 Tracking Stock, symbol QQQQ. The
objective of this fund is to provide investment results that generally
correspond with the price and yield performance of the largest 100
stocks that trade on the NASDAQ. This index fund accomplishes its
mission but is not a good proxy for the new economy because the
NASDAQ 100 index excludes several important new-economy companies that trade on the NYSE.

Many people believe that the NASDAQ 100 of leading NASDAQ
stocks is an important benchmark of stock prices because the
media has the bad habit of telling what the level of that particular
index is. When the media quotes the NASDAQ 100, it makes no
sense because they rarely quote that market alongside the NYSE
and AMEX indexes. Without quoting a broader index, the public
does not get a good sense of what is happening to general stock
prices. Unfortunately, I have no say in what is reported in the
press. At least for this book, know that the NASDAQ is a market,
not an index.

A relevant market index does not have exchange bias. It cuts
across all markets and is not restricted to one exchange or another.
The Standard & Poor's, MSCI, Russell, and Dow Jones Wilshire
indexes are more relevant indexes in that they are not biased as to
where a stock trades. Those index providers represent stocks listed
on all major exchanges within a country. In this book, we will concentrate only on those relevant indexes that cut across all markets
and will ignore most exchange-specific indexes.

INDEXES AS PORTFOLIO BENCHMARKS

Indexes are useful in a variety of ways. They can be used to gauge
the general wealth of a nation. They can be used to track the mood
of consumers, which helps economists forecast sales, profits, and
overall economic growth. Indexes can be compared with one another,
and the spread between them may indicate the attitude of investors

and a possible trading opportunity. Although all those uses are important, the most important use of an index in this book is how they act as a benchmark for mutual fund management.

Guidelines have been established by the CFA Institute regarding the creation of benchmarks. The CFA Institute is an organization of more than 80,000 investment professionals that leads the investment profession globally by setting the highest standards of ethics, education, and professional excellence. To summarize those rules, a good index has the following characteristics:

Relevance: An index should be relevant to investors. At a minimum, it should track those markets and market segments of most interest to investors.

Comprehensive: An index should include all opportunities that are realistically available to market participants under normal market conditions while measuring the performance of new investments and existing holdings.

Replicable: The total returns reported for an index should be replicable by market participants. It must be fair to investment managers who are measured against it and to sponsors who pay fees or award management assignments based on performance relative to it. Furthermore, over time, an index must represent a realistic baseline strategy that a passive investor could have followed. Accordingly, information about index composition and historical returns should be readily available.

Stability: An index should not change composition very often, and all changes should be easily understood and highly predictable. It should not be subjected to opinions about which bonds or equities to include on any particular day. However, index composition must change occasionally to ensure that it accurately reflects the structure of the market. A key virtue of an index is to provide a passive benchmark; investors should not be forced to execute a significant number of transactions just to keep pace.

Barriers to entry: The markets or market segments included in an index should not contain significant barriers to entry. This guideline is especially applicable to an international index in which an included country may discourage foreign ownership of its bonds or participation in its equity market.

Expenses: In the normal course of investing, expenses related to withholding tax, safekeeping, and transactions are incurred. For a market or market segment to be included, these ancillary expenses should be well understood by market participants and should not be excessive. For example, if expenses are unpredictable or inconsistently applied, an index cannot hope to fairly measure market performance.

Simple and objective selection criteria: There should be a clear set of rules governing inclusion of bonds, equities, or markets in an index, and investors should be able to forecast and agree on changes in composition.

Nearly all investment portfolios are benchmarked to one or more market indexes. By comparing the risk and return of a portfolio to an appropriate index or set of indexes, we have a gauge to measure performance of that portfolio. Assume that you owned a portfolio of large U.S. stocks that went up by 10 percent last year. That might seem to be a good return; however, without measuring that against an appropriate benchmark, we cannot know. The S&P 500 is a likely index against which to measure the return of a large U.S. stock portfolio. If the S&P 500 gained 5 percent during the year, your 10 percent return was outstanding. On the other hand, if the S&P 500 gained 20 percent, your 10 percent return was dismal. A portfolio's performance is deemed good or bad depending on how the benchmark performed.

Benchmarking should be done on a quarterly basis. Any more than that may give you erroneous results. On a week-to-week and month-to-month basis, there are inconsistencies between the return of a market index and the cash flow return of a portfolio. Those inconsistencies tend to cancel out over an entire quarter.

Benchmarks should be designated in advance and should be provided by the investment firm managing the portfolio. Investors ask the investment firm to "pick their poison" and tell exactly what benchmark they are trying to meet or beat. If a mutual fund manager is not keeping up with his or her benchmark, it may be time to look for a new manager. Each year many portfolio managers of actively managed funds lose their jobs because they fail to keep up with their predesignated benchmark.

MUTUAL FUNDS AND INVESTMENT ACCOUNTS

Before continuing with a discussion on index funds, we need to get back to basics about what a mutual fund is. There a great deal of misunderstanding in investment terminology among the public. Consider the following conversation that I have had with several people over the years:

> "Rick, should I invest in index funds or put my money in an IRA account?"
>
> "You should buy index funds in an IRA account."
>
> "I don't understand. How can I do both? What is the difference?"
>
> "An IRA is a type of account, just like a savings account or a checking account. Once you open an IRA and put money into it, then you can buy index funds as an investment."

Before you buy a mutual fund, you must open an account to put that investment in. The account will have a title, such as a rollover IRA, Roth IRA, joint, trust, or 401(k). After you open the account and fund it with money, you can then buy a mutual fund.

How Mutual Funds Work

Mutual funds are a wonderful investment idea. They offer diversification, ease of management, and tax simplification, all at a reasonable fee.

There are three different types of mutual funds: open-end funds, closed-end funds, and exchange-traded funds. The most common is an open-end fund. There are about 11,000 of those outstanding. The general concept behind an open-end mutual fund is as follows: A large group of investors pools its money in an account that is held in trust. A professional money manager is hired to pick stocks or bonds that go into the account. The trust is divided into shares, and each investor owns shares based on the amount of money he or she put into the trust. If investors want to sell shares, they can sell back to the trust at the end of each trading day. At that time, the fund manager will sell stocks or bonds to raise the cash needed to pay off the investors. If a new investor wants to buy shares, or old investors want to buy more shares, money is deposited in the trust, new shares are created, and the portfolio manager uses the money to buy more securities. The price to buy and sell is the valuation price, also known as the net asset value (NAV).

The primary difference between an open-end fund and closed-end funds and exchange-traded funds is that the shares of closed-end funds and exchange-traded funds trade on a stock exchange during the day rather than with the fund company at the end of the day. There are several other differences that will not be discussed here. More information on closed-end funds and exchange-traded funds can be found in Chapter 4.

The manager of any type of mutual fund has the right to buy and sell stocks or bonds as he or she sees fit as long the manager follows the strict guidelines that are laid out in the fund prospectus. This legal document explains in nauseating detail how the money in the trust account will be allocated among various securities. For example, the prospectus of a large U.S. stock fund may dictate that the manager can buy only the stock in U.S. companies worth $20 billion or more and restricts the manager from placing any more than 10 percent of the fund in one industry group, such as technology. Some funds forbid managers to have less than 95 percent of the money invested in stocks, regardless of how badly the manager thinks the stock market may perform in the future.

The prospectus is free to all investors, even if they do not own or are considering buying a mutual fund. It should be read prior to purchase because it will give you a detailed description about how your money will be managed. An annual update of the prospectus is mailed to all shareholders. The board of directors must approve major changes to the fund. Sometimes those changes need the approval of a majority of shareholders. All of this information is available to the general public free of charge, and most are filed in electronic format with the U.S. Securities and Exchange Commission (www.sec.gov).

Mutual fund companies (or the brokerage firm that holds a fund) send their investors a Form 1099 at the end of each year that summarizes each fund's cash distributions and tax liability. The securities in a mutual fund may pay dividends or interest during the year, and the buying and selling of securities within the fund may create capital gains or capital losses. Form 1099 is a standardized document that lists all of these items and makes year-end tax preparation almost bearable.

Are Mutual Funds Safe?

Let me be clear in saying that mutual funds do not protect you from a bad stock or bond market. Any notion to the contrary should immediately be dismissed. If you own shares of a stock mutual fund, you own partial shares of many different stocks. As a result, a rising market lifts most funds and a falling market sinks them. There is no free lunch on Wall Street.

It is true that some mutual fund managers have the authority to reduce the amount of stocks or bonds in a fund if they think a bear market is coming. But most fund managers are reluctant to act on that hunch, and rightly so. The ability to identify successfully the tops and bottoms of the market is a rare trait indeed. Mutual fund managers who are wrong on their predictions can cost shareholders a lot of money, and that could cost the manager his or her job. Consequently, mutual fund managers tend to ignore their hunches and remain invested during all market conditions. Of course, that also means a vast majority of funds will go down when the markets go kaput.

Three Good Reasons to Own Mutual Funds

If mutual funds offer no protection when the stock market goes down, then why do people invest in them? There are three good reasons to own mutual funds:

1. Diversification
2. Professional management
3. Convenience

"A little knowledge about the markets is a dangerous thing," says Jeremy Siegel of the Wharton School of Business.[2] Most people do not have the time or expertise to investigate fully the merits of each stock or bond they buy, so diversification among many securities is prudent. The average stock mutual fund contains about 145 securities according to Morningstar Principia. An investor can achieve instant diversification by purchasing almost any mutual fund.

A second reason to buy mutual funds is professional management. Mutual fund managers are generally well educated in the fields of economics and finance. Many hold advanced college degrees and about half have earned the prestigious title of Chartered Financial Analyst (CFA).[3] There is no guarantee a mutual fund manager will earn an acceptable return because they have a lot of education, but they have a better chance at it than most individual investors who do not have training, experience, or immediate access to pertinent market information.

There is a third compelling reason to own mutual funds: your time. It is a rare individual that has the time to sift through 5,000-plus stocks, read numerous financial publications, listen to analysts' research calls, and tune into CNN for breaking news. Let a mutual fund manager do that work. Mutual funds are one of the most convenient investments a person can make. They offer a clean, simple, diversified solution. The only problem is that there are so many mutual funds to choose from, it is difficult to pick the best ones. Index funds can narrow the search.

ALL ABOUT INDEX FUNDS

An index fund is a type of mutual fund. Most index funds are open-end although exchange-traded funds are the new preferred structure. The primary difference between an index fund and any other mutual fund is the way the portfolio manager selects stocks or bonds for the portfolio. An index fund manager has far less discretion regarding the individual investments that go into a fund. In a nutshell, the manager buys what is in the benchmark.

Recall our discussion about the management of mutual funds. A manager of a fund is tasked to buy and sell stocks or bonds as they see fit as long as those securities follow the guidelines laid out in the mutual fund prospectus. In an actively managed fund, a portfolio manager has the right to buy Google and sell Microsoft if they believe Google has better return potential. The portfolio manager takes an active role in the fund in an attempt to beat the stock market. All the rules for a fund are laid out in the prospectus. The prospectus may even allow the active portfolio manager to reduce the overall stock position in the fund if they believe the prospects for the stock market look dim.

Index funds are different than active funds. The prospectus of a stock index fund does not allow the portfolio manager to use his or her own judgment to decide which stocks will go into the fund and which ones will come out. Index fund managers must follow the benchmark index composition as closely as possible. That means holding a proportionate share of each stock or bond held in the index. The prospectus does not allow the portfolio manager to "time" the market by moving in or out of stocks based on a market forecast. The fund must stay as close to 100 percent invested as possible.

Index funds are not meant to beat a benchmark, they merely mirror it. Thus, how do you judge how well a manager is performing? Index fund managers are graded based on how closely they perform to a predetermined benchmark rather than how much they beat it by. The difference in performance between an index fund and its benchmark is called *tracking error.* The ideal index fund has a zero tracking error with the benchmark. Unfortunately, zero tracking error is nearly impossible to achieve because of costs to operate the fund, commissions paid to trade stocks, and operational inefficiencies that occur as a result of cash inflows and outflows from dividends and investor activity. Depending on the index, a tracking error of approximately 0.25 percent per year below the benchmark is generally acceptable.

An Example

The best way to illustrate the mechanics of an index fund is to provide an example. The Vanguard 500 Index Fund is the oldest and largest index fund available to the public today. It began operations in August 1976 with a few million dollars under management. At first, asset growth was slow. It took the fund more than 10 years to reach $1 billion in assets. Since 1986, the fund has grown to nearly $110 billion in all share classes and is now one of the largest mutual funds on the market (Figure 1-2).

The Vanguard 500 Index Fund is benchmarked to the S&P 500 index. Vanguard attempts to replicate the S&P 500 index by investing substantially all of its assets in the stocks that make up that index. Each stock is represented in proportion to its market value.

Standard & Poor's maintains the S&P 500 index, and the Investment Committee at S&P decides which changes will take place in the index. Those changes are made for a number of reasons, including corporate mergers and acquisitions. If a stock is taken out of the

FIGURE 1-2

The Growth of Assets in the Vanguard 500 Index

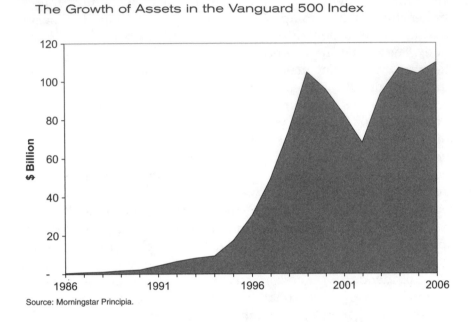

Source: Morningstar Principia.

index, another is added. For example, Realogy Corp. was added in July 2006 at the same time that Gateway Inc. was removed.

The portfolio management team at Vanguard is responsible for adjusting the holdings of the Vanguard 500 Index Fund to match the additions and deletions. The portfolio management team must decide when to add or remove a stock to avoid the market impact of their trading during an adjustment. Trading may occur over period of time to minimize the market impact cost. A gradual adjustment may create some tracking error in the fund, but that is better than bidding up the price of a new entry or collapsing the price of a dropped stock for the sake of filling the allocation quickly.

Vanguard pays a licensing fee to Standard & Poor's for use of the S&P 500 name and access to detailed index data. Because Standard & Poor's had no precedent on what to charge Vanguard in 1976 when the Vanguard 500 Index Fund was developed, Vanguard negotiated a very low fee in comparison with what Standard & Poor's now charges for index licensing. Over the years, index licensing has become an important source of revenue for Standard & Poor's and other index providers.

A PROLIFERATION OF INDEXES AND SPINDEXES

As you read through this book and observe the marketplace, you might wonder why so many similar indexes exist and why there is some much apparent redundancy among index funds. The answer is licensing fees. Index investing has become a very popular strategy over the years with both institutional investors and the public. As a result, competition for index licensing fees has become a big business. The more money that is benchmarked to a particular index, the greater fee that index provider receives.

In the fight for investor attention, each index provider claims that they have the best indexing methodology and put out the best indexes. The truth is some of those products are worth looking at, whereas others border on the absurd. A few investment companies have created portfolio strategies that I describe as *spindexes*. A *spindex* is a managed portfolio of stocks that is created using a quantitative screening process, and then stocks in the portfolio are weighted based on various factors rather than market weight. Periodically, the portfolio is reconstructed according to published rules. These spindex portfolios are created for the sole purpose of marketing to a mutual fund company for a licensing fee.

In this author's opinion, companies that create and maintain spindexes refer to those portfolios as indexes for the media play and marketing hype. Those portfolios have almost nothing in common with index construction guidelines outlined earlier in this chapter. A good index can be used as a measurement to track the performance of a market or segment of a market. A good index can also be used to compare the performance of active managers. The new-fangled spindexes have rapid turnover of stocks, measure nothing of importance, and are not used as benchmarks for active management.

In a crowded mutual fund marketplace, marketing is everything, especially when a company is trying to promote a mutual fund strategy that can cost more than 10 times that of a comparable market-weighted index fund. Thus, we have seen a proliferation of active strategies being called index benchmarks and active mutual funds being titled as index fund. That is spindexing.

Perhaps the most absurd spindex is the StockCar Stocks index, which is the benchmark for the very-high-cost StockCar Stocks index fund. The annual expense ratio for the fund is 1.50 percent, which is almost as absurd as the index itself. The core holdings of the portfolio include official NASCAR sponsors and suppliers such as General Electric, Kellogg's, Speedway Motorsports, and makers of various sex-enhancing drugs. There is no analytical thought behind the companies that go into the portfolio except to add the ones that become sponsors of auto racing and drop those that drop out of sight.

There is no government rule on what can be called a market index and what cannot. Consequently, several fund companies have ignored CFA Institute guidance to promote their active funds as index funds. After reading this book, you can make an informed decision regarding which funds are benchmarked to legitimate indexes and which are not.

CHAPTER SUMMARY

> The greatest results in life are usually attained by simple means and the exercise of ordinary qualities. These may for the most part be summed up in two—common sense and perseverance.
>
> *Owen Flethman*

In this chapter, you learned the difference between a market and an index. A market is an exchange where stock and bond trading is conducted. A broad market-weighted index measures the value of a group of stocks or bonds and cuts across all markets. Indexes have a variety of useful purposes. In this book, indexes are used as a benchmark for the formation of index funds. The less tracking error an index fund has to its benchmark, the better the fund has been managed.

There are hundreds of indexes measuring the performance of stocks and bonds around the globe. As of this writing, in the Morningstar database there were more than 550 distinct index funds benchmarked to various stock and bond indexes (a distinct fund counts all share classes of the same mutual fund as one fund). That number may seem small compared with nearly 6,200 distinct active funds. However, index funds represent almost 25 percent of all money invested in mutual funds in aggregate. That is clear evidence that many wise investors have embraced the low-cost index fund revolution.

NOTES

1. The Dow Jones Industrial Average is a registered trademark of Dow Jones & Company, New York.
2. See Jeremy Siegel's *Stocks for the Long Run* (3rd edition; McGraw-Hill, 2002) for a long-term prospectus about the U.S. stock market.
3. The chartered financial analyst (CFA) program is a globally recognized designation earned by financial analysts and portfolio managers. It is administered by the CFA Institute, Charlottesville, Virginia.

CHAPTER 2

Why Index Funds Beat Most Other Funds

Key Concepts
- Searching for superior active funds is an inferior strategy.
- In the long run, index funds beat most active funds.
- The index fund advantage extends to all markets.
- Low costs are critical in all mutual fund investing.

Index funds are based on a simple concept. Each fund attempts to replicate, as closely as possible, the securities and structure of a market benchmark, such as the S&P 500. In line with this goal, index funds are expected to earn a return equal to their benchmark, less a small fee for administrative and management costs.

There is nothing mysterious or complex about index fund investing, and there should be no surprises in performance. When the S&P 500 index goes up, index funds benchmarked to that index should go up by nearly an identical amount, and vice versa. Because index funds are designed to mirror the movement of a market, they are evaluated based on tracking error, or how closely a fund matches its benchmark. The smaller a fund's tracking error is to its benchmark, the better the performance of the fund manager.

Index funds are a simple concept to understand and can easily be added to an existing investment portfolio. Although these are good reasons to own index funds, the best reason is consistent performance. Over time, index funds achieve higher returns than a vast majority of actively managed funds that try to beat a benchmark. Why is this true? The short answer is that index funds have considerably lower expenses. The cost to manage an index fund is far lower than the cost to manage an active fund because there are no stock analysts to pay, no research to buy, and no excessive commission payments to Wall Street brokerage firms for access to information and initial public offerings of new stock.

The average cost of an S&P 500 index fund is about 0.2 percent per year compared with an average 1.4 percent cost for a large-cap active mutual fund.[1] The lower cost of an index fund gives it a significant performance advantage over time. Although active fund managers may be able to conduct research that enables them to select stocks that outperform the market, they cannot do it with enough consistency to overcome the higher expenses in those funds. In the final analysis, most people would be better off in a low-cost index fund than trying to beat the stock market. Index funds are a winner's game.

Bond index funds also beat most actively managed bond mutual funds over time because the cost of a bond index fund is considerably lower than the cost of other bond funds. Bond index funds also cost about 0.2 percent per year, and actively managed bond funds cost about 1.0 percent. An active bond manager must consistently earn 0.8 percent in fees each year just to match the return of a bond index fund. That is extremely difficult to do in the bond market because the return of bonds is typically less than the return of stocks. So there is not much room to make up high fees. It is not likely that the cost of active management will come down significantly over the next 25 years. Consequently, it is logical to assume that bond index funds will continue to earn higher returns than a vast majority of actively managed bond mutual funds.

SEARCHING FOR SUPERIOR ACTIVE FUNDS IS AN INFERIOR STRATEGY

Actively managed mutual funds have a very difficult time beating the performance of index funds. There are just not enough talented mutual fund managers or enough opportunities to beat the market. For all practical purposes, the stock and bond market can be considered efficient as far as the general public is concerned. An efficient market is one where all known information is immediately priced into the market, so there is no opportunity for a superior gain over the market.

Finding a talented investment manager who will beat the market is more difficult than picking superior performing stocks yourself. To make an analogy, imagine one year the number of professional baseball teams exploded to 5,000. The fact that there are now 5,000 teams does not mean there are 5,000 great pitchers in professional baseball. The number of great pitchers in all of baseball is small regardless of how many teams there are. The number does not increase simply because there is an increase in the number of teams.

The same holds true for mutual funds managers. There are only a few great managers out there, and increasing the number of mutual funds from 500 to 5,000 does not mean there will be 10 times the number of great mutual fund managers. A vast majority of those new funds will have mediocre managers. Granted, there will always be a few new managers that prove to be superior as Figure 2-1 illustrates. Unfortunately, the only way to profit from those funds is to know the winners in advance, which is impossible to know.

FIGURE 2-1

Probability of an Active Equity Fund Beating the Market

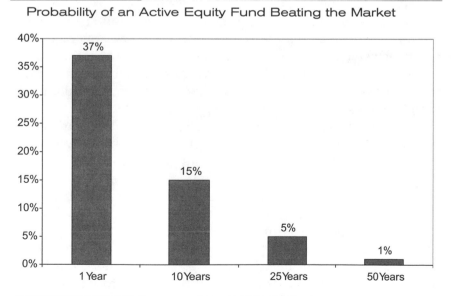

Source: The Vanguard Group (the figure assumes 2 percent in total expenses).

Each year, different active fund managers become stars because of their short-term superior performance. Over the next couple of years, a great majority of these shooting stars burn out. The reversal of fortune occurs for a variety of reasons including (1) the manager's style of investing went out of favor, (2) an over-whelming amount of new money is added to a fund, which changes the dynamics of the fund, and (3) the manager was never good, just lucky, and his or her luck ran out.

The clear mediocrity of the average active manager's perfor-mance has led to a profit-making opportunity for newsletter writ-ers, investment advisors, and magazine publishers. People want to know which funds will beat the market in the future; as a result, an entire industry has evolved that "researches" mutual funds and their managers and recommends funds that are supposed to do that. Don't be misled. A vast majority of the information you hear or read about predicting performance of a mutual fund is pure nonsense. There is no academic evidence that any system of selecting actively managed mutual funds actually works.

Top universities and academic researchers have been search-ing for years trying to find a quantitative method for picking next year's top-performing mutual funds. The best and the brightest financial researchers from colleges across the country have sliced and diced a seemingly endless number of mutual fund factors look-ing for clues to future performance. All of this research has led to two conclusive facts. First, mutual funds that will beat the market next year cannot be identified in advance. Second, mutual funds with lower fees have a greater likelihood of beating mutual funds with high fees.

When you read academic reports, you get the truth about mutual funds and their managers. On the other hand, when you read the research published by mutual fund companies, you get marketing malarkey. The story you hear from the sales side is that their selected fund exhibits impressive growth, rock solid stability, and that the fund manager is a wise decision maker. Most sales liter-ature points to past performance and "star" ratings, although some-times the brochures and ads have to go far back to find a period when the fund actually did beat something. Unfortunately, the future will not be like the past. Regardless of the past history of a fund, it is the future we are concerned about. Neither the fund companies, magazines, nor the financial experts can tell us anything about which active fund will outperform in the future. Hence, we are inundated on a daily basis with irrelevant and useless data.

Many people visit their local financial advisor looking for investment advice. The thinking is that the advisor is an expert, and he or she may have a window to winning investments of the future. Look out! Although these folks mean well, most financial advisors are undertrained salespeople. They do not have years of training in finance or economics. They have not done advanced study outside of the simple study guides that allow them to pass licensing exams.

Advisors who think they can beat the market are a not in short supply, and it is not hard to find one who will gladly sell you market-beating tips for a fee or commission. The next time you are at a social gathering, just mention that you are seeking professional investment advice and you will likely be referred to several local experts. There is even a good chance that an investment expert is already at the event scavenging for business. How do you tell a good advisor from a mediocre one? Ask the advisor how he or she feels about index funds. If they scoff at the idea, you are likely talking to a salesperson, not a *bona fide* investment professional.

The typical way investors and local advisors research mutual funds is to analyze past performance. Unfortunately, that is a dead end street. Past performance is not a reliable method of choosing winning funds in the future. The mistakes made by investors who use past performance cause so many problems that the government requires a warning label on mutual fund advertisements. The U.S. Securities and Exchange Commission requires all sales literature promoting past results to clearly state that "past performance is not an indication of future results." Alas, it is the norm among most investors and local investment experts to ignore that fact.

You shouldn't waste your time or money trying to pick active mutual funds based on past performance, especially when a better alternative exists. In general, the largest advantage one fund has over another is the overall cost to investors in those funds. The evidence is very clear; low-cost funds beat high-cost funds over time. Because index funds have the lowest cost of all funds, control what you can control and buy a diversified portfolio of low-cost index funds.

COMPARING ACTIVE FUNDS TO INDEX FUNDS

I would rather be certain of a good return than hopeful of a great one.

Warren Buffett

The best way to show that index funds perform better than active funds over time is with actual results. It is important to understand that while index funds are consistently good performers over the long-term, they are rarely the best-performing mutual fund in any given category over the short-term. There has always been, and will always be, actively managed mutual funds that beat the return of index funds in any particular category. However, that is irrelevant. You should not be looking for the highest short-term return. You should seek a consistent long-term return. By delivering consistently good returns, index funds become the long-term winner. Over time, the cream floats to the top.

The Vanguard 500 Index Fund

In August 1976, the Vanguard Index Trust became the first index fund available to the general public. The fund is benchmarked to the S&P 500, a broadly diversified index of mostly large, U.S. companies. Vanguard set the management fee very low in comparison with active funds and that meant the company did not have a lot of money available for marketing. At first, the new index fund was sold thought Wall Street brokerage firms, but that did not work well because the commission earned by brokers to sell the Vanguard fund was lower than what they earned selling other equity funds. In addition, Vanguard was ridiculed in the media. After all, who would want a fund that just produced "average" returns? Some called it a fund for "no brainers." One competing mutual fund company labeled indexing as "un-American."

In early 1977, Vanguard changed the name of the fund to the Vanguard 500 Index Fund, dropped the brokerage sale arrangement, and became one of the few direct-purchase, no-commission (no-load) mutual fund companies in existence at the time. The strategy worked. Despite the initial broker boycott and bad press, the public soon began to notice that the average market returns were far superior to most active manager returns. Due to the superior returns of the index over those who tried to beat it, the Vanguard 500 Index Fund has become one of the largest and most successful mutual funds in history.

The analysis of index fund performance starts by comparing the returns of the Vanguard 500 Index Fund to actively managed mutual funds that invest in the same types of stocks. A quick scan of the Morningstar Principia database generates a list of those funds that have been around for 25 years or more. The Vanguard 500 Index Fund is in the Large-Cap Blend Morningstar category and has the prospectus objective of Growth and Index. The Principia search turned up 17 other funds that had the same Morningstar category, the same prospectus objective, and were open to all public investors.

Seventeen funds that are comparable with the Vanguard 500 index may seem like a low number. That is because these are the surviving funds. During the past 25 years, dozens of large-cap blend funds with a growth and income objective came and went. Most of those performed so poorly that they were closed. The rest were merged together when one fund company bought another.

Figure 2-2 compares the load-adjusted returns of the 17 surviving core large-cap funds with the return of the Vanguard 500 Index

FIGURE 2-2

Twenty-five–Year Returns of U.S. Growth and Income Funds

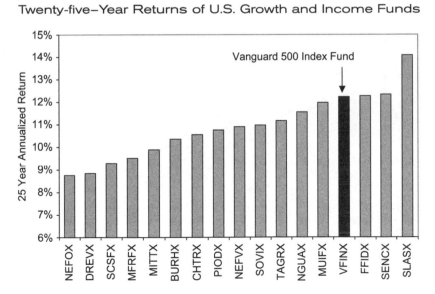

Source: Morningstar Principia (June 2006).

Fund through December 2005. Thirteen of the funds had 25-year annualized returns below the Vanguard 500 Index Fund, two funds had comparable returns, and only one fund, Selected American (symbol: SLASX) beat the index fund by a considerable amount. Load-adjusted return takes into consideration commissions and other sales charges that would have been paid to purchase the funds.

A $10,000 investment in the Vanguard 500 index in December 1980 would have grown to $170,900 in 25 years; $10,000 invested in the other 17 funds would have grown to only $130,584 on average. The difference is the price of a luxury automobile. We cannot know the performance of the funds that did not survive. However, it is safe to assume that if the returns could be included, the growth of the $10,000 would have been less than the average surviving fund and significantly less than the Vanguard 500 Index Fund.[2]

Figure 2-3 is a scatterplot that compares the expenses and annualized 25-year returns of the 18 funds including the Vanguard 500 index. The figure illustrates the relationship between costs and fees. As fund expenses increased, fund returns generally decreased.

FIGURE 2–3

Scatterplot of Fund Expenses and Returns

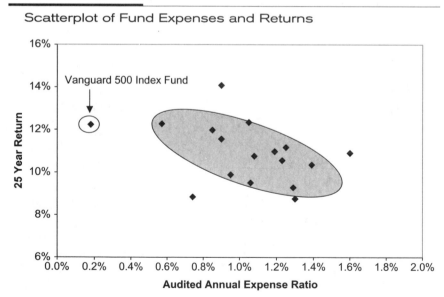

Source: Morningstar Principia (June 2006).

It is very difficult for active mutual fund managers to beat the stock market because of the drag from expenses. In aggregate, they can only perform as well as the market, less fees and commissions. Real-world operating costs of active funds drag down portfolio performance to the point where talented fund managers cannot make up the difference. In the short-term, Wall Street tries to convince us that near-term returns matter. However, in the long-term it is costs that matter most. Because the Vanguard 500 Index Fund has the lowest cost of all its peers, it is no surprise that the fund outperformed most of its surviving peers and all of the funds that did not survive. Costs matter.

THE INDEX FUND ADVANTAGE EXTENDS TO ALL MARKETS

The benefit of low-cost indexing has extended to all categories of the stocks and bonds across the globe. Based on the following three assumptions, it is logical to believe that the return benefit will continue in the future:

1. The aggregate performance of all mutual funds within a category will equal the benchmark index, less all investment expenses.
2. Mutual funds with the lowest overall expenses have a significant advantage over high-cost funds.
3. Index funds are the lowest cost funds in every category. As a result, it is logical to assume that index funds will continue to have superior performance over the category average in the long-term.

Several independent market research companies publish free comparisons of index performance relative to the performance of active funds across several categories. Each year, Morningstar publishes the *Morningstar Indexes Yearbook* featuring three-year track records of active funds to indexes. For a quarterly update, you can also view *Morningstar's Market Commentary*. Both reports are available for free at www.indexes.morningstar.com. Standard & Poor's posts five-year trailing results of active funds relative to their indexes in the quarterly *Standard & Poor's Indices Versus Active Funds Scorecard*. It is available for free at www.standardandpoors.com.

Each report has interesting characteristics. The Morningstar results measure the performance of active funds to the Morningstar indexes. Those indexes are based on Morningstar "style boxes." The methodology behind the Morningstar indexes is covered in Chapter 6. Each fund in the Morningstar report is treated equally (i.e., one vote for each fund regardless of the size of the fund).

Figure 2-4 is an example of a Morningstar active versus passive report over the trailing 30-year period ending in December 2005. Over that period, the Morningstar index beat active funds in all but two categories; large core and large growth. It is typical to see active funds beating the indexes in a few categories over each independent period, although it is impossible to predict where the next outperformance will take place. The category where active funds do beat indexes shifts among styles in a nonpredictive manner, and you would need to be precise in timing. It rare to see active funds achieve higher returns in a majority of categories.

Many mutual funds drift between style boxes over time. Morningstar presents a drifting fund's results using a best-fit method. If

F I G U R E   2–4

Morningstar Active versus Passive Report,
Trailing Three Years

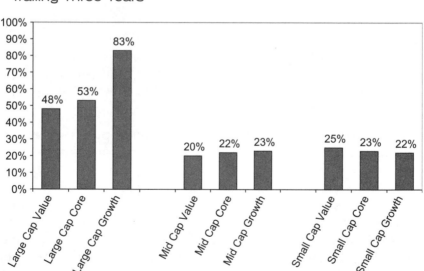

Source: *Morningstar Indexes Yearbook*, 2005.

a fund was in the mid-cap value range on quarter and then moved to the large-cap core range the next quarter, Morningstar would fit the fund to the appropriate style box each quarter and report it only in one type of box.

One element of the *Standard & Poor's Indices Versus Active Funds Scorecard* that is interesting is that they report the percentage of funds that have drifted out of style during the period measured and the percentage of funds discontinued. S&P measures performance during several periods with five years as the longest interval. Table 2-1 lists the percentage of active funds that beat the S&P index benchmark for the trailing five years ending in June 2006, the percentage that drifted off style, and the percentage of funds discontinued. The methodology behind S&P indexes is covered in Chapter 6.

Another interesting element of the Standard & Poor's report is that they measure results two ways. One method assumes all mutual funds are equal weighted (i.e., one vote for each fund), which is similar to Morningstar. In contrast, the second methodology

TABLE 2-1

S&P U.S. Active versus Passive, Trailing Five Years, in Percent

U.S. Fund Style	Beat the Index (Equal Weight)	Beat the Index (Asset Weighted)	Surviving Funds	Style Consistent
All domestic funds	38%	NA	72%	42%
Large-cap value	13%	NA	76%	63%
Large-cap blend	30%	33%	63%	26%
Large-cap growth	46%	NA	67%	50%
Mid-cap value	21%	NA	84%	29%
Mid-cap blend	18%	24%	72%	28%
Mid-cap growth	5%	NA	74%	45%
Small-cap value	40%	NA	86%	61%
Small-cap blend	19%	23%	77%	28%
Small-cap growth	6%	NA	73%	42%

NA, not applicable.
Source: *S&P Indices Versus Active Funds Scorecard* (July 19, 2006).

TABLE 2-2

S&P Active versus Passive, Trailing Five Years in Percent

Fund Style	Beat the Index (Equal Weight)	Surviving Funds	Style Consistent
Global (U.S. & international)	35%	70%	62%
International	20%	69%	67%
International small-cap	22%	75%	75%
Emerging markets	12%	66%	65%

Source: *S&P Indices Versus Active Funds Scorecard* (July 19, 2006).

assigns weights to funds based on the amount of money in each fund. Active funds performed slightly better using a market-weighted methodology, but not by a meaningful amount.

International stock index funds are also gaining prominence in the mutual fund marketplace. They are also significantly less expensive than their actively managed counterparts. Not surprisingly, the June *Standard & Poor's Indices Versus Active Funds Scorecard* results in Table 2-2 points to better five-year performance by indexes over actively managed accounts.

Fund expenses are the number one driving factor of fund performance over the long-term. So it should be no surprise that low-cost bond funds are big winners. Table 2-3 compares the performance of fixed income index funds against the returns of active index funds. The expected performance of fixed-income funds is lower than stock funds. Any amount of fee reduction is going to shine through in the performance numbers. *Standard & Poor's Indices Versus Active Funds Scorecard* results in Table 2-2 points to significantly better five-year performance by comparable Lehman Brothers indexes over high-cost, actively managed, fixed-income funds, with the notable exception of emerging market, fixed-income funds. The methodology behind Lehman Brothers fixed-income indexes is covered in Chapter 10.

A study of the Morningstar and Standard & Poor's results conclusively shows that investors have been better served in low-cost index funds than higher cost actively managed funds. The advantage of low-cost indexing has extended to almost all stock and

TABLE 2-3

S&P Active versus Passive Fixed Income, Trailing Five Years, in Percent

Fixed-Income Style	Beat the Index (Equal Weight)	Surviving Funds	Style Consistent
Government intermediate	25%	76%	57%
General intermediate	26%	82%	76%
High yield	16%	89%	89%
Mortgage backed	11%	92%	85%
Global fixed income	31%	91%	89%
Emerging markets	65%	89%	89%

Source: *S&P Indices Versus Active Funds Scorecard* (July 19, 2006).

bond categories in the United States and internationally. Costs matter. A low-cost indexing approach to portfolio management is a powerful philosophy to live by. It will pay lifelong rewards.

OUTFOX THE BOX

Over time, low-cost index funds deliver higher returns than most mutual funds but never the best returns. Should you go for the reliability of an index fund or take your chances finding a better performing active mutual fund? If you haven't decided yet, one unique way to answer this question is to play a game called "Outfox the Box." Bill Schultheis described this game in his delightful little book, *The Coffeehouse Investor: How To Build Wealth, Ignore Wall Street, And Get On With Your Life* (Palouse Press, 2005). Here is the game:

> You visit a local investment firm and ask them to invest $10,000 for your benefit and give them full discretion to make decisions. They agree and you go about your business. Ten years later, you go back to the investment house and ask for the money. An executive leads you into a room and shows you 10 boxes arranged on a table. Each box has money inside. The executive gives you a list showing the amount of money contained in each box. The list looks like this:

Next, the executive asks you to leave the room. After about five minutes, you are allowed to go back in. The 10 boxes are still on the table, but this time only box no. 8 with $25,000 is open. The rest of the boxes are closed, and the box numbers are covered. The order of the boxes on the table has also been changed. The order now looks like this:

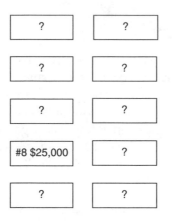

The executive says, "None of the money in the boxes has been touched," and then asks, "Without opening or touching the boxes, you may choose one box as your investment return, including box number eight. Which box do you choose?"

Do you pick box no. 8 with $25,000 in it, or do you forfeit the $25,000 and take your chances on the $26,000 and $30,000 boxes? It is a mathematical puzzle. Let's break it down:

> There are 10 boxes. The one you know contains $25,000. You have a 2 in 9 chance of bettering yourself by picking the box with $26,000 or $30,000. The average amount in those two boxes is $28,000. That means you have a 22 percent probability of gaining an extra $3,000. On the other hand, there is a 7 in 9 chance of picking a box with less money in it. The average amount in those boxes is only $20,000. That means you have a 78 percent probability of earning $5,000 less than a guaranteed $25,000.

What would you do? When I tell this story at seminars, nearly everyone in attendance picks the $25,000 box. Their reasoning is simple. Although it is possible to pick a box that contains more money, it is not a lot more money, and the probability of success is low. In other words, the extra reward is not justified by the extra risk. If you picked the $25,000 box, then you are a perfect candidate for the wonderful world of index fund investing. With an index fund mindset, as long as the markets do well, you are guaranteed a good return. That is better than taking considerably more risk and praying for the remote possibility of a great return.

CHAPTER SUMMARY

> Great rewards grow from small differences in cost.
>
> *John C. Bogle, founder of the Vanguard Group*

Index funds perform well relative to actively managed mutual funds because the costs are lower. Although it is true that some actively managed funds will beat index funds every year, those winning funds cannot be identified in advance, and it is costly and time consuming to guess which ones will be the winners next year. In every global stock and bond market where index funds are available, the costs of those funds is considerably less than the costs of competing active funds. As a result, it is prudent and logical to conclude that in the future, index funds will continue to outshine active management.

In closing this chapter, I will leave you with this thought: do you remember when you were a teenager and dreamed of owning a really cool automobile? You didn't care if the car cost too much and didn't run well, as long as you looked good driving it. Later in life, things changed. You wanted a reliable car that didn't cost you a lot of money. People seem to take the same path with their investment decisions. Early in life, they want fast-moving active mutual funds that will beat the market. Later in life, experienced investors realize that reliability and economy are the keys to success, and they switch to index funds. In the long run, low costs drive investment performance. Keep your portfolio costs low with index funds.

NOTES

1. The expense ratio of the average active equity mutual fund is 1.4 percent according to Morningstar. However, there are other costs not measured in the expense ratio. They are trading expenses, cost of holding cash for redemptions, possibly a sale charge paid to brokers (loads), and possibly a fee to an intermediary such as a financial advisor.
2. Several academic and industry reports have been published that estimate the impact of nonsurviving funds on long-term category returns. On average, those studies find that survivorship bias in mutual fund composites inflates the category returns by more than 1 percent annually.

CHAPTER 3

The History Behind Indexing

Key Concepts

- ◆ Index funds were not available prior to 1976.
- ◆ The Vanguard Group introduced the first index fund.
- ◆ There are approximately 550 index funds on the market.
- ◆ Exchange-traded funds are a growing presence.

In 1896, Charles Dow published the first stock market indicator, and shortly thereafter the Dow Jones Industrial Average (DJIA) became the benchmark for all stock investors. Several competing research firms have established numerous U.S. stock indexes since that time. In 1924, Massachusetts Investors created the first U.S. mutual fund in which people were able to buy and sell shares on a daily basis. Over the next 50 years, hundreds of investment companies established mutual funds. However, it was not until 1976 when John Bogle established the Vanguard Group that the first index fund became available to the public. What took so long?

This chapter takes you on a short history of the mutual fund business. We have to look back at the mutual fund industry since its inception in the early 1920s and work up to the era of exchange-traded fund issuance today. During this journey, we will look at the reasons why it took 80 years to launch the first index fund after the establishment of the DJIA.

Much of the credit for the success of indexing can be directed to one man, John Bogle, the founder of the Vanguard Group. Bogle's dedication to indexing has done more good for individual investors than any other person in modern finance. He has done so much that many investors refer to him as Saint Jack. Now, I don't know if he is a real saint, but we can thank God for John Bogle.

EARLY MUTUAL FUNDS, 1920–1970

In the early 1900s, the U.S. economy was transforming rapidly from agrarian-based to an industrial powerhouse. The change accelerated in the 1920s because American factories had not been damaged during World War I, whereas Europe's infrastructure lay in ruins. In addition, the political atmosphere in Washington, D.C., was particularly favorable toward economic growth. "The chief business of the American people is business," President Calvin Coolidge asserted in 1925.

The economic boom of the Roaring Twenties resulted in a spectacular bull market in stocks, and the invention of the ticker tape brought that excitement to the general public. The excitement on Wall Street was fueled by the growth of large "investment trusts." For the first time, every individual could participate in the market's advance without having to have a large sum of money.

Investment trusts were a collection of capital from various public and private investors. People could participate with as little as $100. The money was pooled together in an account at a trust company for the purpose of investing in the stock market. Each investor in the trust was issued a *pro rata* number of shares representing their portion. After the shares were issued, investors could buy and sell shares on the stock market in the same way stocks trade.

Unfortunately, many problems occurred, and small-trust investors were often defrauded of their money. For example, the shares of the trust were a *free-floating* security on the stock market. That means the shares could trade at a price premium or discount that was different from the actual value of the investments in the trust. The net asset value of a trust share could be $10 while the market price of a trust share was only $9. The spread between actual value and trade value created some unethical practices on the part of traders and issuers who often took advantage of small public investors.

There were several other reasons investment trusts developed a bad name on Wall Street during the 1920s. Many pools were established for unethical purposes such as the attempted monopolization of an industry or as a dumping ground for unwanted investments held by institutional investors. Banks were particularly notorious for establishing investment trusts and using them as a waste disposal for stocks in the banks' private portfolios that went sour. To add insult to injury, many banks encouraged the public to borrow money to invest in these trusts, and the same banks extended up to 90 percent credit. After collecting a pool of capital, many of the trusts borrowed more money internally, thus leveraging the investors even further.

Securities and antitrust laws were virtually nonexistent in the early part of the century, so unchecked speculation and shady financing among trusts were common. If word got out about questionable dealings in a trust, there was a mad rush to sell shares on the open market, and that caused the market value to collapse. Some of these rumors were falsely started by people trying to manipulate the price of a trust for personal gain.

The investment trust was a great idea that would have worked if all the participants stayed honest, but that was not going to happen because there was too much money to be made and too little governmental oversight.

The First Mutual Funds

By 1923, a new idea was buzzing around Wall Street that solved the problem associated with investment trusts. It was a way to keep the market value of a trust in line with its net asset value so that the share price would not collapse due to manipulation. The idea was an open-end trust. An open-end trust differed from a traditional trust in three critical ways. First, it would invest only in publicly traded common stock so that investors could accurately track the value of the fund on a daily basis. Second, it would not borrow money to leverage the portfolio holdings. Third, shares would be redeemed by the trust itself at the net asset value each day at the end of the day rather than having shares trade at a discount or premium in the open market.

In March 1924, the first *mutual fund* was established using the new doctrine. It was called the Massachusetts Investment Trust, also known as MIT. The fund held a diversified portfolio of 46 stocks ranging from insurance companies to railroads. True to the idea, no leverage was used in MIT, and fund shares could be redeemed on demand from the trust at net asset value. MIT was an immediate success with the public, and it brought trust and confidence in the system.

Within one year of the formation of MIT, there were three mutual funds available to investors. They were MIT, Putnam Investors, and State Street Investment Corporation. MIT is now known as MFS Massachusetts Investment Trust while Putnam Investors maintained its original name. The State Street Research Investment fund survived until its 100th birthday in 2004 and then fell out of the Morningstar database. As a matter of record, the two existing funds have performed well over the past 80 years. Neither one beat the stock market, but they did produce similar returns on par with the market average less expenses. That is much better performance than a typical investor would have earned picking stocks on his or her own.

Early Calls for Indexing

Professional researchers recognized the advantage of an index-type portfolio in the early 1930s, when mutual funds were just getting their start. In 1933, Alfred Cowles published an in-depth report about the futility of using Wall Street research to beat the stock market. He believed the market was much too dynamic for any one person on Wall Street to figure out. The Cowles Commission Index tracked all the stocks that traded on the New York Stock Exchange since 1871, not just the Dow 30. In the 1960s, the Cowles index was reengineered and reintroduced as the Standard & Poor's 500 index.

Alfred Cowles was not alone in the call for greater prudence on Wall Street. In the 1950s, academic researchers began to search for "efficient" portfolios of stocks and found that the most efficient portfolio was the market itself. Efficient portfolios are groups of stocks that earn the highest return per level of risk. Harry Markowitz, Paul Samuelson, Irving Fisher, and A.D. Roy conducted much of the early research on efficient portfolios, and some of these people went on to win the Nobel Prize in Economics for their efforts. All of the research seems to point to the same conclusion. There was little reason to invest in any portfolio except an index portfolio.

Over the next 20 years, extensive work was conducted on the concept of an index fund, but no fund was created. In 1973, Princeton University Professor Burton Malkiel published his classic book, *A Random Walk Down Wall Street* (W.W. Norton, 1973). Malkiel called for "a no-load, minimum management fee mutual fund that simply buys hundreds of stocks making up the stock market averages and does no trading." It was clear to Malkiel and others that actively managed funds were not keeping up with the market benchmarks. Charles Ellis highlighted the shortfall of active managers in his widely regarded article, "The Loser's Game," published in the *Financial Analyst Journal* (July/August 1975). Ellis reported that over the prior decade, 85 percent of all institutional investors who tried to beat the stock market had underperformed the S&P 500 index.

Despite repeated calls by academia for an index fund, there were several reasons why the first one did not appear until the mid-1970s. First, whereas the concept of an index-based portfolio is a simple idea, the actual management of a fund is sophisticated. By their nature, index funds hold hundreds of securities, and daily cash-flows into and out of the portfolio make daily balancing a complicated process. Needless to say, computers must be at the heart of every index fund, but readily available computing power was prohibitively expensive until the mid-1970s. Thus, index funds had to wait. A second reason index funds did not make an earlier appearance was that they were cost prohibitive. Prior to 1976, Wall Street was on a fixed commission rate system, which means fund managers could not negotiate lower trading costs with brokers. Index funds make a lot of small trades, and a high commission rate would wipe out any advantage. After 1976, commission costs were deregulated and rates came down considerably. Distribution was a third roadblock. For most of the 20th century, mutual funds were distributed through stockbrokers who were paid an 8 percent commission or more. The very idea of paying a broker a large commission simply to buy an index fund did not sit well with investors. The fourth reason index funds did not exist prior to 1976 was the reluctance of the mutual fund industry to accept the idea. Fund company executives wanted to prove their firm could beat the market, and they viewed indexing as a personal insult to their intelligence. In addition, the fund managers did not want to give up their hefty salaries and bonuses. Low-cost index funds simply did not fit the business models of established fund companies.

THE FIRST INDEX FUND

The first market-weighted S&P 500 index strategy was made available by Batterymarch Financial Management. The firm presented the idea at a Harvard Business School seminar in 1971, although they did not attract clients until 1974.

The first live index account was also established in 1971 by Wells Fargo Bank. The company constructed a $6 million index account for the pension fund of Samsonite Corporation, the luggage people. The strategy was to buy all the stocks on the New York Stock Exchange in equal proportions, thus creating the first equal-weighted index fund. The equal-weight concept was sound in theory, but actual execution of the account was a nightmare. Wells Fargo found that trying to keep the portfolio equally balanced between all stocks was extremely difficult and the commission cost was exorbitant. The equal-weighted strategy was abandoned after a few years, and Samsonite adopted a market-weighted S&P 500 index strategy. That cut down on the maintenance in trading 10-fold.

The popularity of indexing increased in the institutional marketplace after deregulation of commission costs in 1976 and the passage of the Employee Retirement Income Securities Act (ERISA). Pension regulation put new fiduciary requirements on the trustees of retirement accounts, and indexing was one way of eliminating the liability of choosing poor active managers.

The year 1976 was also the year it became overwhelmingly obvious that a publicly available index fund was badly needed. The question was which mutual fund company would put their business model on the chopping block by lowering fees? It was not likely to be an established mutual fund company whose fund managers and corporate officers were getting fat on high management fees. What was needed was an entirely new fund company with a mandate of lower management fees, lower trading costs, and direct distribution to the public.

Along Came John

In 1950, undergraduate students at Princeton University were required to write a senior thesis, and John C. Bogle was no exception. Bogle had not given much thought to the fledgling mutual fund industry as a topic until he read an article in the December 1949 issue of *Fortune* magazine. The article was entitled "Big Money in Boston," and it highlighted the "rapidly expanding and somewhat contentious [mutual fund] industry." He knew he had found his topic.[1]

During the next 18 months, Bogle meticulously researched the mutual fund industry and wrote a thesis entitled *The Economic Role of the Investment Company*. A copy of the thesis has been reproduced in *John Bogle on Investing, the First 50 Years* (McGraw-Hill, 2001). In his 100-page senior thesis, Bogle covered the history and dynamics of the fund industry. He also made the following recommendations to fund companies to increase sales: first, explicitly state a fund's objective; second, reduce sales loads and management fees; and third, make no claim to superiority over the market averages. The insight in Bogle's thesis would have been hailed as revolutionary if written by a seasoned veteran in the mutual fund industry, let alone a 21-year-old college student with no prior experience.

In 1975, Bogle had a chance to put all his ideas into action. As the chairman of the newly formed Vanguard Group, he set the ship's course squarely on low-cost investing. Bogle was resolute that Vanguard was going to be the first company to offer a low-cost index fund to the public. One reason the company was able to follow the mandate of low-cost investing was because of its unique corporate structure. The Vanguard Group is owned by the shareholders that invest in its mutual funds rather than by a private for-profit investment group. The company operates much like a co-op, where lower fees benefit all investors. This "mutual" mutual fund organization was a novel concept in the fund industry, and the Vanguard Group is still one of the only fund companies that operate under the structure that recognizes fund shareholders as company shareholders.

During May 1976, the Vanguard Group board of directors approved an index-style mutual fund, and a prospectus was filed with the U.S. Securities and Exchange Commission (SEC). The fund was called the First Index Investment Trust. The SEC approved the fund, and an opening date was set for August 31, 1976. The only thing missing from the equation was money. The fund needed an initial outlay of cash to get started.

In 1976, all mutual funds were still being sold through commission brokerage firms. Wall Street had the marketing clout, and Vanguard had no other alternative. Bogle needed a burst of assets to come into the new fund to get it rolling, so Vanguard solicited four large brokerage firms to act as its initial sales force. The goal was to bring in between $50 and $150 million in assets during the pre-opening road show. The commission to buy the fund was 6 percent.

Vanguard had the support of brokerage firm management, but the brokers themselves were less enthusiastic. Why should they sell a 6 percent commission mutual fund when they could make 8 percent selling another fund? The fact that the Vanguard fund was a good investment was irrelevant (this attitude still prevails at brokerage firms today). By August 30, 1976, only $11.4 million was raised for the new fund. That was a far cry from $50 million but enough to get started. As an aside, in February 1977, Vanguard dropped all sales agreements with brokerage firms and permanently eliminated all sales loads in their funds. In 1980, the name was changed from the First Index Investment Trust to the Vanguard 500 Index Fund.

From $11 Million to $110 Billion

The road to success was not easy. Right from its beginning, a deluge of critics assaulted the concept, particularly Vanguard's competitors. It was described as "Bogle's Folly" by one company's chief executive. Fidelity Chairman Edward Johnston told the press, "I can't believe that the great mass of investors are going to be satisfied with just receiving average returns." Another competitor put out a poster labeling the index fund as "un-American." Others asked who would want to do business with an average doctor, an average lawyer, or an average mutual fund. I was a stockbroker in the 1980s. We were told to tell clients who brought up the subject of index funds that "Average returns are for average investors, and we think our clients are above average."

Despite the overwhelming negative publicity, assets in the Vanguard 500 Index Fund began to grow as the fund's low fees led to above-average mutual fund category returns. Today, the Vanguard 500 Index Fund has nearly $110 billion in its two public share classes (Investors and Admiral).

THE GROWTH OF INDEX FUNDS

After the introduction of the Vanguard 500 Index Fund, seven years passed before a second index fund was established. In 1984, Wells Fargo introduced the Stagecoach Corporate Stock Fund, which was benchmarked to the S&P 500. Unfortunately, the fund had a 1 percent management fee, so it did not survive in the marketplace. By 1986, nine more index funds were offered by various companies; however, two funds covered obscure international markets, and a third fund was so expensive that it put itself out of business by 1993.

One of the new funds offered in 1986 was the Vanguard Bond Market Fund. It was benchmarked to the Lehman Brothers Aggregate Bond index. This was the first index fund devoted exclusively to the bond market, and Bogle was sure it was going to be a success. With a fee of only 0.25 percent per year, the index fund had a great cost advantage over actively managed bond funds that charged an average 1.0 percent per year. Since its inception, the Vanguard Total Bond Market Index Fund (renamed) has grown to more than $11 billion in assets. That is a phenomenal accomplishment for a bond fund.

A third index fund was added to the Vanguard quiver in 1987. The Extended Market Fund was designed to complement the Vanguard 500 index. It was benchmarked to the Wilshire 4500, an index of small- and medium-sized companies. Because it was not economical for Vanguard to invest in all 4,500 stocks, the Extended Market Fund invested in 2,000 of the largest companies in the Wilshire 4500 and another 800 small- and medium-sized companies based on a statistical sample. The result was a fund that performed very close to the Wilshire 4500 with very low costs. Thus, an investor in both the Vanguard 500 Index Fund and the Extended Market Fund had a full range of market exposure.

The 1990s

Vanguard accelerated the number of index funds in the family in the 1990s. Vanguard added index funds benchmarked to the Russell 2000 Small-Cap index as well as the Morgan Stanley Europe and Pacific Basin Indexes. The first competition also came into the marketplace in 1990. That year Fidelity started two index funds, one that modeled the S&P 500 index and one that modeled the Lehman Brothers Aggregate Bond index. By the end of 1990, there were 43 index funds available from several mutual fund companies. Most of these funds had little capital, and Vanguard stood as the undisputed leader with nine funds and nearly $5 billion in assets. The average expense ratio for the competitors was 0.5 percent versus 0.2 percent for Vanguard. The fact that competition was trying to imitate Vanguard was a triumph for John Bogle and the Vanguard team.

Through the remainder of the 1990s, Vanguard added 20 more index funds to bring the total at the end of the decade to 29. These funds included a large assortment of stock, bond, balanced, and real estate investment trust index funds. Vanguard was not alone in the growth. Due to a few good years for large-cap U.S. stocks, the popularity of mutual funds indexed to the S&P 500 exploded. The total number of index funds on the market expanded rapidly, from 43 in 1990 to 272 at the end of 1999. From 1997 to 1999, there were 40 new index funds benchmarked to the S&P 500.

It is strange how the world turns. All the major brokerage firms and mutual fund companies now compete against Vanguard with their own version of index funds, albeit at a higher cost. Even Fidelity reluctantly gave in. Most of these firms conceded in a desperate attempt to stop assets from transferring to Vanguard rather than out of a burning desire to serve their customers.

2007 AND BEYOND

The total amount in all index funds has growth to more than $1 trillion, which is about 25% of the amount invested in all mutual funds in aggregate.

The growth of index funds has been phenomenal. According to Morningstar Principia, by year-end 1986 there were 13 index funds available to the public. By 1996 there were 128 index funds. By mid-2006 there were 550 index funds. Even more phenomenal is the asset growth in those funds. The total amount in all index funds has grown from $11 million in 1976 to more than $1 trillion today. That is about 25 percent of the amount invested in all mutual funds in aggregate.

The number of new index funds is only limited by the number of new indexes that are created. Collecting index fund royalties has become a big business for the market index providers, such as Standard & Poor's, so it is not likely we will see a slowdown in new indexes occurring anytime soon.

Since 2002, most of the growth in index funds has occurred in exchange-traded funds (ETFs). These special index funds are benchmarked to the same indexes as open-end index funds, however they trade interday on a stock exchange rather than at the end of the day with the issuing mutual fund company. ETFs have become the central platform for issuing new index funds and for that reason warrant a chapter devoted exclusively to the topic (see Chapter 4).

TRANSPARENCY IS CRITICAL

The mutual fund industry has had a long and often uncomplimentary history in the United States. Recent media accounts of fraud, corruption, and cronyism are only the latest phase in a history of scandals. The mutual fund industry has provided an enormous service to society by enabling the average investor to participate easily in the financial markets. Unfortunately, during that past century Congress had to write thousands of regulations requiring fund managers and fund company executives to behave ethically. Since 2001, the pace of regulation has accelerated.

Index funds seem to be one bright spot in an otherwise questionable mutual fund marketplace. With index funds, investors know exactly what they are buying and why a particular fund is performing one way or another. The transparency of index funds and ETFs is refreshing and liberating, as are the lower costs. Accordingly, growth in popularity of index funds continues, and the issuance of new funds in new markets is almost guaranteed for years in the future.

CHAPTER SUMMARY

You can't buy the averages, but it is about time the public could.

Burton Malkiel, Princeton University, 1973

Index funds were born out of necessity. Poor investment returns, high fees, and questionable loyalties by the purveyors of active mutual funds caused an outcry from the academic community for a low-cost index solution. However, operational constraints were one reason index funds did not debut until late in the 20th century, and the reluctance of mutual fund companies to reduce fees was also a major stumbling block.

In 1976, John Bogle ended the wait for public index funds by steering the Vanguard Group in the direction of fund shareholders as company owners. That opened the door for considerably lower fees within the mutual funds under management. In August 1997, Vanguard introduce the first modern index fund benchmarked to the S&P 500 index. The novel concept revolutionized the investment industry and forced many competitors to create competing low-cost funds.

Today there are more than 600 index funds traded in the United States, and the list grows longer every year. The newest and most exciting type of index fund structure is called an exchange-traded fund, or ETF, and this is the topic of the next chapter.

NOTES

1. "The First Index Mutual Fund: A History of Vanguard Index Trust and the Vanguard Index Strategy," by John C. Bogle, 1997, available at www.JohnCBogle.com.

CHAPTER 4

Exchange-Traded Funds

Key Concepts

- Exchange-traded funds (ETFs) are index funds that trade like stocks.
- ETFs are bought and sold through a brokerage firm over a stock exchange.
- Commissions and trading spreads are added costs of ETFs.
- There are unique tax features of ETFs.

Exchange-traded funds (ETFs) are a growing phenomenon in the mutual fund industry. Like traditional open-end index funds, most ETFs track the performance of a specific market benchmark. Unlike traditional index funds, ETFs can be bought or sold like a stock anytime the stock market is open.

The unique blend between an index fund and a stock has gained rapid acceptance in the marketplace. Trading flexibility is only one of the unique advantages that make ETFs the index fund of choice for many individuals and professional money managers. As a result, most new index funds are being introduced in an ETF format.

How and why ETFs came into existence has an interesting history. Mutual funds have been around since the 1920s. ETFs entered the marketplace in the 1990s. The events that occurred between those launches make the concept unique. Those events will be explored in this chapter.

There is some misunderstanding in the marketplace about what ETFs are and what they are not. Some market gurus have written that ETFs are a revolution in the investment industry. One market newsletter writer even went as far as saying that open-end mutual funds are a dangerous investment and warned readers to sell their open-end funds in favor of ETFs. That line of thought is complete nonsense. The fact is ETFs *are* mutual funds. They are just a different structure of mutual funds. ETFs are vanilla ice cream smothered with a new flavor topping.

I believe it is helpful to think of ETFs as an evolution in the mutual fund industry, not a revolution. ETFs are another tool to put in your investment toolbox. They are one more avenue to explore when piecing together a well-balanced mutual fund portfolio.

OPEN-END AND CLOSED-END FUNDS

In the early 1990s, before ETFs appeared on the market, there were two types of mutual funds available to investors: open-end and closed-end. Each structure has its advantages and disadvantages. ETFs were created to combine the best of both worlds.

Morningstar Principia lists 23,080 mutual funds in the September 2006 database. The database can be divided between 6,858 distinct portfolios and 16,222 alternative share classes of those distinct portfolios; that is, A, B, C, and Z shares with different fees, commissions, and restrictions on purchase. ETFs are in their infancy. Slightly more than 304 ETFs on the U.S. markets and another 150 are in some stage of U.S. Securities and Exchange Commission (SEC) registration. That number is with minuscule in comparison with open-end funds. Nonetheless, popularity of using an ETF structure is exploding. Since 2005, more than 25 percent of all new mutual funds launched were ETFs.

An open-end mutual fund structure allows a fund company to create or redeem shares as necessary based on investor demand. It also means that trading is restricted to one buyer and one seller. The SEC allows open-end funds to create and redeem its shares only once per day, at the end of the day, based on the market close price.

Each day after the markets close, open-end mutual fund companies compute the true underlying value of the stocks and bonds in their funds and determine a fair per-share price for each fund.

This amount is called the net asset value (NAV), and its price per share is quoted in the newspaper. After fund NAVs are calculated, fund companies use this price to buy shares from investors who are redeeming and sell shares to investors who are buying. If there are more buyers than sellers, fund companies have the authority to create new shares at the NAV. If there are more sellers than buyers, funds can retire shares. The important point to remember about an open-end mutual fund is that all share creation and redemption is done at the closing NAV priced by the fund company itself.

Closed-end mutual funds were popular in the 1980s, but high initial commissions, ongoing expenses, and pricing inconsistencies held closed-end funds back from achieving mass investor appeal. Unlike open-end funds, the trading of closed-end funds takes place on a stock exchange during the day. The open market determines the price of a closed-end mutual fund, not the mutual fund company. Consequently, the market price of a fund can vary considerably from its NAV.

Unlike open-end funds, closed-end funds cannot issue more shares to new investors or easily redeem shares from a willing seller. Nor can the fund company trade shares on the stock exchange if the market price for the fund is less than or greater than the NAV of the fund (thus creating a risk-free profit). In fact, closed-end fund companies are prohibited from participating in the daily buying and selling of their own closed-end fund shares without specific approval from the SEC, and that is a rare event. Thus, the number of shares of a closed-end fund is typically fixed. The only way a fund company can issue shares is through a secondary offering, which requires SEC approval and shareholder consent. Secondary offerings take time to prepare, and it costs the fund money to issue new shares through an underwriter.

Because the number of shares is basically fixed, frequently the market price of a closed-end fund will trade at a large premium or discount price to its actual underlying NAV. Those discounts and premiums may last several months or years because the company has no share issuance or redemption "arbitrage" mechanism to bring the market price in line with the underlying NAV. If there were a way for the fund company to immediately issue new shares or redeem existing shares, discounts and premiums would be arbitraged until the spread went away. Unfortunately, closed-end funds are locked into an archaic structure. The commission costs, high fees, and persistent disparity between market price and NAV make closed-end funds an undesirable structure for indexing a market.

THE FIRST EXCHANGE-TRADED FUND

In 1990, the SEC issued the Investment Company Act Release No. 17809. This act granted the law firm of Leland, O'Brien, Rubinstein Associates, Incorporated (LOR) the right to create a new hybrid security called a SuperTrust. The SuperTrust had the share creation and redemption characteristics of an open-end fund and traded on the stock exchange like a closed-end fund. On November 5, 1992, after additional tweaking and a few regulatory delays, LOR introduced the revolutionary new product called the Index Trust Super-Unit. The SuperUnit was an index fund of sorts designed to give institutional investors the ability to buy or sell an entire basket of stocks in one trade on the stock exchange. The 1992 SuperTrust had a "maturity" of three years, at which time a new SuperTrust was to be introduced in 1995 to replace maturing units.

The SuperUnit was unique because institutional investors could trade the units for the actual shares of stock in the underlying investment. SuperUnits traded on an exchange, just like closed-end funds. Unlike closed-end funds, if SuperUnits started selling at a discount to their NAV, investors could profit risk-free by purchasing the underpriced units while simultaneously selling the underlying shares in the unit. They would then turn in the unit and would be issued stocks. These stocks would replace the stocks that they sold. This entire transaction created a risk-free profit for the institutional investor. If the SuperUnits were selling at a premium, there was a reverse trade that allowed investors to profit risk-free. Although the arbitrage of SuperUnits sounds like a lot of work, institutional investors could accomplish the task with a few keystrokes. The redemption feature built into SuperUnits neatly eliminated the discount and premium problem that plagued closed-end funds.

The SuperTrust was launched in 1992 with $1 billion in assets. It was a three-year trust that terminated in 1995. The idea was to issue replacement units in 1995, but that never materialized. The cost, complexity, and adverse rulings by the Internal Revenue Service (IRS) precluded any trading from developing or occurring in the retail marketplace, which meant no demand from individual investors. In addition, the SuperTrust idea was pursued after the 1987 crash as a way for institutions to hedge stock portfolios with one simple trade. By the time LOR received regulatory approval (five years in the making), the over-the-counter (OTC) market was developing a simpler product.

SPIDERS CREEP IN

The American Stock Exchange (AMEX) took advantage of the SuperTrust Act of 1992 and petitioned the SEC to allow the creation of the first Standard & Poor's Depositary Receipts (SPDRs) in 1993. The official name of the product was SPDR Trust Series 1, however they are better known as "Spiders" (symbol: SPY). The fund is benchmarked to the S&P 500 index and has the same redemption feature as SuperUnits. However, the structure was simpler than its predecessor SuperTrust and shares were affordable. That meant individual investors and investment advisors could participate in the market.

Each SPDR unit trades at approximately one-tenth the index value of the S&P 500 index. For example, if the S&P 500 were quoted at 1,200, the price of one SPDR unit would be within pennies of $120. The low price per unit of Spiders gave it broad investor appeal. Individuals could buy as few as one unit if they preferred. The low cost of Spiders also allowed them to compete head to head with the open-end index funds, such as the Vanguard 500 Index Fund. Stockbrokers now had an attractive alternative for clients considering transferring to Vanguard. The fees and expenses of SPDR units were only slightly higher than Vanguard 500 Index Fund shares.

The market value of Spiders is kept very close to the underlying index through an arbitrage mechanism similar to SuperUnits. Institutional investors profit from a small mismatch in price between the market value of Spiders and the stocks in the underlying S&P 500 index. If one value is greater than the other, the expensive one is sold and the cheap one is bought. This "risk-free" arbitrage trade is repeated until there is a near equilibrium in price. The two prices will get to within a penny of each other but are rarely the same price because arbitrage will stop when the transaction costs become greater than the risk-free profit. According to the AMEX, actively traded ETFs trade within a few pennies of the underlying index more than 80 percent of the time.

S&P 500 SPDRs are still one of the most popular ETFs on the market today. There are currently $60 billion worth of SPY shares in circulation.

Riding high on the success of S&P 500 SPDRs, the Bank of New York introduced the MidCap SPDR in 1995 (symbol: MDY). This security is nicknamed "Middies" and was the first ETF created to track the performance of the S&P MidCap 400 index. The MidCap 400 index is a composite of stocks that have market values between $2 billion and $10 billion. The structure of the MidCap SPDR is similar to the S&P 500 SPDR and was also widely accepted by individual and institutional investors.

ADVANCES IN ETF DEVELOPMENT

In 1996, Morgan Stanley joined forces with Barclays Global Investors and the American Stock Exchange to create World Equity Benchmark Shares (WEBS). This series of ETFs was benchmarked to 13 different world equity markets from Australia to Belgium.

The structure of WEBS was considerably different than the structure of SPDRs. The latter was organized as a unit investment trust (UIT), which by SEC standards meant it must replicate an index exactly. Consequently, there can be no variation in the holdings of S&P 500 SPDRs and the S&P 500 index. WEBS was organized as an investment company rather than a UIT. A major difference in the two structures is that an investment company does not require that managers of index funds match the indexes exactly. That variation gave WEBS fund managers some discretion to modify the funds as needed to work around difficult operational and trading demands associated with foreign indexes. Some stocks in foreign indexes are simply hard to trade. In some countries, the stocks of one or two companies dominate an index, and the SEC mandates that no one issue may be larger than 25 percent of the portfolio. Also, securities that are greater than 5 percent of a portfolio may not be more than 50 percent of the entire portfolio in aggregate. As an investment company, WEBS managers could maneuver around these issues by "sampling" an index in an attempt to create an optimized portfolio that tracks an index as best as can be expected.

The second difference between SPDRs and WEBS was the way dividends were handled. Under the unit investment trust structure of SPDRs, cash dividends paid by the underlying stocks are retained in a non-interest-bearing account until the end of the quarter and then they are paid out to shareholders as one lump sum. WEBS had more flexibility in dividend payments. The investment company structure allowed WEBS to reinvest dividends in more stocks immediately after they are received by the fund. WEBS still paid dividends like a traditional mutual fund, however the reinvestment feature in-between quarterly dividend payment allows for a closer tracking to the indexes.

WEBS are responsible for other important innovations in ETFs. They made a specific advance in a method of arbitrage that acts to reduce the tax liability for investors holding WEBS in a taxable account. SPDRs initially did not petition the SEC to use this tax-reducing trading strategy, but they eventually changed. We will discuss the tax benefit of ETFs in more detail later in this chapter and in Chapter 5. In a final innovation, WEBS were allowed to use the terms *index fund* and *ETF* together in their marketing literature, a combination the SEC had not allowed previously (and one that has gotten out of hand in this author's opinion).

Diamonds, Sector SPDRs, and Cubes

In 1997, the SEC issued an order covering "Diamonds," which is an ETF based on the Dow Jones Industrial Average (DJIA) and is managed by State Street Global Advisors. Diamonds incorporate the tax benefits of WEBS although created in a unit investment trust structure. I personally believe the 30-stock DJIA is too narrow of a benchmark to invest in, but the cachet of the name makes it attractive to many self-directed retail clients. As a result, Diamonds has become the fifth largest ETF on the market with $2.8 billion in assets and 2 million shares traded daily.

State Street changed ETF structures in 1998 when they filed for Sector SPDRs. The firm opted to organize Sector SPDRs as an investment company. This change allowed the new funds to have all the tax benefits and dividend reinvestment benefits of WEBS. The nine ETFs were benchmarked to nine S&P 500 sectors, and only stocks included in the S&P 500 are included. The sectors are materials, health care, consumer stables, consumer discretionary, energy, financial, industrial, technology, and utilities (see Chapter 7 for more information). In 1998, the SEC also issued an order allowing the older SPDRs to incorporate the same favorable tax treatment as the new funds.

During March 1999, the Bank of New York introduced the NASDAQ 100 Trust under the unit investment trust structure. The NASDAQ 100 index is made up of the largest 100 nonfinancial companies (based on their market capitalization) that trade in the NASDAQ marketplace. The trust was nicknamed "Cubes" because it traded on the AMEX under the trade symbol QQQ. In the late 1999, technology made up almost 70 percent of Cubes, and a bubbling hot technology market allowed the security to gain a massive following by institutional and individual investors. As of June 2006, technology still accounts for 55 percent of the trust. When trading of shares moved from the AMEX to the NASDAQ exchange in 2004, NASDAQ added another Q to the symbol. The current NASDAQ symbol is QQQQ.

Barclays Global Investors Makes a Big Move in 1999

Barclays Global Investors (BGI) created the first index strategy in 1971. The firm was also the first to launch an ETF under the Investment Company Act structure with the creation of WEBS in 1996. Soon after, BGI recognized the tremendous potential for ETFs and decided to greatly expand its ETF product offering.

During 1999, BGI petitioned the SEC for an order covering 50 indexes with 50 new ETF products. The new iShares cover a wide variety of U.S., international, and global stock benchmarks including S&P, Russell, Morgan Stanley Capital International (MSCI), and Dow Jones indexes, among others. The funds cover market capitalization, style (value and growth), sectors or industries, and single countries or regions.

BGI launched their salvo of new ETF funds into the marketplace in May 2000, and those funds were an immediate hit with investors. With the extensive selection within the iShares fund family, in 2000 BGI became the undisputed ETF leader as measured by the number and depth of funds.

The success of BGI's ETF offerings opened the floodgates for more innovation from mainline mutual fund companies to start-up firms. Despite a bear market in stocks that lasted three years, ETF creation and issuance became one of the few bright spots in the mutual fund industry during the early 2000s.

The New, New Thing

Vanguard introduced its first ETF in 2001 and called the product Vanguard Index Participation Equity Receipts (VIPERs). The VIPERs concept was unique in that it was structured as a share class of an existing mutual fund. Up until this point, the only ETFs were new funds.

Vanguard Total Stock Market VIPERs was the first offering as a share class of an existing open-end mutual fund. The difference between Vanguard's open-end Total Stock Market Index Fund and the new VIPERs share class is that the ETF trades when the stock market is open and the open-end fund shares trade after the market is closed.

In January 2002, Vanguard launched its second ETF offering, the Vanguard Extended Market VIPERs. This fund tracks the performance of the S&P Completion Index, which includes all stocks except those in the S&P 500. VIPERs are a unique twist to the ETF marketplace and may prompt other open-end mutual funds to issue ETFs.

During 2006, Vanguard dropped the VIPERs name from all their ETFs and now refer to those funds as simply ETFs. Vanguard also has four fixed income index funds in registration with the SEC that are class shares of the existing Vanguard fixed income funds. Consequently, the word VIPERs will no longer fit because the E stood for *equity*.

No other mutual fund has launched an ETF share class on an existing index fund. Perhaps the reason why is that they would have to pay Vanguard a royalty on the product because Vanguard owns a patent on the structure.

ETF Products in the United States and Abroad

More than 300 ETFs have been issued on the U.S. exchanges and 700 have been launched worldwide (Figure 4-1). As of December 2006, there are also more than 200 new funds in registration worldwide.

FIGURE 4-1

Worldwide ETF Growth

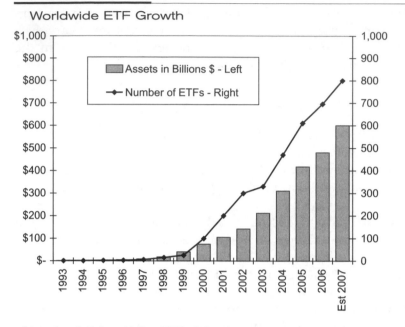

Source: *Journal of Indexes*, July/August 2006, vol. 8, no. 4.

The value of all ETFs combined totals nearly $500 billion as of mid-2006. That amount is expected to reach $1 trillion in assets by 2010.

The vast majority of funds are benchmarked to U.S. and international stock indexes, and a few to the bond markets. However, the marketplace is expanding rapidly. ETFs exist that are benchmarked to individual commodities, such as gold, silver, and a barrel of oil. For more commodity diversification, ETFs are also available that are benchmarked to one of several commodities indexes such as the Goldman Sachs Commodities Index. There are also foreign currencies ETFs. If you are planning on buying a castle in Europe next year, you can hedge the value of your purchase with an ETF benchmarked to a Euro denominated short-term fixed-income fund.

The distinction between index funds and actively managed funds is being blurred by the issuers of ETFs. Over the past few years there has been a rash of new ETFs that have greater resemblance to quasi-active management than passive index investing. Although the issuing companies called their products index funds, the method by which most securities are chosen for those funds in no way resembles any index methodology to speak of. In this author's opinion, the only reason the issuers call those ETFs index funds is to create marketing spin. See Chapter 9 for more information on "spindexes."

The next major innovation in ETFs will be actively managed funds. The SEC is reviewing several proposals for the structure of the product and should approve one or more of those structures in the coming years. The stumbling block for actively managed ETFs is how the fund manager would disclose the holdings of its portfolio as needed each day without inviting front-running of trades by hedge funds. ETF creation requires the holdings of a portfolio be disclosed daily so that authorized participants can turn in stocks and receive new shares, and that leads us into our next section on the mechanics of ETFs.

HOW ETFs WORK

The underlying structure of an ETF is different from the structure of an open-end index fund. As an index fund investor, it is important to understanding those differences because there are certain costs associated with ETFs that can be minimized if traded correctly.

At the end of each trading day, open-end fund companies offer mutual fund shares directly to the public for cash and redeem shares directly from the public for cash. The exchange price is always the net-asset-value, or NAV. Buyers and sellers exchange at the same NAV price. Open-end funds are distributed either through a direct sale, as in the case of a no-load fund company such as the Vanguard Group, or through a brokerage firm that charges a commission, as in the case of American Funds. The commission is added onto the NAV price.

ETF shares are not sold directly to the public for cash. Instead, fund companies exchange large blocks of ETF shares called creation units for actual shares of stock turned in by "authorized participants" such as Goldman Sachs, Smith Barney, and Merrill Lynch. These are not small exchanges of common stock for ETF shares. Most transactions are at least 50,000 ETF shares or multiples thereof.

Participants turn in the exact names and quantities of the underlying stocks that make up an ETF block plus a cash component, which represents the accumulated stock dividends that have yet to be paid. They then receive one *creation unit*, which is a block of ETF shares. After an ETF creation unit is issued, the institutions either hold the unit in their own portfolio or break it up into individual shares and sell those individual ETF shares to the general public via the stock exchange. When an institution redeems an ETF creation unit, everything happens in reverse. An authorized institution turns in one creation unit, and in return they receive individual securities plus a cash portion from unpaid dividends.

As an individual investor, you cannot transact directly with the mutual fund company. Rather, all trades must go through a stock exchange. That means if you were interested in buying a single ETF share, you need to contact a brokerage firm to purchase the share on a stock exchange. That share would be from a creation unit that was broken up by an institutional investor and is offering individual ETF shares on the open market. It does not matter which creation unit your share comes from or which authorized participant created it because they are all exactly the same.

The market price of a single ETF share usually trades close to its NAV but rarely at NAV. That is because of dividend accruals, the bid-ask spread in the underlying securities that make up the fund, and noise created by short lags in trading information.

Different ETFs have different pricing structures. For example, the NAV of a fund could be targeted at one-tenth of the index value, one-twentieth of the index value, or some other set fraction depending on the fund. The NAV of S&P 500 SPDRs (symbol: SPY) should trade at one-tenth of the index value of the S&P 500. The NAV of the United States Oil Fund (symbol: USO) is meant to mirror the price of a barrel of oil.

The value of ETF shares should closely track their NAV price but will not likely match. The difference between NAV and price creates a market premium or discount. If the ETF shares are trading at a large enough discount or premium to their NAV, this is where institutions can make a risk-free return. If market forces have caused the price of an ETF to be less than the price of the underlying stocks and cash in a fund, institutional investors will trade in common stocks and buy creation units. Conversely, if the price of an ETF is trading at a price higher than the underlying stocks and cash, institutions can trade back ETF blocks and receive higher priced individual stocks. Institutional investors continuously monitor ETF prices and underlying securities looking for a risk-free return. The arbitrage mechanism of ETF shares eliminated the persistent premiums, and discounts are common in the closed-end mutual fund marketplace.

ETF ARBITRAGE CREATES A TAX BREAK

The next few paragraphs explain a specific tax benefit that is unique to ETF investors, and Chapter 5 covers the tax benefits of index funds in general. People who buy equity ETF shares in taxable accounts, such as a joint account or trust account, will find their tax bill may be slightly lower at the end of the year than if they had purchased the same amount in a comparable open-end index fund. This tax break is a benefit created from the arbitrage mechanism described above.

As explained earlier, authorized participant investors turn in a predetermined portfolio of individual securities and are issued a new creation unit by the fund company. When the fund manager brings in the new stock, each stock is assigned a *cost basis* based on the market price of the stock when it came into the fund. For example, whatever the market price of Microsoft (MSFT) was at the time it was turned into the fund is the cost of those particular MSFT shares in the fund. These new MSFT shares are added to the already existing shares of MSFT stock in the fund but accounted for separately for tax reasons. Every time a new creation unit is formed, more MSFT stock is turned in, and those shares are given a different cost basis.

When institutions redeem a creation unit, they turn in a unit and receive common stock back, but not necessarily the same shares they turned in. The ETF fund manager can issue out different shares that may have a lower cost basis than what the institution originally turned in. For example, there are many different tax lots of MSFT in the fund, and the manager of the ETF can choose which tax lot of MSFT shares to send back to the redeeming institution. If the manager issues the lowest cost MSFT shares back to the redeeming institutions, they reduce the unrealized capital gains that remain in the fund. The redemption of creation units by authorized participants creates a huge tax benefit to the holders of ETFs because it rids the fund of gains that may otherwise eventually have to be distributed to shareholders, which they would pay taxes on. As long as there is an active market for creation units, most of the unrealized capital gains of an ETF can be erased.

The tax strategy within ETFs is no different than an individual investor making a gift from a stock portfolio. If a taxable investor bought 100 shares of MSFT at two different times and at two different prices, and both "tax lots" are at a profit, one of the 100-share lots will have a different unrealized profit than the other 100 shares. If the investor chooses to gift 100 shares of MSFT to a charity, they should gift the lowest cost shares first because that offers the investor the best long term tax advantage.

Table 4-1 illustrates the tax advantage of ETF shares over an open-end mutual fund. In the 1990s, when stock returns were up significantly, S&P 500 SPDRs issued minimal realized capital gains to investors, whereas the Vanguard 500 Index Fund issued capital gains to investors, each year.

Since the 1990s, greater volume in all ETFs has allowed managers to be very efficient in historically tax-inefficient investment styles. For example, small-cap value funds traditionally have high turnover of stocks resulting in large capital gain distributions. The buildup of capital gains does not occur in small-cap value ETFs because fund managers are able to push out low cost-basis stocks to authorized participants during the redemption process.

TABLE 4-1

Capital Gain Distributions as a Percentage of NAV

	S&P 500 SPDRs	Vanguard 500 Index Fund
1993	0.07%	0.07%
1994	0.00%	0.47%
1995	0.02%	0.23%
1996	0.16%	0.36%
1997	0.00%	0.66%
1998	0.00%	0.37%
1999	0.00%	0.74%

Source: Bloomberg, Morningstar Principia.

Vanguard Uses ETFs to Lower Taxes
in Open-End Funds

Open-end stock index funds have no way to rid themselves of unrealized capital gains that built up in a fund. Eventually, those gains will have to be distributed to shareholders, and those investors that hold the funds in a taxable account will have to pay taxes on the gains. The Vanguard Group has developed a unique way to help reduce that problem. Vanguard ETFs are a share class of an existing open-end fund. This allows a Vanguard manager to take advantage of the arbitrage mechanism in ETFs to reduce the capital gains embedded in the existing open-end share classes. As arbitrage of Vanguard ETFs occurs, the fund manager can distribute some of the low cost-basis stock built up over the years in the open-end fund and distribute it to the authorized participants. That lowers the unrealized gain in the fund and will ultimately benefit all classes of shareholders.

It would not be a surprise if other large mutual fund companies follow Vanguard's lead and offered ETF shares in addition to open-end shares. This strategy would help lower the capital gain tax liability that has built up in existing open-end shares. The disadvantage of using ETFs on open-end funds is the royalty those fund companies would have to pay to Vanguard to use the patent.

THE COST OF INVESTING IN ETFs

There are four potential costs individual investors face when investing in ETFs. First, the management charge in all mutual funds; second, the brokerage commission to buy and sell ETFs; third, the spread between the true underlying value of the fund and the market value of ETF shares; and fourth, the dividend drag of holding cash in an ETF that has a UIT structure.

Internal Expenses

An ETF's annual expense ratio is an internal fee that is paid to the fund sponsor. It covers portfolio management, accounting, legal expenses, advertising, and other miscellaneous charges. In addition, ETFs must pay a licensing fee to the index provider firm whose index it uses. All S&P 500 index funds pay Standard & Poor's a negotiated royalty each year. The expense ratio is typically expressed as a percentage of assets of the fund. However, in a new fund, it is common for a portion of the management fees to be waved until the assets in the fund build to critical mass. That holds the fund expenses down and attracts new investors.

Table 4-2 presents a sample cost comparison of Vanguard open-end mutual fund Investor share class to their ETF share class. In addition to lower expense ratios on ETFs, Vanguard charges purchase and redemption fees on several open-end funds. There are no extra fees on Vanguard ETFs although there is a brokerage commission cost to buy and sell shares.

Why do Vanguard ETFs charge lower fees than the open-end shares? It is because ETF shares cost Vanguard less money to administer. The brokerage firms bear almost all the administrative costs. When an investor buys a Vanguard ETF, they do so through a brokerage firm. That alleviates Vanguard from the administrative tasks of individual shareholder record-keeping, sending monthly account statements and year-end tax reports. The savings is passed on to ETF shareholders in the form of lower fees.

On average, the fees of ETFs are similar to low-cost, open-end index funds. However, that is not true of all funds. Some ETFs are very expensive in comparison with open-end funds. Individual

TABLE 4-2

A Comparison of Vanguard Fees

Vanguard Fund	Investor Class Expense Ratio	Other Open-End Fees	ETF Expense Ratio	Other ETF Fees
Total Stock Market Index	0.19%	None	0.07%	None
REIT Index	0.21%	1% fee if held <1 year	0.12%	None
European Stock Index	0.27%	2% fee if held <2 months	0.18%	None
Emerging Markets Index	0.45%	0.5% to buy and sell	0.30%	None

Source: The Vanguard Group.

investors should avoid these higher cost ETFs. A complete list of current ETF fees is available at www.IndexUnivierse.com.

Commission Costs and Market Spreads

The expense ratios of the popular ETFs are on par with the expenses of open-end index funds, but there are other costs to buy and sell ETF shares that are not associated with open-end funds. ETFs trade on stock exchanges and that implies trading commissions. All ETF trading is conducted through brokerage firms, and the commission you pay depends on where you trade. In addition to commissions, there is a second cost inherent in all exchange transactions. That is the trading spread. The spread is the difference between a stock's ask price (what you can buy it for) and its bid price (what you can sell it for). Spread costs can vary. With ETFs, there are several factors that influence the spread. First, the less trading volume that occurs in an ETF, the larger the spread between the bid and ask. Second, the larger the average spread in the individual securities that make up the ETF, the larger the spread in the ETF itself. Third, the exchange you trade on has a determining factor in the spread. Your broker is required to get the best execution on your trade, meaning they are supposed to find the best market to trade in. However, I do not believe that always occurs, particularly for smaller trade amounts.

Let's look at an example of an ETF trade using Spiders to show the impact of commissions and the bid-ask spread. Suppose it is midday and you heard the S&P 500 was down about 50 points and is trading at 1,200.00. Your hunch is that the market will recover the loss by the end of the day, so you call your broker and place an order to buy 100 Spiders at the current market price. Your broker immediately executes the trade at $120.05 per share, which is approximately one-tenth the value of the S&P 500 at the time. The total cost to trade 100 Spiders is $12,055 including a $50 commission. The extra $5 represents the spread between the bid of $120 and the ask price of $120.05. If you are right about the market and the S&P 500 recovers all the loss, the value of your 100 Spiders increases to $12,500. If you sell at $125, you will pay another $50 commission, and your total gain will be $395. The $105 given up to Wall Street is more than 20 percent of the investment's profit potential. That is quite a bit less than the theoretical no-commission, no-spread gain of $500. Obviously, the more you trade, the more you lose to commissions and spreads, which is one reason I advocate keeping your trades to a minimum.

More on Premiums, Discounts, and Stale Prices

ETF shares trade independently of the securities they are composed of. This means the market value of an ETF share can differ from the underlying NAV of the stocks and cash that make up that share. Premiums and discounts create an arbitrage opportunity for institutional investors, but they also add an element of risk for individuals. If an ETF is trading at a premium when you buy shares, you paid more than it was worth. If you sell at a discount, you sold at less than the shares were worth.

Most prices that individuals get on their home computers are 20-minute delayed. You must pay the exchanges to access real-time quotes. That means individual investors trading from work or home have no idea what the true underlying value of an ETF should be at the time they trade. Your broker can get better information for you before trading, but unfortunately even the brokers do not have up-to-the-second information because a listing exchange disseminates NAV information every 15 seconds. Finally, the underlying trading value of many international ETFs is not readily available when overseas exchanges are closed. See Table 4-3 for an example of NAV symbols.

TABLE 4-3

A Sampling of ETF Price and Interday NAV Symbols

ETF Name	Price Symbol	Interday NAV Symbol
S&P 500 SPDRs	SPY	SXV
Vanguard Total Stock Market	VTI	TSJ
NASDAQ 100	QQQQ	QXV
iShares Mid Cap 400	IJJ	NJJ
United States Oil LP	USO	UOI
Source: The Vanguard Group.		

Dividend Drag

A second hidden cost of UITs is called dividend drag. As underlying stocks in an ETF pay dividends, those dividends accumulate in the fund over a period of time. The fund management deducts fees and expenses from the dividend, and the remaining cash is passed through to shareholders on a quarterly basis. Once an ETF dividend is distributed, investors can automatically reinvest the cash in more shares through their broker. Due to different dividend payment dates by companies, there is always a small *cash component* of the ETF that is not invested in stocks. Because cash generates less return than stocks (most of the time), it creates a slight drag on the performance of the fund.

Dividend payments are also treated differently by index providers who calculate an index return. S&P assumes that stock dividends are automatically reinvested in the stock of the companies on the index on the ex-dividend date. Unfortunately, the actual dividend payment date can occur several days or weeks after the index goes ex-dividend. Because dividend reinvestment only occurs after cash is paid, it is technically impossible for any index fund, including ETFs, to attain the exact performance of the benchmark index.

There are also differences in ETF structures that affect cash flow and performance. The iShare structure allows BGI to reinvest dividends and interest back into the market while waiting for the next ETF dividend payment date. Conversely, the UIT structure of SPDRs prohibits the reinvestment of dividends paid by securities in the funds. SPDRs hold company dividends in cash for up to three months before the quarterly ETF payment to shareholders. The drag affects the performance of SPDRs. When the market goes up, SPDRs lag the market, but when the market goes down, the cash can help performance. During the bull market in the 1990s, the cash drag of S&P 500 SPDRs was about 0.25 percent per year. On the other had, cash drag helped SPDRs outperform most other S&P 500 index funds during down-markets from 2000 to 2002.

CHAPTER SUMMARY

There are many benefits and several disadvantages of using ETFs in a portfolio. The benefits include the flexibility to trade anytime the markets are open and the inherent tax advantage that institutional arbitrage creates. The disadvantages include the extra layer of cost caused by commissions, market spreads, and potential dividend drag. Depending on your objective, ETFs may be the best way for you to invest in index funds.

ETFs are an exciting area of the index fund marketplace. Each year the structure and depth of this marketplace expands exponentially. Today, over 700 ETFs trade worldwide, and the pace of new issuance is accelerating. It is my belief that there will be more than 1,000 ETFs available by 2010 holding more than $1 trillion in assets. ETFs are a growth market for index fund investors.

CHAPTER 5

Tax Advantages of Index Funds and Exchange-Traded Funds

Key Concepts

- One should understand the taxation of mutual funds.
- It is important to compare the tax efficiency of index funds to active funds.
- Mutual fund managers can reduce your taxes.
- Tax swapping can increase your after-tax total return.

All mutual fund investors pay expenses. The cost of investing in mutual funds includes management fees, legal fees, administrative charges, and sometimes sales commissions and 12b-1 (marketing) fees. Investors who buy mutual funds in a taxable account incur another fee that can dwarf all others, which is the cost of taxation. If you are considering investing taxable money in an open-end mutual fund or exchange-traded fund (ETF), pay close attention to this chapter. It highlights one of the great advantages that open-end index funds and ETFs have over actively managed mutual funds. Index funds are very tax-efficient, and that can save you a bundle of money.

THE MECHANICS OF MUTUAL FUND TAXATION

There are four events that can trigger a tax consequent for mutual fund shareholders. Three of those events are direct cash distributions by a mutual fund, and the fourth is triggered by investors selling appreciated shares of a fund.

Each year, all mutual funds are required to distribute ordinary income, dividends, and realized capital gains to shareholders. Those distributions are subjected to personal income tax, even if the shareholder automatically reinvests the cash in more shares. Most mutual fund managers do not hesitate to distribute all income and capital gain earnings to shareholders because the fund itself would have to pay a 35 percent tax if they were not passed along.

All income and capital gain distributions are reported to shareholders annually on Form 1099-DIV. The form is sent in late January for the previous tax year. Form 1099-DIV is compiled and sent by the brokerage firm or the mutual fund company that holds your fund shares, otherwise known as the custodian. The form will list all taxable distributions by type so there is no misunderstanding between ordinary income, short-term capital gains, and long-term capital gains. Capital gain distributions that are short-term are taxed the same as ordinary income, whereas long-term gains are taxed at lower capital gains rates.

Not all cash distributions are taxable. Municipal bond funds distribute mostly tax-free interest income. In addition, some non-taxable mutual fund distributions are considered a return of principal on your original investment. All nontaxable and taxable distributions will be listed on Form 1099-DIV that you receive from the mutual fund company or brokerage firm that holds your mutual funds.

A fourth event that may trigger a tax liability is the personal sale or exchange of mutual fund shares. Thus, keep good records. Even if you exchange one mutual fund for a different mutual fund of the same fund family, you are still liable to pay capital gains tax if there was a gain. At a minimum, you should keep a separate folder for each mutual fund and at the end of each year match up any share sales with a purchase price. Any gain or loss should be reported on Schedule D of your tax return.

The Internal Revenue Service (IRS) has stated that it is your responsibility to track gains and losses on the sale of mutual fund shares, not the mutual fund company or brokerage firm. However, starting in 2007, mutual fund companies and brokerage firms will be required to report the cost basis of shares to the IRS to discourage cheating. That is true even if the mutual fund was not purchased though your current broker. The original cost basis must now stay with the fund shares as they transfer from one brokerage firm to another.

The Taxation of Ordinary Income Dividends

Whether you buy a stock mutual fund or bond mutual fund, the securities in the fund will likely pay some type of cash income. "Ordinary" dividend income represents the distribution of all dividend and interest income earned from stocks, bonds, and cash equivalents in a mutual fund. Shareholders must report all ordinary income the tax year for which they are generated.

Unless otherwise designated by the fund, ordinary dividends are reported as "dividend income" on Form 1040 of an individual tax return. Dividend income is taxed as ordinary income by the IRS, which means it is taxed at the same rate as your earned income from employment. Ordinary income tax is based on a progressive, tiered system. The more ordinary income you make, the higher your tax rate bracket. The Tax Act of 2001 lowered the ordinary income tax rate from 39.5 percent to 35 percent.

There is little a mutual fund company can do to reduce the effect of taxes on ordinary dividend income. Most mutual funds draw their management fees and expenses from dividend and interest income earned, which reduce the amount of the distribution. However, I do not see paying high fees to lower income as a tax benefit. Index fund expenses are typically low, so the dividend and interest income are generally greater than the cost of running the fund, and ordinary income taxes must be paid to Uncle Sam.

The Taxation of Capital Gain Distributions

The underlying holdings of all mutual funds change each year as assets are bought and sold or companies are bought out or merged. This is true for index funds as well as actively managed accounts. Some of these occurrences result in a realized capital gain, whereas other transactions result in a realized capital loss. At the end of the year, realized losses are offset against realized gains, and if there is a gain for the year, the realized capital gain is distributed as cash to shareholders. Shareholders who hold mutual funds in a taxable account must pay a capital gains tax on these distributions.

There are two types of capital gains distributed by mutual funds and two tax rates. The first type of capital gain is a short-term gain. These are the net gains on securities held less than one year. The short-term capital gains tax is the same as your ordinary income tax rate. For example, if you are paying 35 percent in income tax on ordinary income, you will also pay 35 percent on short-term capital gain distributions. The second type of capital gain distribution is a long-term gain. This is reported to you in a different block on Form 1099-DIV. Long-term capital gains are taxed at a lower rate than short-term gains. For example, you may have to pay 35 percent on short-term gains but only 15 percent on long-term gains. Depending on an investor's ordinary income tax rate, 15 percent is the highest tax rate the individual would pay on long-term capital gain distributions.

Reducing Capital Gain Distributions

Because mutual fund managers must pay net capital gains each year, and taxable shareholders must pay taxes on these gains, it seems logical that the fund manager would try to reduce the amount of realized gains by holding the winning stocks in the mutual fund rather than selling them—but sometimes logic does not prevail in the investment industry. On average, mutual fund managers do not manage portfolios for maximum tax-efficiency. The average equity mutual fund has more than 60 percent turnover of stocks, which can create a heavy tax burden for some investors.

After-tax returns of mutual funds are almost always lower than pre-tax returns. For example, Table 5-1 illustrates the average effect of taxes on mutual fund returns. It assumes that all funds are sold at the end of the period ending June 2006. The after-tax return is the actual after-tax in pocket return an investor subjected to the highest tax rates would have achieved. The tax ratio is computed by Morningstar and represents the average tax drag on the funds during the period measured.

According to the data from Table 5-1, the 10-year after-tax median performance of U.S. Growth & Income equity funds has been approximately 1.8 percent less than their pretax returns. Much of the difference is the result of capital gains tax created from portfolio turnover. The median portfolio turnover of funds in the study was 55 percent. That creates a lot of short-term capital gains that are taxed at

TABLE 5-1

Ten-Year After-Tax Returns of U.S. Large Core Growth
and Income

	10-year Pre-tax Returns	Percent of Gain Lost to Taxes	10-year After-Tax Returns
Vanguard 500 Index Fund (VFINX)	8.9%	15%	7.5%
S&P 500 SPDRs (SPY)	8.8%	16%	7.4%
Median US Growth & Index Large Core Fund	7.9%	23%	6.1%
Source: Morningstar Principia (June 2006).			

a higher ordinary income tax rate. Paying 23 pecent of your gains to
Uncle Sam in the form of taxes is a significant penalty.

Low turnover creates a large tax advantage in index funds. The
Vanguard 500 Index Fund and S&P 500 SPDRs had turnover in
those portfolios averaging only 7 percent per year. Lower turnover
ensured that long-term capital gains rates applied to most securities
in those funds. Subsequently, investors pay less taxes overall and
experience a higher after-tax performance. On a pretax basis, the
Vanguard 500 Index Fund outperformed the median fund in its category by 1 percent. After tax, the Vanguard 500 Index Fund outperformed the median fund in its category by 1.4 percent.

Note that the performance of the Vanguard 500 Index Fund
was higher than the performance of SPDRs. The return was in part
a result of dividend reinvestment. The Vanguard 500 Index Fund
was able to reinvest company dividends as they were paid, whereas SPDRs were not able to reinvest. See Chapter 4 for a detailed
explanation.

Tax-Managed Funds

If mutual fund managers were able to eliminate or defer realized
capital gains by reducing the amount of trading, investors would
pay less tax and have more money to spend or invest. A few mutual fund companies have introduced *tax-managed* funds, sometimes

referred to as *tax-sensitive* or *tax-efficient* funds. These mutual funds employ an investment strategy designed to minimize the effects of capital gains on a fund, including reducing portfolio turnover, mitigating the effect of realized capital gains by taking offsetting losses in other securities, and tilting the portfolio toward growth stocks that have a lower dividend payout.

The amount of buying and selling that occurs in a mutual fund is called portfolio turnover. Most active fund managers buy and sell stocks on a regular basis, sometimes holding onto a position for only a few days. High turnover tends to generate a lot of realized capital gains in a portfolio. Part of the gain from heavy turnover is short-term, which means taxable shareholders are subjected to ordinary income tax rates on that amount.

Low turnover is typically better for taxable fund investors. The less a fund manager trades, the less realized capital gains are generated, and less tax is paid by shareholders. Unrealized stock gains can stay in a fund indefinitely, and those gains will not be taxable to shareholders until the fund manager sells the position.

In addition to low turnover, mutual fund managers can reduce capital gains distributions by selectively choosing which shares of a stock position to sell. As new contributions come into a fund, the manager adds to the current stock positions. The periodic buying of shares creates different "tax layers" of cost basis for each stock position. As investors begin to redeem shares, the manager can choose which layer to sell first. The manager should sell the highest cost shares of a stock first, leaving the low-cost stock in the fund. This technique reduces realized capital gains and saves taxes. Fund managers who employ good tax-management techniques can avoid capital gains distributions for a long time.

If a large number of shareholders decide to redeem a tax-managed fund at the same time, a fund must sell a large enough amount of each security to meet shareholder redemption. Some tax-managed mutual funds charge a fee to shareholders for redemption if they do not hold a fund for a specified period of time. That redemption fee is slapped on exiting share to deter people from redeeming those shares during adverse market conditions. Depending on the mutual funds company, sometimes the redemption fees goes back into a mutual fund to compensate the remaining shareholders who are adversely affected by trading caused by redemptions.

Tax-managed funds have had varying success depending on the type of fund being managed. Broad market funds have better tax-management opportunities in a niche market such as small-cap value. In a niche market, the manager will eventually face tracking error against the fund's benchmark. For example, in a successful tax-managed small-cap value fund, the stocks become mid-cap growth stocks. That means they should be sold. Either the manager of a small-cap value tax-managed fund sells the stocks and distributes capital gains or the fund risks losing its status as a small-cap value fund.

There is a way around the catch 22 of tax-managed niche funds. When choosing a niche fund with high turnover in a taxable account, ETFs make for better after-tax investments. In an ETF, the manager can rid the fund of capital gains through the redemption described in the next section. That eliminates most capital gain distributions to fund shareholders and increases after-tax returns.

ETF Advantage

ETFs are index funds that trade during the day on one of the major stock exchanges. Individual investors can buy and sell ETF shares just like they buy and sell individual shares of common stock. There are a number of different ETFs on the market covering different indexes. See Chapter 4 for a broader explanation of ETFs.

One advantage of the ETF structure over an open-end fund format is that its structure creates an extra tax benefit for taxable investors. Capital gains that build up in an ETF can be "pushed off" onto institution investors rather than distributed to individual shareholders. In fact, many actively traded ETFs have never paid a capital gain distribution. This is possible through the share redemption mechanism built into ETF structure. ETFs are created when a large institution exchanges individual stocks of companies for a creation unit composed of 50,000 ETF shares. Those ETF shares are either held for investment or broken apart and resold on the stock exchange.

Frequently, creation units are redeemed by institutions and reissued as individual stocks, and during this redemption process an ETF fund manager can purge the fund of low-cost stock. By assigning lower cost stock to redeeming institutions, the fund permanently reduces the tax liability in the ETF. Table 5-1 highlighted the tax advantage that an S&P 500 ETF format may have had over actively managed funds and an open-end S&P 500 index fund for 10 years ending in 2005. The return of the S&P 500 ETF is simulated. Table 5-1 assumes the fund is sold at the end of 10 years. Although the extra tax advantage of ETF shares is not huge, every little bit helps.

Tax on a Sale or Exchange of Fund Shares

When you sell shares of any mutual fund in a taxable account, you will incur either a taxable gain or tax loss. Very rarely are shares sold at the exact price they were purchased. To measure the gain or loss accurately, you need to keep good records of the cost basis. Three accounting methods are acceptable when tracking the cost basis of an open-end mutual fund: the average cost method, the first in, first out (FIFO) method, and the actual cost method. If you sell a partial position in an open-end mutual fund and report the gain or loss to the IRS, you cannot switch from one method to another. ETFs are handled somewhat differently. Because they trade like stock, you need to account for them like stock, which means tracking every new purchase and assigning a cost to those shares individually.

Average cost accounting means using the average price of all open-end mutual fund shares to compute a gain or loss, including the reinvestment of dividends. This method may seem simple, but it can be a tax nightmare. You must keep track of when you purchased individual shares to determine if you are selling long-term shares or short-term shares. There are two steps involved in the process. First, you add all the money you invested to purchase shares held for more than a year, including the cash from dividend reinvestment, and divide that amount by the number of shares you owned for more than one year. This gives you the average cost per share on long-term investments. The second part of the equation is to add all the shares you owned for one year or less, including the reinvestment of dividends, and divide that amount by the number of shares held for less than one year.

When selling shares under the FIFO inventory accounting method, your oldest shares are sold first, and the newest shares are sold last. The profits from shares you held for more than one year are taxed at a long-term capital gain rate, and the profit for shares held one year or less generate short-term capital gains, which are taxed at your higher ordinary income rate. If you do not know when you purchased your shares, contact the mutual fund company or your broker. They are required to keep records of share purchase dates and trade amounts.

The last accounting method is actual cost. This is similar to FIFO, only you can designate which shares are being sold. For example, assume you bought 100 shares of a mutual fund in 2000, another 100 shares in 2001, and a third 100 shares in 2002. Then in 2007 you decided to sell 100 shares. For tax and accounting purposes, you can designate the 2000 shares, the 2001 shares, the 2002 shares, or any combination thereof. Under most circumstances you would choose the tax lot with the highest cost basis to reduce your taxable gain and save money on April 15.

The actual cost method of share accounting gives you the most tax flexibility, but it is also the most time consuming. When you call your broker or mutual fund company to sell shares, make sure you tell them which shares you are selling. Some firms will print that information in the trade ticket, which makes your accounting easier.

Overall, I do not recommend the average cost method of mutual fund accounting in a taxable account. It is too restrictive, and you may end up paying more in taxes than you should. FIFO accounting is better, and the actual cost method is best.

Mutual fund companies give you the option to automatically reinvest dividends and capital gains. Automatic reinvestment is not recommended in a taxable account. The bookkeeping that is required to track dividend reinvestment data is not worth the aggravation or the expense, and you lose the ability to choose which tax lots to sell if you needed to raise cash or do a portfolio rebalancing. Instead of doing automatic reinvestment of dividend and capital gains, accumulate cash from all mutual fund distributions and reinvest the total amount in one mutual fund and in one lump sum. Tax-lot buying makes accounting much simpler and that saves your CPA time and you money. See Chapter 15 for more details on these and other portfolio strategies for taxable accounts.

TAX SWAP TO REDUCE CAPITAL GAINS TAX

Your goal as an investor is to keep as much as possible of what you earn. Therefore, tax efficiency is an important concept. To add another dimension to tax management, I have included a section on tax swapping index funds. Most of the advanced portfolio management techniques are found in Part III of this book; however, the strategy of tax swapping fits best in this chapter.

The Concept of Tax Swapping

Tax management is as important to a financial plan as choosing the right investments. A dollar saved in taxes is a dollar increase in your wealth. One way to increase your total return is to use tax swapping in a portfolio of index funds. The idea is buy stock index funds on different dates throughout the year and establish multiple tax lots. As the stock market moves up and down during the year, these tax lots can be selectively sold and simultaneously replaced by a similar index fund. This creates a realized capital loss but never puts you out of the stock market. Using this tax-swap strategy, you will increase your overall net worth due to a tax deduction from the realized loss. It is important to understand that the money invested in stocks will always stay in stocks. This strategy is designed to lower your tax bill, not your allocation to the stock market.

The best way to explain the concept of tax swapping is by reviewing how it is done in a bond portfolio. Bond swapping is an established tradition among taxable fixed-income investors. Tax-swapping bonds involves selling one issue for the tax loss and simultaneously buying another issue that is very similar but not "substantially identical." For instance, you would sell a 5-year, 7 percent yield General Motors bond and buy a 5-year, 7 percent yield Ford Motors bond. Those bonds are very similar in rating and maturity, but are issued by different companies. As a result, they are not substantially identical.

A bond swap creates a tax loss while not affecting the total return of the bond portfolio. In the GM for Ford bond swap, let's assume we have realized a $3,000 loss on the trade but are still earning the same 6 percent yield on the new bond, so your total return has not changed. However, the $3,000 loss can be used to offset a $3,000 realized capital gain that may be in your portfolio. That gain may have come from another bond trade, a stock trade, a mutual fund trade, the sale of real estate, or the sale of a business. If there are no realized gains, the loss can be used to reduce your adjusted gross income up to a maximum of $3,000 per year. However you use the loss, it will reduce the amount of tax you owe. Swapping is a very useful strategy for reducing taxes.

It is important not to swap into a security that is substantially identical to the one sold. If the new security is substantially identical, the transaction will be considered a *tax wash* by the IRS, and the loss would not be allowed. For example, if you sold Intel (INTC) stock at a loss and bought the shares back the next day, the loss would not be allowed. Tax-wash rules state that you need to wait 30 days before buying back a substantially identical security to take a tax loss. The definition of substantially identical is in the gray area in the tax code. Tax courts have ruled that if you swap the stock of one company for the stock of an unrelated company, then there is no tax wash. For example, it is not a tax wash to sell Intel and buy Advanced Micro Devices (AMD).

Let's apply the tax-swapping strategy to index funds. If you had a loss in a broad-based U.S. stock index fund issued by one mutual fund company and simultaneously bought a broad-based U.S. stock index fund issued by a different mutual fund company, a legitimate tax loss has been created. This also means you never missed a day in the market. As long as two unrelated mutual fund companies manage the two funds, no tax wash has occurred. There are several broad-based U.S. stock index funds to choose from, so creating this transaction is easy. Now, I must warn you, to date the IRS has not contested tax swapping of index funds, but that does not mean they will not contest the practice in the future. Consult your tax adviser before proceeding.

Setting Up for Tax Swapping

Most people put money into the markets over time. They invest a little here and a little there. Rather than simply investing when you have the money on hand, I recommend saving your taxable dollars and making regularly scheduled quarterly investments. For example, instead of investing $1,000 one month, $500 the next, and $1,500 the next, I recommend investing $3,000 once per quarter. This strategy is commonly known as dollar cost averaging. One reason dollar cost averaging makes sense is because it establishes different tax lots for your shares. Each quarter you will buy index fund shares at different prices, thereby establishing different tax positions.

To see how tax swapping works, let's look at an example using the two funds in Table 5-2. Assume you are buying $3,000 per quarter in Vanguard Total Stock Market ETFs (VTI) on the first day of each quarter (for an explanation on Vanguard ETFs, see Chapter 4). From January through July, the purchases would be as follows:

Assume that during the third quarter the stock market suffers a 10 percent correction, and on August 1 the price of the Total Market ETF is trading at $108 per share. Your account value and tax lot values are now as follows:

The overall account has a gain of $180. However, the 25-share tax lot bought on July 1 has a loss of $300. If you decide to take the tax loss and sell 25 shares, you will need to designate the shares to be sold. If you do not, your broker will assume the shares being sold were the ones bought on January 1. Remember, tax selling goes first in, first out unless you designate otherwise. By designating for sale the tax lot bought on July 1, the portfolio would realize a loss of $300. This tax loss would reduce your tax liability for the year by about $105, assuming a 35 percent tax bracket.

Immediately following the sale of the 25 ETFs share tax lot, you buy $2,700 of the iShare Russell 3000 ETF (IWV). The Russell 3000 is very similar to the Vanguard Total Stock Market ETF but is not substantially identical because it is based on a different market

TABLE 5-2

Calendar Year Returns of VTI and IWV

	Vanguard Total Market ETF (VTI)	iShare Russell 3000 (IWV)
2002	−20.9%	−21.6%
2003	31.4%	30.8%
2004	12.6%	11.8%
2005	6.1%	6.0%
June 2006	2.6%	2.6%

Note: On April 22, 2005, the Vanguard Total Stock Market ETF switched benchmarks from the Dow Jones Wilshire 5000 Index to the MSCI US Broad Market Index (BMI). The MSCI BMI differs from the DJ Wilshire 5000 Index by reducing the number of micro-cap holdings in the portfolio. That put the BMI closer in comparison with the Russell 3000 than the DJ Wilshire 5000 as evidenced by the 2005 and 2006 returns.
Source: Morningstar Principia.

index and issued by a different fund company (see note below). The net result of this transaction is a tax loss that you can write off against income taxes while remaining 100 percent invested in a broad market index. This transaction is easily accomplished through any discount brokerage firm at a nominal commission rate.

Let's look a little closer at the total economic impact of this index fund swap. On August 1 you had an overall unrealized profit of $180 in the account. That is a gain of 2 percent on the original $9,000 invested. Assuming you are in the 35 percent tax bracket and take a $300 tax loss, your federal income tax saving amounts to $105. This increases your overall return on the portfolio from $180 to $285, which is an extra gain of 1.1 percent. Your portfolio did not increase in value by an extra $105, but your net worth did because of a $105 tax savings. A dollar saved on taxes is a dollar added to your wealth. That is the advantage of tax-swapping index funds.

There are a few warnings about tax swapping. Depending on where you trade, commissions and other fees may reduce the effectiveness of a tax swap. Seek low-commission rates on ETF trades and stick with no-load mutual funds. Finally, this is not a book about income taxes. Always consult your tax adviser before using tax swaps in your portfolio. There is no clear definition of what is considered a substantially identical index fund. Your accountant's interpretation of the tax code may differ from my own.

CHAPTER SUMMARY

The avoidance of taxes is the only intellectual pursuit that carries any reward.

John Maynard Keynes

Mutual fund investors pay a variety of expenses, but none cut as deep as the tax that Uncle Sam can levy on your portfolio. Pay close attention to the tax efficiency as you invest your taxable money. Select low-cost, low-turnover index funds and practice good tax-management techniques.

You have worked hard for the money and need to work hard to keep it in your pocket. Know how the taxation of mutual funds

works and understand the tax benefits of ETFs in a taxable portfolio. Track capital gains that have been paid from a fund you own,
and attempt to offset those gains with realized losses through tax
swapping. Uncle Sam wants your money, but you do not have to
pay more than you legally owe.

PART TWO

Guide to Indexes and Index Funds

CHAPTER 6

Broad U.S. Equity Market Funds

Key Concepts

- There are many index providers.
- Each provider has a different selection methodology.
- Size and value styles categories are also available.
- S&P index holdings are managed by a committee.

The index fund revolution had it roots in the U.S. stock market. During 1976, the Vanguard Group introduced the first index fund available to the general public. The fund was benchmarked to the S&P 500 index. The fund was ahead of its time and misunderstood. Brokers would not sell it, competitors bashed it, and investors had doubts whether a market-based mutual fund was the right move for their portfolio. Investors back then (and now) are brainwashed by Wall Street into believing that anyone can beat the market. The Vanguard 500 Index Fund survived through perseverance and a solid investment performance over its peer group. Today the fund is one of the biggest success stories in mutual fund history.

Success breeds imitation, and index funds are no exception. It did not take long for competitors to challenge Vanguard by launching their own index funds. As of this writing, there are approximately 550 open-end and exchange-traded index funds offered through various mutual fund companies. In total, more than $1.2 trillion is invested in index funds by individual investors. About 42 of these funds are distinct portfolios benchmarked to the S&P 500, and the amount in those funds exceeds $800 billion. These figures do not include index funds sold through insurance company products like variable annuities. Nor do the figures include institutional investors who have enough assets to create a private index fund. When all the money is added, the total amount of money indexed in the S&P 500 index approaches $1.5 trillion.

S&P is only one of several broad U.S. stock indexes available to individual investors. Other research companies offer competing U.S. equity indexes. Major index providers include Frank Russell & Company, Dow Jones & Company, Morgan Stanley Capital International Inc. (MSCI), and Morningstar, Inc. To limit the length of this chapter, only market-weighted U.S. stock indexes that have at least one low-cost index fund benchmark are listed.

There is tremendous competition among index providers for index recognition on Wall Street because royalties and licensing fees are a big business. Every time a new index fund is launched, the index provider receives an annual fee from a mutual fund company. The fee is paid by the fund and is part of the expense ratio. The more money an index fund attracts, the larger the fee to the index provider.

It is important to compare and contrast the U.S. equity indexes before deciding which index fund fits your needs. In this chapter, we explore several competing broad market-weighted U.S. stock indexes by size, style, and structure, so you can visualize the underlying strengths and weaknesses of each methodology. Chapter 7 continues an analysis of U.S. equity benchmarks by analyzing industry sector indexes and reviewing low-cost index funds based on those sectors.

SIZE AND STYLE

"Style boxes" popularized by Morningstar can help investors visualize the difference between different U.S. equity indexes and styles. The Morningstar equity "tic tac toe" style box appearing in Figure 6-1 is a nine-box matrix that displays a fund's investment methodology based on the size of the companies in which it invests and the fund's style. Across the top are the three styles of a fund (value, core, and growth) and down the side are the average size of stocks in a

Figure 6-1

Morningstar Style Boxes with Micro-Cap Added

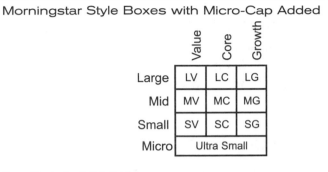

Source: Morningstar, Portfolio Solutions.

fund (large, mid, and small). A micro-cap section was added to the bottom by the author and is not part of the original Morningstar diagram. Morningstar does have funds benchmarked to its indexes, and they will be discussed later in this chapter.

Market Capitalization

U.S. equity index funds can be categorized by the average size of the companies they hold. Index funds that invest in predominately large company stocks are classified as large-cap funds. Those that invest in smaller companies are labeled mid-cap funds. Those that invest in the small companies are small-cap funds. Funds that invest in the smallest companies available on listed exchanges are called micro-cap funds.

A few years ago, nearly all index providers used a total market cap methodology to construct indexes. In essence, all shares of stock for each company counted in the index regardless of who owned it. Today, most index providers use a *free-float* methodology. The free float is typically defined as a company's outstanding shares adjusted for block ownership to reflect only shares available for investment. The types of block ownership that are considered during float adjustment are

- Cross-ownership (shares that are owned by other companies)
- Government ownership

- Private ownership
- Restricted shares (shares that are not allowed to be traded during a certain time period)

Closely held stock can account for up to 80 percent of a small publicly traded company. Institutional investors' holdings such as pension funds, mutual funds, and other financial institutions are not considered closely held, cross-ownership, or restricted stock.

Carving Up the Markets by Size

All the major index providers use roughly the same company size criteria to divide large-, mid-, small-, and micro-cap stocks. However, some index providers use hard rules and move companies up and down the size scale, whereas others slowly morph companies gradually into different market cap categories. The methodology used by each provider is discussed in this chapter.

Figure 6-2 represents the major market indexes and the number of stocks in the investment universe of those index providers. Each index provider divides its universe of investable stocks into

Figure 6-2

Major Market Index Penetration

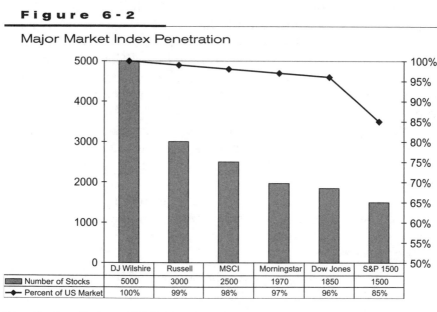

	DJ Wilshire	Russell	MSCI	Morningstar	Dow Jones	S&P 1500
Number of Stocks	5000	3000	2500	1970	1850	1500
Percent of US Market	100%	99%	98%	97%	96%	85%

Source: Dow Jones, Morningstar, MSCI, S&P, Russell, and Wilshire.

size and style categories. The Dow Jones Wilshire 5000 is the most complete universe covering more than 5,000 stocks and 100 percent of stocks that trade on major U.S. exchanges, and the S&P 1500 covers 1,500 stocks and only 85 percent of the market.

The market value of stocks in large-cap indexes are typically more than $10 billion in size. Only about 5 percent of all U.S. stocks can be classified as large-cap, yet they make up nearly 80 percent of the dollar value of the entire U.S. stock market. These stocks include General Electric, Microsoft, and ExxonMobil.

The next level of size is mid cap. The market value of mid-cap stocks generally falls between $2 billion to $10 billion. About 12 percent of all U.S. stocks are classified as mid cap.

Index funds that hold companies that have a market value of $600 million to $2 billion each are generally classified as small cap. More than 80 percent of public U.S. companies by number are small cap, yet their aggregate market value equals only about 8 percent of the value of the broad U.S. market.

Micro-cap stocks have a market capitalization below $600 million and represent less than 2 percent of the total market capitalization. Although there are thousands of micro-cap stocks, there are only a few micro-cap mutual index funds in comparison with hundreds of large-cap index funds. Many micro-cap stocks do not trade with enough volume or with enough consistency to make them a suitable style for wide-scale mutual fund exploitation.

If you put all sizes of stocks together in a market-weighted portfolio, you end up with an all-cap index or total market index. The most complete total market index that measures the wealth of the entire stock market is the Dow Jones Wilshire 5000 index, which holds more than 5,000 large-, mid-, small-, and micro-cap stocks. The next most complete index is the Russell 3000 index, which holds 3,000 stocks based on market capitalization.

Growth and Value Styles

The division of stocks between growth and value companies is more difficult to comprehend than size differences, and value methodology varies between index providers. As a result, the composition and performance of growth and value index funds will vary depending on the index that they are benchmarked against. Examples of growth stocks typically include Microsoft and Cisco Systems, and examples of value stocks include General Motors and CitiGroup.

Depending on the index provider, the style categories of stocks are not cut in stone. Valuations change daily, and what was a value stock one day may be categorized as a growth stock the next. To add more confusion, not all stocks are classified as growth or value. One index provider may classify a stock as both value and growth, and another index provider may classify the same stock as neither value nor growth but rather in a third category called core.

To give you an idea of the growth and value differences between index providers, here is a quick snapshot. DJ Wilshire and Russell use price-to-book (P/B) ratio and incorporate a forecasted earnings growth rate. Dow Jones uses six factors to classify style: projected price-to-earnings (P/E) ratio, projected earnings growth, trailing P/E, trailing earnings growth, P/B, and dividend yield. MSCI incorporates eight factors and Morningstar methodology uses ten. Which is better? One is not better than the other, just different. It is for you to decide which is right for you.

Style allocation rules are confusing, but don't become frustrated. Most professional investment advisors don't know the differences between index methodology and style rule, and they are the people giving you recommendations!

THE INDEX PROVIDERS

The major index providers for the U.S. equity market are Frank Russell & Company, Standard & Poor's, MSCI, Morningstar, and Dow Jones & Company. In this chapter, each provider is analyzed for portfolio structure, ongoing management, and completeness of their indexes. No performance data are provided because it is counterproductive to the discussion. One company's method is not better or worse than another, just different.

We will look at the Dow Jones Wilshire index methodology first because that firm offers the most complete market index, meaning they publish an index that holds the largest number of U.S. securities. Next we will look at the Russell indexes and funds, MSCI indexes and funds, Morningstar funds, and finally Standard & Poor's indexes and funds. In addition to each provider's broad market index methodology, their size and style indexes are also discussed. Mirco-cap indexes and funds are discussed in a separate section at the end of the chapter.

Keep in mind that one index methodology is not better or worse than another, just different. Not all indexes were designed to be made into index funds. Trying to force a square peg into a round hole has been challenging for mutual fund companies that chose to create an index fund to that benchmark. Traditional indexes such as Russell Indexes were created as yardsticks by which to measure active managers against. They were not designed to be used as an index fund. Only since 2000 were new indexes created for the sole purpose of making them into efficient index funds.

Part II of this book will provide you with meaningful information about different index methodologies so you can make an informed decision about which index funds are right for your portfolio.

Dow Jones Wilshire U.S. Equity Indexes

Wilshire Associates is a privately owned investment firm headquartered in Santa Monica, California. Since its founding in 1972, Wilshire Associates has evolved from an investment technology firm into a global investment advisory company specializing in mutual funds, consulting services, and financial data. Since 2004, Wilshire began cobranding its index data with Dow Jones & Company.

Dow Jones Wilshire 5000 Composite Index

Over the years, Wilshire Associates has developed a wide variety of U.S. indexes. The Dow Jones Wilshire 5000 was the first U.S. equity index to capture the return of the entire U.S. stock market. When originally introduced in 1974, the index held 5,000 stocks, thus the name. The name does confuse many people who think Wilshire has a goal to maintain the index at 5,000 stocks. That is not the case. The actual number of stocks in the DJ Wilshire 5000 varies from week to week depending on the number of new issues, mergers, buyouts, and bankruptcies.

There are two different measures of the DJ Wilshire 5000 index. One is full market capitalization and the other is float-adjusted market capitalization. The DJ Wilshire 5000 (Full Cap) measures the market value of all stocks outstanding, and the DJ Wilshire 5000

(Float Adjusted) excludes the value of privately held shares, restricted stock, shares held by other companies, and other stock blocks not available on the open market. A block of stock is considered at least 5 percent of all shares outstanding.

The DJ Wilshire 5000 Total Market Index represents the broadest index for the U.S. equity market, measuring the performance of all U.S. headquartered equity securities with readily available price data. No other index offers its comprehensiveness. When the index was created in 1974, Wilshire's founder took advantage of then-new technologies that made it possible to collect stock prices and calculate returns for a volume of issues never before brought together.

According to the Wilshire Associates' Web site at www.Wilshire .com, the construction methodology of the 5000 index includes the rules below. For complete information, visit the Web site.

Membership

- The company is headquartered in the United States.
- The security trades in the United States.
- The issue is the primary equity issue for the company.
- Equity issues include common stocks, real-estate
- investment trusts (REITs), and limited partnerships.
- Primary equity issue selection criteria include volume, institutional holdings, and conversion criteria.
- Shares outstanding for multiple classes of stock are combined into the primary issue's shares outstanding to reflect the total market capitalization of the firm.

Exclusions

- Very small "bulletin board" issues are excluded from the monthly addition process by the assumption that they do not have consistent, readily available prices.
- Nondomiciled U.S. stocks, foreign issues, and American Depositary Receipts (ADRs) are excluded.

Adjustments and Maintenance

- Stock additions and deletions are made after the close of trading on the third Friday of each month.
- The additions include all companies that met inclusion

standards during the previous calendar month, whether from Initial Public Offerings (IPOs) and other new exchange listings.

◆ Issues spun off from index members will be added to the index as soon as prudently possible.

◆ A security will be removed from the index on the day it fails index inclusion guidelines.

◆ A security will be removed from the index on the day it stops trading but may reenter the index when it resumes trading.

◆ Shares outstanding may be adjusted to reflect corporate events during the month; otherwise, shares outstanding are updated once a month.

Investors who want the broadest possible breadth of stocks in the U.S. market will find that an index fund benchmarked to the DJ Wilshire 5000 provides it. However, you will not be able to invest in an index fund that holds all stocks in the index because some of the smallest stocks in the index do not have enough liquidity. That means some stocks in the index rarely trade in enough volume to be bought by a large index fund.

Because the DJ Wilshire 5000 cannot be fully replicated in an actual portfolio, an index fund manager will work around the problem by sampling the smaller stock universe. The logic behind sampling is to buy an assortment of liquid small stocks representing different industries, trying to develop a portfolio that replicates the movement of the small-cap portion of the index without owning all stocks in the group. The typical index fund benchmarked to the DJ Wilshire 5000 is composed of about 3,000 stocks. Table 6-1 lists low-cost index funds benchmarked to the DJ Wilshire 5000 index and whether those funds follow the full-cap or free-float methodology.

The DJ Wilshire 5000 index is a perfect example of an index that was not designed to be an index fund. But that is not why indexes were designed back in 1974. The DJ Wilshire 5000 index was designed to be a measure of the wealth of the U.S. stock market in aggregate, and in that capacity, it does a good job.

Dow Jones Wilshire 4500

The DJ Wilshire 4500 was created on December 31, 1983, and measures the performance of small- and mid-cap stocks in the DJ

TABLE 6-1

Dow Jones Wilshire Index Funds

DJ Wilshire U.S. Indexes	Fund Name	Class	Fee	Symbol	Minimum
W5000	Fidelity Spartan Total Market	Open-End	0.10	FSTMX	$10,000
W5000	streetTRACKS DJ Wilshire Total Market	ETF	0.20	TMW	None
W5000	T. Rowe Price Total Equity Market	Open-End	0.40	POMIX	$2,500
W5000	Vantagepoint Broad Market I	Open-End	0.45	VPMIX	None
Large Cap	streetTRACKS DJ Wilshire Large Cap	ETF	0.20	ERL	None
Large Value	streetTRACKS DJ Wilshire Large Value	ETF	0.20	ELV	None
Large Growth	streetTRACKS DJ Wilshire Large Growth	ETF	0.20	ELG	None
Mid Cap	streetTRACKS DJ Wilshire Mid Cap	ETF	0.25	EMM	None
Mid Value	streetTRACKS DJ Wilshire Mid Value	ETF	0.25	EMV	None
Mid Growth	streetTRACKS DJ Wilshire Mid Growth	ETF	0.25	EMG	None
Small Cap	streetTRACKS DJ Wilshire Small Cap	ETF	0.25	DSC	None
Small Value	streetTRACKS DJ Wilshire Small Value	ETF	0.25	DSV	None
Small Growth	streetTRACKS DJ Wilshire Small Growth	ETF	0.25	DSG	None
W4500	Fidelity Spartan Extended Market	Open-End	0.10	FSEMX	$10,000

Wilshire 5000. Essentially, it is the DJ Wilshire 5000 index with all the companies in the Standard & Poor's 500 index removed. The approximately 4,500 stocks left over provide an excellent benchmark for "extended" market performance, or how the non–S&P 500 stocks are fairing.

Membership and Exclusions

- All stocks in the DJ Wilshire 5000 excluding stocks in the S&P 500.
- Issues spun off from the S&P 500 index members will be added to the DJ Wilshire 4500 as soon as prudently possible if they are not staying in the S&P 500.
- All else is the same as the DJ Wilshire 5000 index methodology

DJ Wilshire Micro-Cap Index

All stocks that are in the DJ Wilshire 5000 index below the 2,501 rank. The index follows DJ Wilshire 5000 membership guidelines. The index consists of approximately 2,600 stocks from size 2,500 and below, although the smallest companies have limited liquidity and cannot be efficiently indexed in a fund.

Dow Jones Wilshire Style Indexes

Dow Jones Wilshire's style indexes are benchmarks used to evaluate the performance of active managers. They separate the Dow Jones Wilshire 5000 into four capitalization groups (large, small, mid, and micro), and then divide the large-, small-, and mid-cap issues by float-adjusted capitalization equally into growth and value indexes.

Growth and value is defined by looking at six factors: projected price-to-earnings ratio, projected earnings growth, price-to-book ratio, dividend yield, trailing revenue growth, and trailing earnings growth. The purpose of the Indexes is to help fund sponsors measure the performance of managers relative to their respective investment management style.

There are many index funds benchmarked to the Dow Jones Wilshire indexes. The funds with the lowest cost are listed in Table 6-1.

Russell U.S. Equity Indexes

In 1984, Frank Russell & Company of Tacoma, Washington, created the Russell family of stock indexes. Russell calculates the value of 21 indexes daily, from the largest 200 growth companies to the smallest capitalization value companies. Today, several hundred billion dollars are benchmarked to Russell's 21 U.S. stock indexes. Return data on those indexes is available at www.Russell.com.

Each year Russell constructs its primary U.S. index by ranking the 3,000 largest U.S. stocks using their market values on May 31. These 3,000 stocks are selected and ranked strictly by size, and the list does not reflect any subjectivity. Companies that started in the index at the beginning of a year may leave the index during the year due to mergers or bankruptcies, although replacements for these securities do not occur until the annual rebalancing in June.

The Russell U.S. indexes are market cap–weighted and include only common stocks domiciled in the United States and its territories. The indexes represent the free-float value of U.S. stocks rather than all shares outstanding.

All Russell indexes are subsets of the Russell 3000 index, which represents approximately 98 percent of the investable free-float U.S. equity market. The rules below are a guide to how Russell indexes are constructed. A more in-depth description of the index methodology is available at the Frank Russell & Company Web site.

Membership

- Rank the U.S. common stocks from largest to smallest market capitalization at each annual reconstitution period (May 31).
- The top 3,000 stocks are included in the Russell 3000 index.
- The largest 1,000 stocks are included in the Russell 1000 index.
- The next 2,000 stocks are included in the Russell 2000 index.

Exclusions

- Stocks trading below $1 on May 31 of each year.
- Pink sheet and bulletin board stocks (not traded on a major exchange).

- Closed-end mutual funds, limited partnerships, royalty trusts.
- Berkshire Hathaway, Inc. (considered an investment company).
- Non–U.S. domiciled stocks, foreign stocks, ADRs.

Adjustments and Maintenance

- Adjust shares outstanding for cross-ownership and privately held shares to reflect shares available for trading.
- Adjust book value due to writeoffs when determining price-to-book ratio for style classification.
- Stocks deleted between reconstitution dates are not replaced.
- Spin-offs are the only additions between reconstitution dates.
- Dividends are reinvested on the ex-date.

Determining Style Index Membership

- Rank each stock in the Russell 1000 and Russell 2000 by price-to-book ratio and forecast long-term earnings growth averages.
- Combine variables to create a composite value score (CVS) for each stock.
- Rank the stocks by their CVS and apply a mathematical formula to the distribution to determine style membership weights. Of the stocks, 70 percent are classified as all value or all growth, and 30 percent are weighted proportionately to both value and growth and are listed in both indexes.

Russell 3000 Index

The Russell 3000 index measures the performance of the 3,000 largest U.S. companies based on total market capitalization, which represents approximately 98 percent of the investable U.S. equity market. As of July 31, 2006, the average weighted market capitalization of companies included in the index was approximately $74 billion, and the median market capitalization was approximately $1.1 million. The companies had a total market capitalization range of approximately $410 billion (largest) to $95 million (smallest).

TABLE 6-2

Russell Index Funds

Russell U.S. Indexes	Fund Name	Class	Fee	Symbol	Minimum
R3000	TIAA-CREF Equity Index	Open-End	0.26	TCEIX	2,500
R3000	iShare R3000 Index	ETF	0.20	IWV	None
R3000 Value	iShares Russell 3000 Value	ETF	0.25	IWW	None
R3000 Growth	iShares Russell 3000 Growth	ETF	0.25	IWZ	None
R1000	iShares R1000 Index	ETF	0.15	IWB	None
R1000 Value	iShares Russell 1000 Value	ETF	0.20	IWD	None
R1000 Growth	iShares Russell 1000 Growth	ETF	0.20	IWV	None
R2000	E*Trade Russell 2000 Index	Open-End	0.22	ETRUX	5,000
R2000	iShares R2000 Index	ETF	0.20	IWM	None
R2000 Value	iShares Russell 2000 Value	ETF	0.25	IWN	None
R2000 Growth	iShares Russell 2000 Growth	ETF	0.25	IWO	None
Mid Cap	iShares Russell Midcap Index	ETF	0.20	IWR	None
Mid Cap Value	iShares Russell Midcap Value	ETF	0.25	IWS	None
Mid Cap Growth	iShares Russell Midcap Growth	ETF	0.25	IWP	None
Top 50	Rydex Russell Top 50	ETF	0.20	XLG	None
Micro Cap	iShares Russell Micro Cap Index	ETF	0.60	IWC	None

Russell 1000 Index
The Russell 1000 index measures the performance of the 1,000 largest companies in the Russell 3000 index, which represents approximately 92 percent of the total market capitalization of the Russell 3000 index. As of July 31, 2006, the average weighted market capitalization was approximately $81 billion with a median market capitalization of approximately $4.8 billion. The smallest company in the index had fallen to an approximate market capitalization of $1.0 billion. On that date, the Russell 1000 index represented approximately 92 percent of the total market value of the Russell 3000.

Russell 2000 Index
The Russell 2000 index measures the performance of the 2,000 smallest companies in the Russell 3000 index, which represent approximately 8 percent of the total market capitalization of the Russell 3000 index. As of July 30, 2006, the weighted average market capitalization was approximately $1 billion and the median market capitalization was approximately $570 million. The largest company in the index had grown to an approximate market capitalization of $2.4 billion and the smallest had an approximate market capitalization of $95 million. On that date, the Russell 2000 index represented only 8 percent of the total market value of the Russell 3000.

Russell Top 50 Index
The Russell Top 50 index offers investors access to the 50 largest companies in the Russell 3000 index. As of July 30, 2006, the weighted average market capitalization was approximately $410 billion and the median market capitalization was approximately $87 billion. The largest company in the index had grown to an approximate market capitalization of $410 billion and the smallest had an approximate market capitalization of $50 billion. On that date, the Russell Top 50 index represented 41 percent of the total market value of the Russell 3000.

Russell Mid Cap Indexes
The Russell Mid Cap indexes measure the performance of the 800 smallest companies in the Russell 1000 index, which represent approximately 25 percent of the total market capitalization of the Russell 1000 index. As of July 31, 2006, the average weighted market

capitalization was approximately $7.5 billion and the median market capitalization was approximately $3.8 billion. The largest company in the index had an approximate market capitalization of $16.6 billion.

Russell Micro Cap Index
The Russell Micro Cap index measures performance of the micro-cap segment, representing less than 3 percent of the U.S. equity market. The index includes the smallest 1,000 securities in the small-cap Russell 2000 index plus the next 1,000 securities. In aggregate, the index covers stocks 2,000 to 4,000.

Russell Style Indexes
The Russell style indexes divide the Russell size index into growth or value categories by ranking stocks according to their price-to-book ratio and forecast earnings growth rate. Each stock is then given a score and allocated to the growth or value index accordingly. Each index represents 50 percent of the total market value of its respective Russell size index. For example, market values of stocks in the Russell 1000 index are equally divided between the Russell 1000 Value index and the Russell 1000 Growth index.

Russell splits the market capitalization of many stocks that have both growth and value characteristics. Of the stocks in a Russell index, about 30 percent have a percentage weighting allocated to both the value index and the growth index depending on the style score. These allocations do not overlap, and there is no double counting. For example, in aggregate the combined market value of the Russell 1000 Value and Russell 1000 Growth indexes will equal the market cap of the Russell 1000 index.

Morgan Stanley Capital International Indexes

Morgan Stanley Capital International (MSCI) is the new index kid on the block. In 2002, MSCI adopted a broad index structure that reflects the full breadth of investment opportunities across market capitalization size in the U.S. equity markets in which companies and their securities are categorized into different market capitalization segments and indexes that are defined by a fixed number of companies.

Mammoth index fund firm Vanguard has adopted several MSCI indexes as benchmarks for their index funds. In fact, Vanguard's chief investment strategist, Gus Sauter, had a hand in creating the MSCI methodology. Sauter is arguably the most experienced index fund manager in the business.

MSCI U.S. Methodology

MSCI starts with the U.S. equity universe: all listed equity securities, or listed securities that exhibit characteristics of equity securities, of U.S. incorporated companies listed on the NYSE, AMEX, or the NASDAQ (both NASDAQ National Market and NASDAQ Small Cap Market). Shares of non–U.S. incorporated companies, investment trusts (other than REITs), mutual funds, equity derivatives, limited partnerships, limited liability companies, and business trusts that are structured to be taxed as limited partnerships, and royalty trusts are generally not included in the universe.

MSCI then screens securities in the U.S. equity universe for investability using the following factors:

+ Liquidity
+ Length of trading
+ Company and security free float
+ Relative security free-float-adjusted market capitalization

The investable market segment and index is composed of three market capitalization segments and their corresponding indexes— large cap, mid cap, and small cap. MSCI defines the Large-Cap index as consisting of the 300 largest companies by full market capitalization in the investable market segment, the Mid-Cap index as consisting of the next 450 companies, and the Small-Cap index as consisting of the remaining 1,750 companies. The Large-Cap and the Mid-Cap indexes, as defined above, are also combined to create a separate index of the 750 largest companies in the investable market segment ranked by full market capitalization.

MSCI Buffer Zones

Market capitalization is fully reviewed on a semiannual basis, at the end of May and November, and partially reviewed at the end of February and August. During these index reviews, MSCI uses "buffer zones" to manage the migration of companies from one market capitalization index to another. Buffers zones are used to segregate and migrate between indexes the stocks of large-cap, mid-cap, small-cap, and micro-cap companies. Figure 6-3 highlights the buffer zones for Large-, Mid-, and Small-Cap MSCI indexes.

Once the market capitalization subindexes have been constructed according to the design mentioned above, an existing constituent will leave the Large-Cap index when it drops to a market capitalization rank of 451. Similarly, a mid-cap company will enter the Large-Cap index when it reaches a market capitalization rank of 200.

The purpose of the buffer zone is to reflect the evolution of equity markets and equity market segments in a timely fashion. In reviewing its various subindexes, MSCI's goal is to strike a balance between ensuring that the various indexes continue to accurately reflect the different investment styles and at the same time minimize stock turnover.

The buffer zones also help reduce trading losses caused by hedge fund managers and other short-term opportunists that

Figure   6-3

MSCI U.S. Equity Buffer Zones

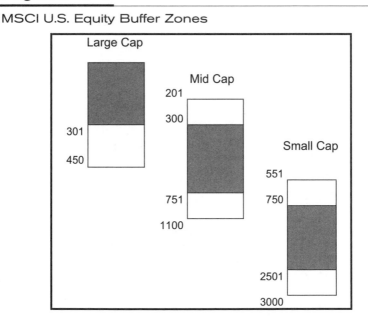

Source: MSCI.

attempt to "front-run" changes to an index. The opportunists try to buy stocks that are added to indexes before index fund managers can buy and sell stocks before an index fund has time to sell. Losses to index funds from front-running depends on the index being benchmarked, however it can be substantial. Older indexing methodologies and particularly older small stock indexes suffer the most.

MSCI Micro-Cap Index

All securities that are included in the top 99.5 percent of the U.S. equity universe and are not part of the 98% Investable Market index will be included in the Micro-Cap index, provided they pass the investability screen. In addition, all new companies and securities that are considered for inclusion in the Micro-Cap index must have a company full market capitalization of at least $20 million. The index consists of approximately 2,000 stocks from size 2,500 and below.

MSCI Multifactor Approach

The value investment style characteristics for index construction are defined using the following three variables:

- Book value to price ratio
- Twelve-month forward earnings to price ratio
- Dividend yield

The growth investment style characteristics for index construction are defined using the following five variables:

- Long-term forward earnings per share (EPS) growth rate
- Short-term forward EPS growth rate
- Current internal growth rate
- Long-term historical EPS growth trend
- Long-term historical sales per share (SPS) growth trend

The objective of the value and growth indexes is to divide constituents of an underlying market capitalization index into a value index and a growth index, each targeting 50 percent of the free-float-adjusted market capitalization of the underlying market capitalization index.

Securities may be partially allocated to both value and growth indexes depending on their score. The market capitalization of each

TABLE 6-3

MSCI U.S. Index Funds

MSCI U.S. Indexes	Fund Name	Class	Fee	Symbol	Minimum
Broad Market	Vanguard Total Stock Market	Open-End	0.19	VTSMX	3,000
Broad Market	Vanguard Total Stock Market ETF	ETF	0.07	VTI	None
Prime Market 750	Vanguard Large-Cap Index	Open-End	0.20	VLACX	3,000
Prime Market 750	Vanguard Large-Cap ETF	ETF	0.07	VV	None
Prime Market Growth	Vanguard Growth Index Fund	Open-End	0.22	VIGRX	3,000
Prime Market Growth	Vanguard Growth ETF	ETF	0.11	VUG	None
Prime Market Value	Vanguard Value Index Fund	Open-End	0.22	VIVAX	3,000
Prime Market Value	Vanguard Value ETF	ETF	0.11	VTV	None
Mid Cap 450	Vanguard Mid-Cap Index	Open-End	0.22	VIMSX	3,000
Mid Cap 450	Vanguard Mid-Cap ETF	ETF	0.13	VO	None
Mid Cap 450 Growth	Vanguard Mid-Cap Growth Index	Open-End	0.25	VMGIX	3,000
Mid Cap 450 Growth	Vanguard Mid-Cap Growth ETF	ETF	0.13	VOT	None
Mid Cap 450 Value	Vanguard Mid-Cap Value Index	Open-End	0.25	VMVIX	3,000
Mid Cap 450 Value	Vanguard Mid-Cap Value ETF	ETF	0.13	VOE	None
Small Cap 1750	Vanguard Small-Cap Index	Open-End	0.23	NAESX	3,000
Small Cap 1750	Vanguard Small-Cap ETF	ETF	0.10	VBR	None
Small Cap Growth	Vanguard Small-Cap Growth Index	Open-End	0.23	VISGX	3,000
Small Cap Growth	Vanguard Small-Cap Growth ETF	ETF	0.12	VBK	None
Small Cap Value	Vanguard Small-Cap Value Index	Open-End	0.23	VISVX	3,000
Small Cap Value	Vanguard Small-Cap Value ETF	ETF	0.12	VBR	None

size index will be fully represented in the combination of the value index and the growth index and will not be double counted.

MSCI constructs and maintains the value and growth indexes by allocating securities and their free-float-adjusted market capitalizations to the appropriate value and growth indexes, during the semiannual style index reviews of May and November.

Morningstar Indexes

Based on the same methodology as the well-known Morningstar style box, as illustrated in Figure 6-4, Morningstar has developed a comprehensive family of 16 size and style indexes that target 97 percent coverage of the free-float U.S. equity market. The style methodology uses 10 factors to identify distinct growth and value attributes, creating an integrated framework for stock research, portfolio assembly, and market monitoring.

Morningstar Index Methodology

Stock in Morningstar indexes are selected from the investable universe. To be included in the investable universe, a stock must be

- Domiciled in the United States or its primary stock market activities are carried out in the United States
- Listed on the NYSE, the AMEX, or
- Have sufficient historical fundamental data available to classify its investment style
- In the 75 percent of companies in the investable universe based on its liquidity score

Figure 6-4

The 16 Morningstar Size and Style Indexes

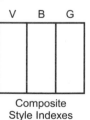
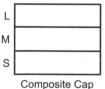

| Broad Market Index | Composite Style Indexes | Composite Cap Indexes | Style Indexes |

Source: Morningstar, Inc.

Stocks are excluded if they:

- Have more than 10 nontrading days in the prior quarter
- Are American Depositary Receipts and American Depositary Shares, fixed-dividend shares, convertible notes, warrants, rights, tracking stocks, limited partnerships, and holding companies

Morningstar divides its U.S. Market index into three cap indexes by defining each as a percentage of the market cap of the investable universe:

- Large cap: largest 70 percent of investable market cap
- Mid cap: next 20 percent of investable market cap
- Small cap: Next 7 percent of investable market cap

Determining a Stock's Style

Within each capitalization class, index constituents are assigned to one of three style orientations—value, growth, or core—based on the stock's overall style score. A stock's value orientation and growth orientation are measured separately using different variables.

Value Factors

- Price/projected earnings (50.0 percent)
- Price/book (12.5 percent)
- Price/sales (12.5 percent)
- Price/cash flow (12.5 percent)
- Dividend yield (12.5 percent)

Growth Factors

- Long-term projected earnings growth (50.0 percent)
- Historical earnings growth (12.5 percent)
- Sales growth (12.5 percent)
- Cash flow growth (12.5 percent)
- Book value growth (12.5 percent)

Style Classification Process

* Determine the value score and the growth score within each cap class.
* Using the value score and the growth score, determine each stock's composite style score.
* Stocks are reclassified in terms of style or capitalization only if they move sufficiently beyond the break point between styles (value-core or core-growth break points) or capitalization (large-mid or mid-small).

Reconstitution and Rebalancing

* Morningstar adds or removes stocks from each index twice annually.
* Morningstar rebalances its indexes quarterly. However, immediate rebalancing occurs when a company's free-float changes by 10 percent or more or when two companies merge even if change in their free-float shares is less than 10 percent.

Buffer zones allow stocks to migrate between size categories and style categories over time without affecting the classification. Short-term movements of stocks into or within the buffer zones do not result in high index turnover.

Nine Morningstar style box index funds are listed in Table 6-4. For a complete description of Morningstar's index eligibility requirements, please refer to the Morningstar Rulebook at www.indexes .morningstar.com.

Dow Jones U.S. Equity Averages and Indexes

Dow Jones launched its first stock indicator in 1884 with an index composed of 12 railroad stocks. This indicator would later become known as the Dow Jones Transportation Average. In 1896, the company introduced the Dow Jones Industrial Average. Better know as the Dow, it is still the world's most widely followed stock market indicator. The Dow is currently composed of 30 large U.S. companies and is supposed to represent the pulse of the market.

Dow Jones & Company has created more than 3,000 proprietary U.S. and international market indexes, including style and

TABLE 6–4

Morningstar Index Funds

Morningstar Indexes	Fund Name	Class	Fee	Symbol	Minimum
Large Core	iShares Morningstar Large Core	ETF	0.25	JKD	None
Large Growth	iShares Morningstar Large Growth	ETF	0.25	JKE	None
Large Value	iShares Morningstar Large Value	ETF	0.25	JKF	None
Mid Core	iShares Morningstar Mid Core	ETF	0.25	JKG	None
Mid Growth	iShares Morningstar Mid Growth	ETF	0.25	JKH	None
Mid Value	iShares Morningstar Mid Value	ETF	0.25	JKI	None
Small Core	iShares Morningstar Small Core	ETF	0.25	JKJ	None
Small Growth	iShares Morningstar Small Growth	ETF	0.25	JKK	None
Small Value	iShares Morningstar Small Value	ETF	0.25	JKL	None

industry indexes. Several of those indexes are replicated in niche index funds. This chapter reviews only a few benchmarks including the not very broad Dow Jones Industrial Average and the broader U.S. Dow Jones Total Market Index.

Dow Jones Industrial Average

No discussion of Dow Jones would be complete without a mention of the Dow Jones Industrial Average (DJIA) and the index funds that are benchmarked to it. The DJIA is a 30-stock index that is followed by more people around the world than any other stock market benchmark. Although the methodology used to construct the index is antiquated and the narrowness of the 30-stock portfolio makes it unsuitable for academic study or performance measurement, it nevertheless commands attention. For that reason, mutual fund companies have stepped up to the plate and created index funds that track DJIA performance.

As an investment, I do not recommend buying Dow index funds because the index is so narrow in scope. That being said, a list of index funds benchmarked to the DJIA is provided in Table 6-5. Notice the expense ratios on a couple of these funds. They are designed for naive investors. If you are going to buy a DJIA index fund, the SPDR Diamonds are the best deal.

Dow Jones U.S. Total Market Index

In 2000, Dow Jones got up to speed with its U.S. indexes and launched the U.S. Total Market Index. The U.S. Total Market Index represents the top 95 percent of the free-float value of the U.S. stock market. The Dow Jones U.S. Total Market Index spans only 1,850 stocks, making it the smallest range of stocks for any index provider using the title of "total market." What about the other 3,000-plus stocks? As you may recall, Dow Jones is now cobranding the Dow Jones Wilshire indexes. That gives the company needed depth in the broad U.S. total market category.

Membership

+ The company must be headquartered in the United States.
+ The issue must trade in the United States.
+ The issue must be the primary equity issue for the company.

TABLE 6-5

Dow Jones Indexes and Averages Funds

Dow Jones U.S. Indexes and Averages	Fund Name	Class	Fee	Symbol	Minimum
Total Market Index	iShares DJ Total Market	ETF	0.20	IYY	None
Dow Jones Industrial Average	Dow Diamonds	ETF	0.18	DIA	None
Select MicroCap Index	First Trust DJ Select MicroCap	ETF	0.50	FDM	None

Source: Morningstar Principia.

- Equity issues include common stocks and REITs.
- Shares outstanding for multiple classes of stock are combined into the primary issue's shares outstanding to reflect the total market capitalization of the firm if both issues are eligible.

Exclusions

- Thinly traded stocks are excluded by the assumption that they do not have liquidity.
- Nondomiciled U.S. stocks, foreign issues, and ADRs are excluded.
- Mutual funds, closed-end funds, ETFs, limited partnerships, and Berkshire Hathaway, Inc., are excluded.

Adjustments and Maintenance

- Additions to the index are made quarterly, effective the Monday after the third Friday in March, June, September, and December.
- Initial public offerings will generally be added at the beginning of the quarter.
- Issues spun off from index members will be added to the index as soon as prudently possible.
- A security will be removed from the index on the day it fails index inclusion guidelines.
- A security will be removed from the index on the day it stops trading but may reenter the index when trading resumes.
- Stocks that are removed will not be replaced until quarterly balancing.
- Shares outstanding may be adjusted to reflect corporate events during the month if they affect 10 percent or more of the stock; otherwise, shares outstanding are updated quarterly.

Dow Jones Select MicroCap Index

The Dow Jones Select MicroCap index represents the "investable" portion of U.S. micro-cap companies. It measures the performance of micro-capitalization stocks traded on the major U.S. exchanges, screening for size, trading volume, and fundamentals. Issues with the smallest market capitalizations and lowest trading volumes are excluded, so the index contains more-investable stocks. In addition, companies with poor fundamentals are excluded by screening out stocks that score worst based on operating profit margin, price-to-earnings ratio, price-to-sales ratio, earnings momentum, and trailing stock-market return. As of June 30, 2006, there were 261 stocks in the index.

Standard & Poor's U.S. Equity Indexes

There is more money benchmarked to the S&P 500 index than all other index funds combined. So did I save the best for last? Not necessarily. All the index providers have their strengths and weaknesses, and Standard & Poor's is no exception. Of all the index providers presented so far, Standard & Poor's has the most subjective stock selection methodology. As a result, the S&P indexes are not "all inclusive," and therefore, they do not represent the entire stock market. Rather, they are hand selected, which adds an element of subjectivity to the process. Standard & Poor's uses a team of analysts to physically pick the stocks that go in their indexes.

Indexes created by Wilshire, Russell, Dow Jones, and others include at least 95 percent of the value of all stocks listed on U.S. exchanges. The S&P SuperComposite 1500 index includes only 85 percent of total market capitalization. Fewer stocks make it into S&P indexes because the selection committee has strict selection criteria. The other index providers just use a straight computer model and thus include nearly all stocks. Because S&P has a subjective process, S&P indexes are often referred to as *actively managed* indexes.

Does the human from the S&P committee provide a better or worse investment result than an unconscious computer? That depends on who you talk with. Many people believe that a committee is a good idea because not all stocks make good investments. Others say that human subjectivity degrades the essence of an unbiased index. In my opinion, it makes no difference once a portfolio gets past a few hundred stocks. If you are going to put 500 stocks in an index, a monkey could pick them by throwing darts at a dartboard and the results of the portfolio would be close to any other broad market index.

There is a second difference between Standard & Poor's and other providers. All other providers start with a total market index and divide it into subindexes. Standard & Poor's starts with subindexes and works up to a total market index. Russell divides its 3000 index into the Russell 1000 Large Cap and Russell 2000 Small Cap indexes. The S&P committee starts by selecting stocks for the S&P 500 Large-Cap, S&P SmallCap 600, and the S&P MidCap 400 and then putting them together in the S&P 1500 SuperComposite.

All S&P indexes consist of hand-selected stocks based on the discretion of the Index Committee. This committee examines several criteria when looking for index candidates (i.e., trading analysis, liquidity, ownership, fundamental analysis, market capitalization, and sector representation). Even then the criteria to get in an index are guidelines and not rules. Occasionally, the committee may go outside the guidelines to include a stock.

Membership

Criteria for Index Additions

- U.S. company: To determine what is a "U.S. company," the Index Committee looks at a number of factors including location of the company's operations, its corporate structure, accounting standards, and exchange listings.
- Market cap in excess of US$4 billion: This market cap minimum is reviewed from time to time to ensure consistency with market conditions.
- Financial viability: This is usually determined by four consecutive quarters of positive as-reported earnings, where as-reported earnings are defined as Generally Accepted Accounting Principles (GAAP) Net Income excluding discontinued operations and extraordinary items.
- Adequate liquidity and reasonable price: The ratio of annual dollar value traded to market capitalization should be 0.3 or greater. Very low stock prices can affect a stock's liquidity.
- Public float of at least 50 percent (S&P indexes use free float).
- Sector representation: The Index Committee strives to maintain a balance for the S&P 500 in line with the sector

balance of the universe of eligible companies greater than US$4 billion.

- Must be an operating company: Closed-end funds, holding companies, partnerships, investment vehicles, and royalty trusts are not eligible. Real estate investment trusts are eligible for inclusion.

Exclusions

- Exclude stocks that trade less than 0.3 percent of shares on average each month on the New York Stock Exchange and American Stock Exchange and trade less than 0.6 percent of shares outstanding per month on the NASDAQ.
- Nondomiciled U.S. stocks, foreign issues, and ADRs are excluded.
- ETFs, closed-end funds, and tracking stocks are excluded.
- There are no IPOs less than 6 months old in the S&P 400 and 600 and no IPOs less than 12 months old in the S&P 500.
- Standard & Poor's will analyze a stock's price history in an effort to limit the single-digit stocks in the indexes.
- No single entity can own more than 50 percent of the stock in a company, and multiple entities cannot hold more than 60 percent, excluding mutual funds.

Criteria for Index Removal

- Companies that substantially violate one or more of the criteria for index inclusion.
- Companies involved in merger, acquisition, or significant restructuring such that they no longer meet the inclusion criteria.

Adjustments and Maintenance

- The S&P indexes are dynamic. Additions to the indexes can occur on an ongoing basis, but most changes are normally made once per month.
- Issues spun off from index members will be added to the index as soon as prudently possible if they qualify.

- A security will be removed from the index on the day it stops trading but may reenter the index when trading resumes.
- Shares outstanding will be adjusted to reflect corporate events during the month.
- Although the committee has set certain market capitalization guidelines for each index, change in market capitalization is not an adequate criterion for removing a company from an index. There are typically more than 100 stocks in each index that are trading above or below the guidelines at any time.

Continued index membership is not necessarily subjected to these guidelines. The Index Committee strives to minimize unnecessary turnover in index membership and each removal is determined on a case-by-case basis.

S&P 500 Index

The S&P 500 index is widely regarded as the professional standard for measuring the performance of the U.S. stock market. The index is used by 97 percent of money managers and pension plan sponsors as a benchmark in one form or another. It is included in the government's Index of Leading Economic Indicators and is widely followed by economists as an early indicator of consumer confidence. The amount of money indexed to the S&P 500 is enormous. More than $1 trillion is invested in S&P 500 index funds by individual investors and institutions.

A popular misconception about the S&P 500 is that it contains only large companies. Actually, there is not a market capitalization limit for inclusion in the index. The guiding principle is that the company must be a leader in an important industry, but that does not mean the company chosen to represent the industry has to be highly valued. Visteon (VC) was a spin-off from Ford and was added to the S&P 500 when it had a market cap of only $1.6 billion. That barely earns the company a mid-cap status. Nevertheless, Visteon made it into the S&P 500 because sales were similar to other companies in the index and it was considered a leader in the auto parts industry. Because most leading companies are large, the average market value for an S&P 500 stock is about $25 billion compared with $2.5 billion for the S&P 400 MidCap 400 index and $700 million for the S&P SmallCap 600 index.

Companies turn over in the S&P 500 at about 5 percent per year. That is the average from its inception in 1926 until 2001. Companies exit the S&P 500 mostly through mergers and acquisitions, and a few fall out of favor. The Index Committee usually replaces a void in the index within 30 days.

S&P 400 MidCap Indexes

More than $25 billion is indexed to the S&P MidCap 400. This index is used by most mutual funds and pension plan sponsors to measure the performance of the mid-size company segment of the U.S. market. Companies in the S&P 400 are split into two groups based on price-to-book ratio to create growth and value indexes (Table 6-6). The value index contains companies with lower price-to-book ratios, and the growth index contains those with higher price-to-book ratios. The indexes are equal weight, so each represents approximately 50 percent of the market cap of the S&P 400.

S&P 600 SmallCap Index

The S&P SmallCap 600 index is gaining wide acceptance as the preferred benchmark for both active and passive small-cap managers due to its low turnover and high liquidity. Approximately $8 billion is indexed to the S&P SmallCap 600. Companies in the S&P SmallCap 600 are split into two groups based on price-to-book ratio to create growth and value indexes (Table 6-6). The value index contains companies with lower price-to-book ratios, and the growth index contains those with higher price-to-book ratios. The indexes are equal weight, so each represents approximately 50 percent of the market cap of the S&P 600 SmallCap Index.

S&P SuperComposite 1500 Index

Combining the S&P 500, MidCap 400, and SmallCap 600 indexes together makes up the S&P SuperComposite 1500. This index represents 85 percent of the total U.S. equity market capitalization (as measured by the Wilshire 5000).

S&P 100 Index

The S&P 100 stock index is better known by its ticker symbol OEX. It is a measure of the largest U.S. stocks. This index is a subset of

TABLE 6-6

Funds Benchmarked to S&P Indexes

S&P Indexes	Fund Name	Class	Fee	Symbol	Minimum
500 Index	Vanguard 500 Index	Open-End	0.18	VFINX	3,000
500 Index	Fidelity Spartan 500 Index	Open-End	0.10	FSMKX	10,000
500 Index	SPDR ETF	ETF	0.10	SPY	None
500 Index	iShares S&P 500 Index	ETF	0.09	IVV	None
500/Citigroup Growth	iShares S&P 500 Growth Index	ETF	0.18	IVW	None
500/Citigroup Value	iShares S&P 500 Value Index	ETF	0.18	IVE	None
MidCap 400 Index	MidCap SPDR Trust	ETF	0.25	MDY	None
MidCap 400 Index	iShares S&P MidCap 400 Index	ETF	0.20	IJH	None
MidCap 400/Citi Growth	iShares S&P MidCap 400 Growth	ETF	0.25	IJK	None
MidCap 400/Citi Value	iShares S&P MidCap 400 Value	ETF	0.25	IJJ	None
600 SmallCap Index	iShares SmallCap 600	ETF	0.20	IJR	None
SmallCap 600/Citi Growth	iShares SmallCap 600 Growth	ETF	0.25	IJT	None
SmallCap 600/Citi Value	iShares SmallCap 600 Value	ETF	0.25	IJS	None
100 Index	iShares S&P 100 Index	ETF	0.20	OEF	None
1500 Composite Index	iShares S&P 1500 Index	ETF	0.20	ISI	None
S&P Completion Index	Vanguard Extended Market	Open-End	0.25	VEXMX	3,000
S&P Completion Index	Vanguard Extended Market ETF	ETF	0.08	VXF	None

Source: Morningstar Principia.

the S&P 500 and is used mainly by institutions that want to hedge a large-cap U.S. stock portfolio. The S&P 100 is a free-float market capitalization–weighted index that is made up of 100 major blue-chip stocks across diverse industry groups. The index represents approximately 40 percent of the market value of all listed U.S. equities.

S&P Total Market Index and Completion Index
The S&P Total Market Index (TMI) is an index representative of the U.S. stock market. It includes all common equities listed on the NYSE, the AMEX, the NASDAQ National Market, and the NASDAQ Small Cap. The S&P Completion index is a subindex of the S&P TMI, including all stocks eligible for the S&P TMI and excluding all current constituents of the S&P 500. Covering more than 4,000 constituents, the S&P Completion index offers broad market exposure to mid-, small-, and micro-cap companies.

S&P/Citigroup Style Indexes
In 1992, Standard & Poor's and Barra began a collaboration to produce growth and value subsets of S&P's equity indexes. Those indexes used a single factor (price-to-book value) to determine growth from value. In December 2005, Standard & Poor's switched to Citigroup Growth and Value series and discontinued the single-factor Barra series. The S&P/Citigroup methodology uses a multifactor approach to separating growth stocks from value stocks.

The style indexes measure growth and value along two separate dimensions, with three factors used to measure growth and four factors used to measure value. The list of factors used is outlined below.

Growth Factors
- Five-year earnings per share growth rate
- Five-year sales per share growth rate
- Sales-to-price ratio

Value Factors
- Book value to price ratio
- Cash flow to price ratio

- Five-year internal growth rate
- Dividend yield

Each stock is assigned a style score and then assigned to a value or growth index. While the choice of the factors offers the advantage of consistency, more importantly, Standard & Poor's believes that once style is determined using multiple factors, the addition or deletion of a factor does little to change the profile of the growth and value index.

S&P/Citigroup uses style factors to construct two sets of complementary index series: Style Index Series and Pure Style Index Series.

- *Style Index Series:* This series divides the complete market capitalization of each parent index approximately equally into growth and value indexes while limiting the number of stocks that overlap between them. This series is exhaustive (i.e., covering all stocks in the parent index universe) and uses the conventional, cost-efficient, market capitalization–weighting scheme.
- *Pure Style Index Series:* This series is based on identifying approximately a third of the market capitalization of the index as pure growth and a third as pure value. There will be no overlapping stocks, and stocks are weighted by their style attractiveness. Pure Style indexes are not market weighted. They are weighed based on the fundamental attractiveness of the stock. Chapter 9 contains a list of S&P/Citigroup style index funds.

S&P size funds and Style Index Series funds are listed in Table 6-6. Only the lowest cost S&P index funds are presented. Fees on a basic S&P 500 index fund can range from a low of 0.09 percent per year to more than 1.00 percent per year for the same investment! Don't pay more than you should for index funds.

Miscellaneous Indexes and Funds

There are a few important miscellaneous indexes that need mentioning due to their importance in academics or to the amount of money benchmarked to them. Below are descriptions of those indexes and the funds benchmarked to them.

NASDAQ 100 and the NASDAQ 100 Trust
The NASDAQ 100 index includes 100 of the largest domestic and international nonfinancial securities listed on the NASDAQ stock market based on market capitalization. The index reflects companies across major industry groups including computer hardware and software, telecommunications, retail/wholesale trade, and biotechnology. It does not contain securities of financial companies including investment companies.

The NASDAQ 100 Trust (symbol QQQQ; fee 0.20) is a unit investment trust that issues securities called NASDAQ 100 Index Tracking Stock. The trust holds all of the component securities of the NASDAQ 100 index. The investment objective of the trust is to provide investment results that generally correspond with the price and yield performance of the index. Although limited in scope because it only covers stock on one exchange, QQQQ is a popular investment with institutions and individual traders. There was close to $20 billion in QQQQ as of June 2006.

Schwab 1000 Index and Fund
The Schwab 1000 Index Fund (symbol SNXFX: fee 0.50) seeks to track the total return of the Schwab 1000 index by investing in the stocks of the 1,000 largest publicly traded U.S. companies. The Schwab 1000 index is similar to the Russell 1000 index; however the fund combines an index model with a management strategy that actively seeks to offset capital gains by realizing corresponding capital losses. In April 2006, the fund celebrated 15 years in a row with no capital gain distributions to shareholders. There was more than $6.5 billion in the Schwab 1000 Index Fund as of June 2006.

Center for Research in Security Prices
The Center for Research in Security Prices (CRSP) is an important source of historical market data favored by academics. CRSP sorts all stocks on the NYSE by market cap and breaks the universe into 10 equal groups by number of names. These are called *deciles*. Decile 1 is the group of the largest stocks on the NYSE, and decile 10 is the

group of the smallest stocks on the NYSE. CRSP then includes all equivalently sized AMEX and NASDAQ (OTC) stocks into the NYSE size decile in which they fit by market cap. All small-cap indexes are rebalanced quarterly.

Deciles are grouped together to form indexes. The CRSP 1-2 is the largest fifth of NYSE stocks by name and all equivalents from other exchanges and makes up the CRSP Large Cap index. The CRSP 9-10 index is the smallest fifth of NYSE stocks by name and all equivalents from other exchanges and makes up the CRSP Micro Cap index. There are approximately 4,270 stocks in the CRSP database, and of those, 2,400 make up the micro-cap index.

The Bridgeway Ultra Small Company Market Fund (symbol BRSIX; fee 0.73) seeks to replicate the total return of the CRSP decile 10 group by investing in a sampling of companies in that decile. As of June 2006, there were approximately 600 stocks in the fund, and total assets were slightly over $1 billion. One problem that all successful small- and micro-cap fund managers face is being flooded with new money coming into a fund. There is not enough stock available to buy. BRSIX has closed to new investors in the past and will close in the future when management believes the fund is at capacity or assets are growing too quickly.

References to CRSP data will become commonplace as you continue your investigation into index funds. That is particularly true if you explore advisor-only funds offered through Dimensional Fund Advisors (DFA), an institutional investment firm headquartered in Santa Monica, California. Several of DFA's U.S. equity funds loosely follow CRSP decile groups.

CHAPTER SUMMARY

This chapter gave you a comprehensive overview of the major U.S. equity indexes and examples of low-cost index funds benchmarked to those indexes. There are many similarities and several differences among the DJ Wilshire, Russell, Morningstar, Dow Jones, MSCI, and Standard & Poor's methodologies. One methodology is not better than another; they are only different. Each index structure has its good points and less desirable points.

In the end, it is very likely that the performance of all competing U.S. stock averages will be very close. Follow the adage "All roads lead to Rome" when you are selecting an index to benchmark. I do recommend selecting one index provider and using only their indexes. That will ensure there is no overlap of stock holdings and will help you organize your portfolio according to one system.

This chapter included many examples of index funds that are benchmarked to broad U.S. equity indexes. These samples do not represent a complete list of index funds available to the public. For a complete list of index funds and their benchmarks, visit www.indexuniverse.com.

CHAPTER 7

U.S. Sector Equity Funds

Key Concepts

- There are differences in industry classification systems.
- Some index funds are benchmarked to industries.
- Real estate investment trust index funds are indirect investments in real properties.
- Socially responsible index funds exclude companies that do not pass certain social criteria screens.

"**D**ivide and conquer" is an ideal strategy in war, but it is a questionable tactic for index fund investors. This chapter explains how index providers divide the stock market into industry classifications allowing mutual fund companies to create index funds benchmarked to those classifications. Industry sector investing has huge appeal to some investors because of the singular industry concentration of these funds. Recall the 80% decline in technology stocks than occurred between 2000 and 2002. Proceed with caution. A successful sector fund investing diversified their portfolio into several sectors so they will not be hurt badly when one sector takes a tumble.

The stock market is made up of thousands of individual companies. Without an orderly way to classify those stocks, the market would be a quagmire of names and symbols. Classifying stocks by industries is a logical way to separate stocks into categories. It allows investors to study different parts of the market and to gauge the movement of capital from one industry to another.

New technology often creates new companies, which are financed in part by an issuance of common stock. The listing of new companies often leads to new industries sectors and subsectors in the market. At the same time new industries are created, established industries fade away. Thus, the industry classification systems used by index providers are constantly evolving.

This chapter is divided into three sections. The first explains the different industry classification systems and the index funds benchmarked to those systems. The second section is specifically on real estate investment trusts (REITs). The last section explores sociably responsible indexes and funds that exclude certain industries.

INDUSTRY CLASSIFICATION SYSTEMS

There are several ways competing index providers slice and dice index data to create industry sectors. Although there are differences in the methodology, in the final analysis the difference in industry classification systems is not drastic. They all hold 10 or 11 basic industry groups, and the names of those industry groups are fairly consistent.

The big difference in the competing classification systems lies mainly in the subgroups. That is which subgroups make up a basic group. In my opinion, there is no need for individual investors to become too concerned with the details of an industry classification if you pick one group of industry index funds and stick with that group. Then you will not have overlap.

The value of each industry group floats with the market, so there can be huge swings in industry valuation, and fortunes can quickly reverse. Figure 7-1 illustrates the changes that can occur in industry group valuations over time. In 1980, energy and basic material stocks lead the S&P 500. By the turn of the century, technology and finance ruled. Of course, nothing is forever. Technology collapsed by 50 percent between 2000 and 2005 while energy and basic material stocks pushed ahead.

Using perfect hindsight, investors would have significantly outperformed the S&P 500 if they sold technology in 1999 and energy companies. Of course hindsight is 20/20, and trying to guess the next hot industry sector is impossible. Nonetheless, large potential gains in industry sectors entice many investors to buy books, magazines, and newsletters that claim to predict the future.

FIGURE 7–1

Changes to Standard & Poor's Industry Leaders from 1980 to 2000

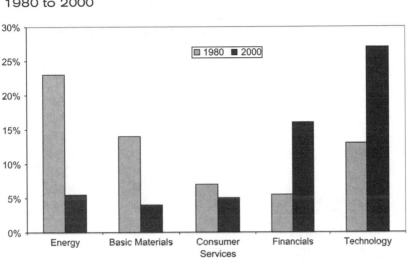

Source: Standard & Poor's.

In this chapter, we compare three industry sector providers and review index funds that are benchmarked against their indexes. This discussion of index providers will help you select a sector index fund series that is right for you. In addition, we will look at index funds outside of the basic industry sectors such as real estate investment trust index funds and a few niche markets.

Global Industry Classification Standard

Standard & Poor's and Morgan Stanley Capital International (MSCI), two leading providers of global indexes, jointly launched the Global Industry Classification Standard (GICS) in 1999. The GICS was developed in response to the global financial community's need for one complete, consistent set of global sector and industry definitions that reflects today's economy and is flexible enough to change as the investment world changes. More than 34,000 active, publicly traded companies globally are currently classified and maintained by S&P and MSCI according to the GICS methodology.

The GICS structure currently has four levels of detail. The GICS structure, which is reviewed annually, is composed of 10 sectors, 24 industry groups, 67 industries, and 147 subindustries. Here is an example of the structure:

Sector: Consumer Discretionary (GICS code: 25)

Industry Group: Consumer Services (GICS code: 2530)

Industry: Hotels, Restaurants and Leisure (GICS code: 253010)

Subindustry: Casinos and Gaming (GICS code: 25301010)

The 10 sectors and examples of industries and subsectors are as follows:

1. Basic Materials: metals, mining, forest and paper products, chemicals
2. Consumer Discretionary: auto, appliances, retail, leisure, homebuilding, media
3. Consumer Stables: food and drug retailing, tobacco, household products
4. Energy: energy equipment, oil and gas exploration, refining, storage
5. Financials: banks, financial services, real estate investment trusts, insurance
6. Health Care: managed care, medical products, drugs, biotech
7. Industrials: capital goods, building, defense, aerospace, all transportation
8. Information Technology: hardware, software, telecom equipment, consulting
9. Telecommunication Services: fixed line, mobile, integrated services
10. Utilities: electric, gas, water, multi-utilities

In the spring of each year, the GICS structure is reviewed and changes are made as needed. In 2006, one industry group was renamed, and 4 new industries and 10 new subindustries were formed. Changes also included discontinuing one industry and two subindustries and making name and definition changes to others.

Select Sector SPDRs are ETFs that unbundle the S&P 500 and

allow you to customize the S&P 500 to better meet your investment goals. There are 9 SPDRs representing the 10 GICS sectors. The Information Technology and Telecommunication Services sectors are lumped together under the Technology SPDR.

In addition to GICS sectors, iShares offers funds covering some industries and subindustries. Table 7-1 gives a list of funds that use GICS.

Vanguard U.S. Sector Index ETFs Also Use GICS

Each issue of U.S. Sector ETFs is designed to give investors exposure to a segment of the U.S. stock market by tracking the performance of

TABLE 7-1

Industry Select Sector SPDRs

	Type	Fee	Symbol	Minimum
GICS Sector Funds				
Consumer Discretionary SPDR	ETF	0.26	XLY	None
Consumer Staple SPDR	ETF	0.26	XLP	None
Energy SPDR	ETF	0.26	XLE	None
Financial SPDR	ETF	0.26	XLF	None
Health Care Select SPDR	ETF	0.26	XLV	None
Industrial SPDR	ETF	0.25	XLI	None
Basic Materials Select SPDR	ETF	0.26	XLB	None
Technology SPDR	ETF	0.26	XLK	None
Utilities SPDR	ETF	0.26	XLU	None
Specialty Funds				
SPDR Biotech	ETF	0.35	XBI	None
SPDR Homebuilders	ETF	0.35	XHB	None
SPDR Metals & Mining	ETF	0.35	XME	None
SPDR Oil & Gas Exploration and Production	ETF	0.35	XOP	None
SPDR Oil & Gas Equipment and Services	ETF	0.35	XES	None
SPDR Pharmaceuticals	ETF	0.35	XPH	None
SPDR Retail	ETF	0.35	XRT	None
SPDR Semiconductor	ETF	0.35	XSD	None

Source: Morningstar Principia.

TABLE 7-2

Funds Benchmarked to MSCI Industry Sectors

MSCI Investible Market Industry Sector Funds	Type	Fee	Symbol	Minimum
Vanguard Energy	ETF	0.25	VDE	None
Vanguard Financials	ETF	0.25	VFH	None
Vanguard Health Care	ETF	0.25	VHT	None
Vanguard Industrials	ETF	0.25	VIS	None
Vanguard Information Technology	ETF	0.25	VGT	None
Vanguard Materials Index	ETF	0.25	VAW	None
Vanguard Telecommunication Services	ETF	0.25	VOX	None
Vanguard Utilities Index	ETF	0.25	VPU	None
Vanguard Consumer Discretionary	ETF	0.25	VCR	None
Vanguard Consumer Staples	ETF	0.25	VDC	None
Source: Morningstar Principia.				

a benchmark index as listed in Table 7-2. The MSCI US Investable Market 2500 index (see Chapter 6) is classified into different sectors according to the GICS. Having 2,000 extra stocks in a universe adds more depth to the Vanguard Sector Index ETFs than Sector SPDRs, which only cover S&P 500 stocks.

Another difference between Vanguard U.S. Sector ETFs and SPDRs is that Vanguard ETFs are formed under the Investment Company Act of 1940. That allows the management to sample their target indexes rather then fully replicate them as with SPDRs. However, that also leads to greater tracking error with the index. Currently, Consumer Staples, Energy, Industrials, and Telecommunication Services ETFs may experience a greater degree of tracking error than other Vanguard ETFs.

Industry Classification Benchmark

Dow Jones indexes and FTSE have created a definitive classification system called the Industry Classification Benchmark (ICB). The system is supported by the ICB Universe Database, which contains more than 40,000 companies and 45,000 securities worldwide from the FTSE and Dow Jones universes. ICB offers broad, global coverage of companies and securities and classifies them based on revenue, not earnings.

For the most part, ICB and GICS are very similar. However, a few important subsectors fall under different categories. For example, airline transportation (Southwest, Delta) is classified as Consumer Services under ICB and is classified as Industrials under GICS.

The structure of ICB is based on 10 industries, 18 supersectors, 39 sectors, and 104 subsectors. Although many names in ICB are the same as GICS, they are not in the same order. What ICB calls an industry, GICS calls a sector, and what ICB calls a supersector, GICS calls an industry group.

There are 10 ICB industries. They are

1. Basic Materials: metals & mining, metals, forest/paper, chemicals
2. Consumer Services: travel, airlines, retailers, leisure, media
3. Consumer Goods: autos, food, beverage, tobacco, cosmetics, homebuilding
4. Energy: oil and gas exploration, equipment, pipelines, distribution
5. Financials: banks, insurance, financial services, real estate investment trusts
6. Health Care: drugs, biotech, health care providers, medical equipment
7. Industrial: defense, aerospace, heavy equipment, construction, shipping
8. Technology: hardware, software, communication equipment, Internet
9. Telecommunications: fixed line, mobile, integrated services
10. Utilities: electric, gas, water, multi-utilities

Since 2000, Barclays Global Investors has introduced a series of sector iShares based on what was then called the Dow Jones U.S. classification structure, now the ICB. Ten of these funds are benchmarked to the 10 primary ICB industries, and the rest are

TABLE 7-3

Funds Benchmarked to Dow Jones Industry Sectors

	Type	Fee	Symbol	Minimum
ICB Industry Funds				
iShares DJ US Basic Material Sector	ETF	0.60	IYM	None
iShares DJ US Consumer Goods Sector	ETF	0.60	IYK	None
iShares DJ US Consumer Services Sector	ETF	0.60	IYC	None
iShares DJ US Financial Sector	ETF	0.60	IYF	None
iShares DJ US Health Care Sector	ETF	0.60	IYH	None
iShares DJ US Industrial Sector	ETF	0.60	IYJ	None
iShares DJ US Energy Sector	ETF	0.60	IYE	None
iShares DJ US Technology Sector	ETF	0.60	IYW	None
iShares DJ US Telecommuni- cations Sector	ETF	0.60	IYZ	None
iShares DJ US Utilities Sector	ETF	0.60	IDU	None
Specialty Index Funds				
iShares DJ US Financial Services Sector	ETF	0.60	IYG	None
iShares DJ US Select Aerospace & Defense	ETF	0.60	ITA	None
iShares DJ US Select Health Care Providers	ETF	0.60	IHF	None
iShares DJ US Select Home Construction	ETF	0.60	ITB	None
iShares DJ US Select Insurance	ETF	0.60	IAK	None
iShares DJ US Select Investment Services	ETF	0.60	IAI	None
iShares DJ US Select Medical Equipment	ETF	0.60	IHI	None
iShares DJ US Select Oil Equipment & Service	ETF	0.60	IEZ	None
iShares DJ US Select Oil Exploration & Production	ETF	0.60	IEO	None
iShares DJ US Select Pharmaceuticals	ETF	0.60	IHE	None
iShares DJ US Select Regional Banks	ETF	0.60	IAT	None

Source: Morningstar Principia.

benchmarked to supersectors, sectors, and subsectors. Table 7-3 is a list of funds that use ICB:

Merrill Lynch HOLDRS

In early 2000, Merrill Lynch introduced a series of unit investment trusts called HOLDRS. These securities are exchange-traded funds that have creation and redemption characteristics similar to other ETFs described in Chapter 5. HOLDRS are included in this chapter because they can come in handy. Not all industry sectors and subsectors of GICS or ICB are available using a full index fund. Table 7-4 provides a list of HOLDRS and the sectors they represent.

There are several unique features of HOLDRS that investors should be aware of:

- HOLDRS invest in the top 20 stocks of industry sectors and subsectors using the GICS, but they do not fit the definition of a true index fund because they do not attempt to replicate an industry group.
- HOLDRS invest an equal amount of money in each stock in the industry sector.
- Existing HOLDRS units are not rebalanced to the index after mergers and acquisitions. When a fund expires, a new HOLDRS is created using new industry data. Old units can be rolled into new units without a tax consequence.
- Individual investors can turn in HOLDRS in round lots in 100 units and receive the underlying stock in return. This allows an investor to sell specific stocks in the fund rather than the entire fund.
- The owners of HOLDRS retain voting rights on the stocks in a fund. This means an investor in one HOLDRS unit will get 20 annual reports and voting proxies stuffed in their mailbox each year.

HOLDRS are nonmanaged unit investment trusts, so there is no ongoing management fee. However, there are still commission costs to buy and sell the units on the market. In addition, there is an annual $2 per 100-unit trustee and custody fee that is paid to the Bank of New York from stock dividends. Because the market price of HOLDRS units varies from fund to fund, the $2 per 100 units fee can represent a varying cost. For example, the $2 charge is only 0.02 percent of a $100 per unit fund, but it is 0.4 percent of a $5 per unit fund. Finally, if you redeem HOLDRS for an in-kind distribution of the underlying stock, which is an option, there is a $10 per 100 unit round lot redemption fee.

REAL ESTATE INVESTMENT TRUST INDEX FUNDS

Real estate should be treated as a different asset class than common stock. The tax accounting is different than common stocks, and the underlying collateral of REITs is considerably different. In addition, REITs do not correlate well with the rest of the stock market, making an investment in real estate a good diversification tool.

Several years ago, the only way you could invest in real estate was through direct ownership or a limited partnership, but not any more. The magic of modern finance now allows us to buy a huge assortment of real estate with a few computer clicks by purchasing a REIT on the stock exchange.

A REIT represents an indirect investment in a group of real properties. You are actually buying a publicly traded management company whose purpose is to acquire and manage commercial real estate. That company collects rents and distributes those rents to shareholders.

REITs are similar to closed-end mutual funds because they can trade at a premium or discount to the underlying value of the assets. Buildings are not appraised on a daily basis. The only time the true value of a piece of property is known is when it is sold. As a result, the market value of a REIT goes up and down with the supply and demand for REIT shares even though the actual underlying value of the properties likely differs from the net asset value of the REIT fund.

There are unique tax benefits that make REITs interesting. Management companies do not pay corporate income tax on any distributions to shareholders as long as 90 percent of the income is passed on to shareholders. At least 75 percent of the income must be from rents, mortgages, and the sale of properties. That makes the dividend income from REIT index funds higher than other equity index funds and also makes REIT funds an ideal choice for investors needing more income.

TABLE 7-4

Merrill Lynch Holders

HOLDRs Sector Funds	Symbol	Minimum
B2B Internet HOLDRs	BHH	None
Biotech HOLDRs	BBH	None
Broadband HOLDRs	BDH	None
Europe 2001 HOLDRs	EKH	None
Internet Arch HOLDRs	IAH	None
Internet HOLDRs	HHH	None
Internet Infr HOLDRs	IIH	None
Market 2000 HOLDRs	MKH	None
Oil Services HOLDRs	OIH	None
Pharmaceutical HOLDRs	PPH	None
Regional Bank HOLDRs	RKH	None
Retail HOLDRs	RTH	None
Semiconductor HOLDRs	SMH	None
Software HOLDRs	SWH	None
Telecom HOLDRs	TTH	None
Utilities HOLDRs	UTH	None
Wireless HOLDRs	WMH	None
Source: Morningstar Principia.		

Adding REITs to a portfolio tends to reduce portfolio risk and increase return. That is due to the low correlation in return between REITs, stocks, and bonds. Having several different types of investments in your portfolio is a good strategy. For detailed information on portfolio management using REITs and other asset classes, read *All About Asset Allocation* by Richard Ferri (McGraw-Hill, 2005).

REIT Indexes

REIT index construction and constituents differ by index provider. For example, some REIT indexes include hospitals and other health care facilities while others do not. Table 7-5 highlight the major differences. Table 7-6 provides a list of REIT index funds available for the different indexes.

The Morgan Stanley US REIT index was designed as a broad representation of REITs. The index represents approximately 85 percent of the US REIT universe. It consists of REITs included in the MSCI US Investable Market 2500 index, excluding specialty equity REITs that do not generate a majority of their revenue and income from real estate rental and leasing operations. The MSCI US REIT index excludes mortgage and hybrid REITs and companies classified under the GICS Real Estate Management and Development subindustry. The index holds approximately 112 companies.

The Dow Jones U.S. Real Estate index seeks to provide a broad measure of the U.S. real-estate securities market. The index currently has approximately 93 companies, which make up the real estate portion of the Dow Jones U.S. Total Market Index. Although the U.S. Real Estate index consists predominately of REITs, it also includes real-estate operating companies (REOCs).

The DJ Wilshire REIT index is a subset of the Dow Jones Real Estate Securities index and includes only REITs. Its objective is to provide a broad measure of publicly traded REITs. The index holds 85 components. The DJ Wilshire REIT index does not hold health care REITs or RECOs .

The S&P REIT Composite tracks approximately 100 REITs on the U.S. markets. The securities are chosen for their liquidity and importance in representing a diversified real estate portfolio. To be included, a REIT must meet the same liquidity guidelines used for the S&P SuperComposite 1500 and must have at least US$100 million in unadjusted market capitalization. Mortgage REITs are not

TABLE 7–5

Major REIT Indexes and Their Constituents

REIT Index Holdings	Health Care Long-term Care Nursing Homes	Commercial Mortgage Lenders	Large Land Tracks and Farming
MSCI US REIT Index	Yes	No	No
Dow Jones REIT Index	Yes	Yes	Yes
DJ Wilshire REIT Index	No	No	No
Cohen & Steers Realty Majors	Yes	No	No
S&P REIT Index	Yes	No	Yes

Source: MSCI, Dow Jones, S&P, Cohen & Steers.

TABLE 7-6

Low-Cost REIT Index Funds

Index	REIT Index Fund	Type	Fee	Symbol	Minimum
MSCI US REIT	Vanguard REIT ETF	ETF	0.12	VNQ	None
MSCI US REIT	Vanguard REIT Index	Open-End	0.21	VGSIX	3,000
DJ Wilshire REIT	streetTRACKS WR REIT	ETF	0.26	RWR	None
Dow Jones REIT	iShares DJ RE Index	ETF	0.60	IYR	None
Cohen & Steers	iShares C&S Realty	ETF	0.35	ICF	None
Source: Morningstar Principia.					

eligible for inclusion. Currently, there are no low-cost index funds benchmarked to the S&P REIT Composite.

Cohen & Steers Realty Majors index tracks the performance of large, actively traded U.S. real estate investment trusts. It is the least diverse of all the indexes holding only about 30 REITs. There are no mortgage lenders in the Cohen & Steers Realty Majors index.

SOCIALLY RESPONSIBLE INDEXES AND FUNDS

Some investors have a moral dilemma with index funds because they include all companies, including those that profit from businesses they disagree with. Socially screened indexes and the index funds benchmarked to them seek to gain broad-based equity or bond exposure while excluding companies that do not pass certain social criteria tests. Examples of screening include eliminating companies in the tobacco, alcoholic beverages, and pornography industries. In addition, social screens may extend into labor practices, human rights, and even animal rights.

Different index providers have different views regarding what is socially responsible. People who desire to follow a socially responsible investment strategy need to study the methodology of each index to determine which fund screens to fit their beliefs. Following in the text is Table 7-7, which provides a list of socially screened index providers and a few low-cost index funds benchmarked to them. For more information on social index funds, visit

TABLE 7-7

Low-Cost, Socially Screened Index Funds

Social Index	Low-Cost Socially Screened Index Funds	Type	Fee	Symbol	Minimum
FTSE4Good US Select	Vanguard FTSE Social Index	Open-End	0.25	VFTSX	3,000
KLD BMS (sampled)	TIAA-CREF Social Choice Equity	Open-End	0.27	TCSCX	2,500
KLD Select Social	iShares KLD Select Social Index	ETF	0.50	KLD	None
Domini 400 Social	Domini Social Equity	Open-End	0.62	DSFRX	2,500
Source: Morningstar Principia.					

www.socialinvest.org. The mutual fund screening tool on the Web site is particularly helpful.

The FTSE4Good US Select index is maintained by FTSE Group (FTSE), a global index. FTSE selects stocks from approximately 700 of the largest public companies in the United States by evaluating each company's performance in the following categories: environmental sustainability, upholding and supporting universal human rights, and developing positive relations with stakeholders. The FTSE index includes companies considered to have superior environmental policies, strong hiring and promotion record for minorities and women, and a safe and healthy workplace. Excluded from the index are companies that are involved with tobacco, alcohol, adult entertainment, firearms, gambling, nuclear power, and those that violate fair labor practices and equal opportunity standards.

The KLD Broad Market Social index (BMS) starts with the Russell 3000 index and disqualifies companies involved in adult entertainment, alcohol, firearms, gambling, military, nuclear power, and tobacco. Then KLD uses an internal ratings system to rank the remaining Russell 3000 companies in relation to their sector peers in the following issue areas: community, corporate governance, diversity, employee relations, environment, product quality, product safety, and human rights. Finally, the index selects the top scores that make up 65 to 75 percent of the market capitalization of each sector.

The KLD Select Social index methodology is less restrictive than the BMS in that only tobacco stocks are excluded from the initial list. Starting with the Russell 1000, KLD evaluates the social and environmental performance of companies in the universe by analyzing community relations, diversity, employee relations, human rights, product quality and safety, environment, and corporate governance. KLD assigns ratings based on specific criteria within each issue. Company ratings are translated into issue scores that are aggregated into overall company scores. An optimization process uses the company scores to determine index holdings and weights. Companies with high company scores have higher weights and companies with low company scores have lower weights compared with the Russell 1000.

The Domini 400 Social Index (DSI) uses the S&P 500 as its core universe in addition to 100 non-S&P companies chosen for sector diversification and market capitalization and 50 additional companies with exemplary social and environmental records. Companies involved in alcohol, tobacco, firearms, gambling, nuclear power, and military weapons are not eligible for the DSI. Companies that do not meet KLD's financial screens (market capitalization, earnings, liquidity, stock price, and debt-to-equity ratio) are also ineligible for inclusion. KLD selects companies for the DSI that have positive social and environmental records based on the following issues: community relations, diversity, employee relations, human rights, product quality and safety, environment, and corporate governance. KLD evaluates companies in the context of their industry and sector as well as in relation to the broader market.

The Calvert Social index starts with 1,000 of the largest U.S. companies and screens for alcohol, tobacco, gambling, nuclear power, and companies that use animal testing. In addition, Calvert's in-house social research department looks for companies that meet its standards on issues such as the environment, workplace issues, product safety, community relations, military weapons contracting, international operations, and human rights. There are currently no low-cost index funds benchmarked to the Calvert Social index.

CHAPTER SUMMARY

The allure of sector funds is tantalizing. All you have to do is figure out which industry investors will embrace next and get in front of an avalanche of cash. Unfortunately, the public is usually too late getting into a sector and too late getting out. In the mid-1990s, a meltdown in emerging country funds claimed a number of greedy souls. In the late 1990s, the investment world was bubbling in tech stocks. At the very peak of the craze, investors poured money into tech funds, only to get wiped out after the millennium. In the early 2000s, energy funds and commodity funds are the rage. Chances are that greedy investors will eventually get hurt in those sectors also.

U.S. sector index funds may have a place in your investment portfolio but a very small one. My advice is to avoid most sector funds with the exception of REITs, which should be part of your long-term buy and hold portfolio.

Part III of this book will help you discover how a moderate investment in industry sector funds may enhance your long-term returns. If you do invest in sector funds, it is better to pick funds that use one industry classification standard methodology, either the GICS or ICB. Selecting one standard ensures that there is no overlap of stocks in the sector funds you own.

CHAPTER 8

Global and International Equity Funds

Key Concepts

- Global index funds offer the broadest diversification.
- International index funds invest outside the United States.
- Regional index funds are confined to one part of the globe.
- Country funds are available but not recommended.

The global equity markets have grown dramatically over the past 50 years. In the early 1970s, the U.S. stock market accounted for more than 70 percent of the global equity market. Today, U.S. companies account for less than 50 percent despite compounding at greater than 10 percent return during the period. International equity markets have grown in number, size, scope, and operational efficiency. In the past decade, the number of index funds benchmarked to the international markets has rapidly expanded.

There are good reasons to consider international exposure in a portfolio of stock index funds. Adding international index funds to an all-U.S. index fund portfolio has historically lowered portfolio risk and increased portfolio returns. A second reason to add international stocks is that they are valued in native currency, which hedges an investor against devaluation in the U.S. dollar. Although some foreign markets have had long periods of poor performance, a globally diversified portfolio has been positive for investors and I believe will be positive in the future.

INTERNATIONAL INVESTING TERMINOLOGY

Before presenting the specifics of the international index funds, it is important to clarify the terminology surrounding global and foreign investing.

- ◆ International indexes are composed of stocks whose corporate main headquarters are located outside the United States. Other names for international indexes are foreign and overseas indexes.
- ◆ Global indexes invest in both international stocks and U.S. stocks. Another name for a global index is a world index.
- ◆ Regional indexes invest in stocks of a specific geographical region, such as the Pacific Rim or Latin America.
- ◆ Regional indexes (X-country or ex-country) invest in stock of a region, minus the X country. For example, Pacific Rim (ex-Japan).
- ◆ Developed market indexes are composed of countries whose economies and governments are advanced; generally, those countries that have per capita gross domestic product (GDP) of at least $10,000 per year.
- ◆ Emerging markets indexes are composed of countries that are less advanced and do not meet the GDP requirement of a developed market yet have a free-market system and active financial markets.

Examples of developed markets include Australia, Germany, Japan, Canada, and the United Kingdom. Emerging markets can be divided into early stage and late stage depending on their stage in the evolution to a free-market system. Examples of early-stage emerging markets include Russia, Turkey, Poland, and Indonesia. Late-stage emerging markets are more developed and include Mexico, South Korea, and India.

This chapter presents global and international investing from the broadest global indexes down to the individual countries. The presentation of indexes and funds is in the following order:

1. Global indexes and funds
2. International indexes and funds (multiregional, including emerging markets)

3. Regional indexes funds (Pacific Rim, Continental Europe, United Kingdom, Latin America)
4. Individual country indexes and country funds

GLOBAL MARKET INDEXES AND FUNDS

If you are going to buy only one stock index fund, you might consider a global developed markets fund. Global index funds invest in the largest companies from around the world, including the United States. The three main providers of global index funds are Standard & Poor's (S&P), Dow Jones (DJ), and Morgan Stanley Capital Investments (MSCI). S&P and MSCI often work together to compile international data and contrast indexes. All of the index providers have at least one global index fund benchmarked to them.

MSCI Global Indexes

The MSCI Global Capital Markets index combines the components of the MSCI All Country World index and the MSCI Global Total Bond index. It is an all-encompassing index that spans the global stock and bond markets. As of March 31, 2006, the total market capitalization of the MSCI Global Capital Markets index was $44.9 trillion, composed of $25.8 trillion in equity and $19.1 trillion in fixed income. U.S. equities account for about 28 percent of the index and U.S. bonds account for about 18 percent. There are more than 11,500 securities in the MSCI Global Capital Markets index.

The MSCI All Country World index is a free-float-adjusted market capitalization equity index that is designed to measure market performance in the global developed and emerging markets. MSCI adjusts the market capitalization of index constituents for free float and targets for index inclusion 85 percent of free-float-adjusted market capitalization in each industry group in each country. Currently, the MSCI All Country World index includes 50 countries. At this time, there are no index funds benchmarked to the MSCI All Country World index.

The S&P Global Indexes

The S&P Global 1200 index combines the features of a broad global portfolio with sufficient liquidity in the underlying equities, making the index ideally suited for index-related investment products. The S&P Global 1200 is a free-float-weighted index constructed in a joint effort with Morgan Stanley (for an explanation of free-float, see Chapter 6). There are no index funds benchmarked to the S&P Global 1200 index, however it is a good place to begin a discussion on global investing.

The S&P Global 1200 index covers approximately 70 percent of the global market capitalization and is composed of the S&P 500 for the United States and five non-U.S. indexes: S&P Europe 350, S&P/TOPIX 150 (Japan), S&P/TSX 60 (Canada), S&P Asia Pacific 100, and S&P Latin America 40. An index committee made up of Standard & Poor's staff worldwide selects companies for inclusion in each index and maintains those indexes on a regular basis.

The S&P Global 100 index consists of 100 leading companies listed in the S&P Global 1200 whose businesses are global in nature and that derive a substantial portion of their operating income from multiple countries. The Global 100 does not represent the largest 100 companies, although it comes very close. Rather, Standard & Poor's selects individual companies for the index based on strong fundamentals, industry leadership, market liquidity, and size. See Table 8-1 for an ETF benchmarked to the S&P Global 100.

Currently, U.S. companies make up about 48 percent of the Global 100 index and Europe makes up 30 percent. Financial companies compose 23 percent of the index and energy companies make up 15 percent. The largest holding is currently ExxonMobil representing about 5 percent of the index, and the largest foreign holding is BP PLC representing less than 3 percent. Currencies are not hedged in the S&P Global indexes. General information on the S&P 100 index follows.

The Dow Jones Global Titans 50 Index

Dow Jones is not a leader in global index construction, but they are trying to catch up. Recently, Dow Jones released a new set of indexes aimed at international markets. As of this writing, the only noteworthy index fund is benchmarked to the Global Titans 50 index (see Table 8-1). It is a global stock index consisting of 50 of the

TABLE 8-1

Global Index Funds and Benchmarks

Index	Global Index Funds	Type	Fee	Symbol	Minimum
S&P Global 100	iShares S&P Global 100	ETF	0.40	IOO	None
Dow Jones Global Titans 50	streetTRACKS DJ Global Titans	ETF	0.51	DGT	None

Source: Morningstar Principia.

world's largest companies. To be included in the index, a stock must be well-established with a solid financial situation and a broad client base, well-known to global investors for its success or widely used products and services, a market leader in its industry with either a dominant position or a competitive advantage, and the largest of the blue-chip companies in the global arena.

Dow Jones uses a multifaceted process for selecting stocks. First, 5,000 global stocks are screened for size and liquidity, creating a pool of 100 companies. Every company in the pool must derive some revenue from foreign operations. Next, the stocks are ranked by four fundamental factors that include asset size, book value, sales, and net profit. The stocks are then divided into industry groups and sorted by market value. The largest stocks in each industry group are determined based on a composite score of their market size and the four fundamental values. Fifty of the largest stocks are included in the Dow Jones Global Titans index.

INTERNATIONAL INDEX FUNDS (MULTIREGIONAL)

International index funds invest in companies whose main headquarters are outside the United States. These companies may do a substantial amount of business in the United States or they may do none at all. Most Americans would be shocked to discover that a number of their favorite brand names are not owned by a U.S. company. For example, Skippy® peanut butter is owned by CPC-Bestfoods, a subsidiary of Unilever N.V., a Dutch firm.

Many times a foreign company will buy a U.S. company to gain global market share and increase distribution. A good example is DaimlerChrysler. Even though a large volume of DaimlerChrysler sales are to U.S. customers, Chrysler stock was delisted from the New

York Stock Exchange, and DaimlerChrysler is listed on the German stock exchange and is a component of the German stock index (DAX). Table 8-2 lists examples of low-cost multiregional index funds.

Developed Market Indexes and Funds

There are several index providers offering competing indexes that track developed international markets. The most widely quoted index is the Morgan Stanley Capital International Europe, Australasia, and the Far East index, better know as the MSCI EAFE index. It is also the index that most developed market index funds are benchmarked to. See Table 8-1 for a representative list of EAFE index funds.

The EAFE index is composed of approximately 1,000 large company stocks from 21 developed markets located in Europe and the Pacific Rim. The EAFE is a float-adjusted index that includes at least 85 percent of the free-float market value of each industry group within each country. The best way to think of the EAFE index is as a big international S&P 500 index that covers all developed countries except the United States and Canada.

MSCI does not attempt to control sector weights, country weights, or regional weights in the EAFE index. As a result, the value of the index can swing dramatically between industry sectors, countries, and regions. In 1990, Japan dominated the EAFE with a weight of 70 percent. However, due to a long bear market in Japan and a bull market in Europe, Japan represents about 2 percent of the index. See Figure 8-1 for an illustration of the regional swings that can occur in the EAFE index.

MSCI divides the EAFE into growth and value styles based on the methodology described in Chapter 6. The objective is to divide constituents of an underlying MSCI standard country index into a value index and a growth index, each targeting 50 percent of the free-float-adjusted market capitalization of the underlying country index. Country value and growth indexes are then aggregated into regional value and growth indexes.

The FTSE International Limited Developed ex-North America index is composed of approximately 1,300 stocks of predominately large companies from about 20 countries including Japan, the United Kingdom and developed countries in Continental Europe and the Pacific Rim.

TABLE 8-2

Multiregion International Index Funds

Index	International Index Funds	Type	Fee	Symbol	Minimum
MSCI EAFE	Fidelity Spartan International	Open-End	0.20	FSIIX	10,000
MSCI EAFE	Vanguard Developed Markets	Open-End	0.29	VDMIX	3,000
MSCI EAFE	iShares MSCI EAFE	ETF	0.35	EFA	None
MSCI EAFE Growth	iShares MSCI EAFE Growth	ETF	0.40	EFG	None
MSCI EAFE Value	iShares MSCI EAFE Value	ETF	0.40	EFV	None
FTSE Dev. X-North America	T. Rowe Price Int'l Equity Index	Open-End	0.50	PIEQX	2,500
Schwab International Index	Schwab International	Open-End	0.72	SWINX	2,500
Total International Composite*	Vanguard Total International	Open-End	0.31	VGTSX	3,000

*A market-weighted composite of the MSCI Pacific, MSCI EAFE, and Select Emerging Markets indexes.
Source: Morningstar Principia.

FIGURE   8 - 1

MSCI EAFE Market Weight by Region

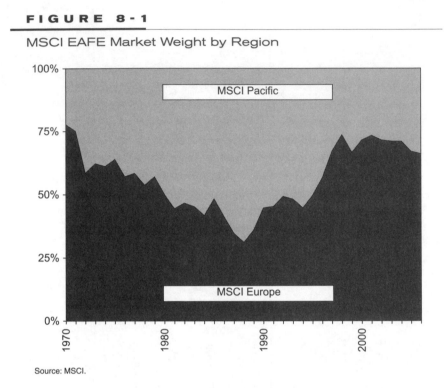

Source: MSCI.

Charles Schwab developed its own developed markets index and called it the Schwab Total International index. The index includes common stock of 15 developed countries outside the United States. Within these countries, Schwab identified the 350 largest companies according to their market capitalization, which became the basis for the index. The Schwab Total International index does not maintain any particular country weighting, although no individual country can make up more than 35 percent.

The Vanguard Developed Markets Fund is composed of a market weighting in the Vanguard Pacific Stock Index Fund and the Vanguard European Stock Index Fund. The fee for the fund is the weighted average charged to the two underlying funds. Because the composition of the portfolio changes with global market conditions, the fee also varies. As of October 2005, the fund cost was 0.29 percent.

If you add the MSCI EAFE index to the MSCI Select Emerging Market index (see next section), you have a "total" international index that covers developed countries and emerging markets. This is precisely what Vanguard did with their Total International Port-folio. It is also a fund of funds. The fund holds a market weighting in the Vanguard Pacific Stock Index Fund, the Vanguard European Stock Index Fund, and the Vanguard Emerging Market Stock Index Fund. The fee for the Vanguard Total International Portfolio is the weighted average charged to the three underlying funds. As of October 2005, the fund cost was 0.31 percent.

One disadvantage of both the Vanguard Developed Markets Fund and the Vanguard Total International Portfolio is that they do not qualify for the foreign dividend tax exclusion. When a foreign company pays a cash dividend, the company's home country often taxes that dividend before the cash is sent overseas. According to the U.S. tax code, investors are entitled to a tax credit for the amount of foreign tax withheld. This is not true for the two Vanguard funds mentioned. U.S. tax rules do not permit the passthrough of foreign dividend tax credits in a fund-of-funds structure.

Emerging Market Indexes and Funds

The phrase *third-world countries* may conjure up images of famine and poverty in your mind. The title did not sit well with the marketing wizards on Wall Street who were trying to sell third-world securities, and they decided to change the name to something that sounded more sophisticated. Thus, the term *emerging markets* was created. Broadly defined, an emerging market is a less fortunate country that is making an effort to change and improve its economy. These countries are going to considerable lengths to make their economies strong, more open to international investors, and more competitive in global markets.

There are two major providers of emerging market index data: S&P and MSCI. Table 8-3 provides a list of funds benchmarked to those indexes.

The S&P Emerging Market indexes and their underlying data-base, which Standard & Poor's acquired from International Finance Corporation (IFC) in 2000, have been maintained since 1975. Since their inception, the indexes, have grown to cover more than 2,000 companies in 53 markets.

The S&P Emerging Market indexes divide into two main families. S&P/IFCG (Global) indexes, the most comprehensive

TABLE 8-3

Emerging Market Index Funds

Index	Emerging Markets Funds	Type	Fee	Symbol	Minimum
MSCI Emerging Markets	Vanguard Emerging Market	Open-End	0.45	VEIEX	3,000
MSCI Emerging Markets	Vanguard Emerging Market ETF	ETF	0.30	VWO	None
MSCI Emerging Markets	Northern Emerging Markets	Open-End	0.85	NOEMX	3,000
MSCI Emerging Markets	iShares MSCI Emerging Markets	ETF	0.75	EEM	None
BNY EM 50 ADR	BLDRS Emerging Markets 50 ADR	ETF	0.84	ADRE	None

Source: Morningstar Principia.

series, are broad market indicators that measure the widest possible opportunity set of investable stocks in each emerging market. S&P/IFCI (Investable) indexes, which are subsets of S&P/IFCG indexes, measure the returns of stocks that are legally and practically available to foreign investors.

All of the S&P Emerging Market indexes are constructed from equities included in the Emerging Markets Database (EMDB). The EMDB, to which index users may subscribe, defines the universe of emerging market stocks. A country is classified as emerging if it has a low- or middle-income economy as defined by the World Bank. In addition, the country's investable market capitalization must be low relative to its most recent GDP figures and its equity market must exhibit substantial features of emerging markets. As of 2006, the database of emerging markets totaled 54 countries.

Indices in S&P/IFCG target an aggregate market capitalization of 70 to 80 percent of the total capitalization of all exchange-listed shares. To qualify for S&P/IFCG, a company typically must be domiciled in an emerging market and among the most actively traded securities in that market. To qualify for inclusion in S&P/IFCI, a company must have a minimum average investable market capitalization of US$125 million and trade at least US$50 million in the 12 months prior to addition.

The MSCI Emerging Markets index is a free-float-adjusted market capitalization index that is designed to measure equity market performance in the global emerging markets. Designation as an emerging market is determined by a number of factors. MSCI evaluates gross domestic product per capita, local government regulations, perceived investment risk, foreign ownership limits, and capital controls.

As of June 2006, the MSCI Emerging Markets index consisted of the following 25 emerging market country indexes: Argentina, Brazil, Chile, China, Colombia, Czech Republic, Egypt, Hungary, India, Indonesia, Israel, Jordan, Korea, Malaysia, Mexico, Morocco, Pakistan, Peru, Philippines, Poland, Russia, South Africa, Taiwan, Thailand, and Turkey.

A minor index that is followed by one index fund is the Bank of New York Emerging Market 50 ADR index (BNY EM 50 ADR). The stocks of most foreign companies trade in United States stock markets as American Depositary Receipts (ADRs).Each ADR is issued by a U.S. depositary bank and represents one or more shares of a foreign stock or a fraction of a share. They are traded in U.S. dollars. A Global form of the security is similar and is also included in the index (GDR). The BNY EM 50 ADR index is a free-float composite of the largest and most liquid ADRs and GDRs that trade on U.S. exchanges.

REGIONAL INDEX FUNDS

MSCI slices the EAFE index into two large geographic regions forming the MSCI Europe index and the MSCI Pacific index. The division of the international indexes into regions allows the formation of index funds benchmarked to those regions.

The MSCI Europe index is made up of approximately 594 common stocks of companies located in 16 European countries, mostly companies in the United Kingdom, France, Switzerland, and Germany (which made up 37, 14, 10, and 10 percent, respectively, of the index's market capitalization as of October 31, 2005). Other countries represented in the index include Austria, Belgium, Denmark, Finland, Greece, Ireland, Italy, The Netherlands, Norway, Portugal, Spain, and Sweden.

The MSCI Pacific index consists of approximately 546 common stocks of companies located in Japan, Australia, Hong

Kong, Singapore, and New Zealand. (As of October 31, 2005, Japan and Australia made up 75 and 16 percent, respectively, of the index's market capitalization.)

The MSCI Pacific Free (ex-Japan) consists of approximately 546 common stocks of companies located in Japan, Australia, Hong Kong, Singapore, and New Zealand. (As of October 31, 2005, Japan and Australia made up 75 and 16 percent, respectively, of the index's market capitalization.)

The word *Free* is used to mean that an index was constituted by free float. Now that all MSCI indexes are free float, the company removed the word *Free* from most index titles. However, the continued use of the word *Free* in the title of certain MSCI indexes recognizes that these indexes have histories different from a similar index that does not have the suffix *Free*. Otherwise, these indexes have the same current constituents and current performance. For example, the MSCI EAFE and EAFE Free indexes now have exactly the same constituents and performance. However, due to investment restrictions on foreign investors in the past, in Singapore, Switzerland, Sweden, Norway, and Finland, which were recognized in EAFE Free, but not in EAFE, the history of the two indexes is different.

The S&P Global 1200 index is also divided into regional indexes. One benchmark is the S&P Europe 350 index. It measures the performance of stocks in continental Europe and the United Kingdom that are in the S&P Global 1200 index. The market capitalization of constituent companies is adjusted to reflect only those stocks available to foreign investors. The stocks in the index are chosen for market size, liquidity, industry group representation, and geographic diversity. Constituent companies are float-adjusted, and reconstitution is a continuous process.

The introduction of the euro as a common currency throughout much of Europe created an opportunity for index providers to create more indexes. Twelve of the 15 states are European Economic and Monetary Union (EMU) member countries. The EMU countries are sometimes referred to as Eurozone or Euroland. The iShares MSCI EMU index seeks to provide investment results that correspond generally with the price and yield performance of the aggregate publicly traded securities in the Eurozone markets, as measured by the MSCI EMU index.

The MSCI United Kingdom index is an index that seeks to provide a benchmark of publicly traded securities in the aggregate in the British markets. The United Kingdom, Sweden, and Denmark are the only developed markets in Europe that are currently not in the Eurozone.

The Dow Jones STOXX 50 index was created to provide a blue-chip representation of Supersector leaders in Europe. Dow Jones STOXX 50 is a subgroup of 50 companies of the Dow Jones European broad index with the aim to mirror the sector leaders. The index includes companies from the countries of Austria, Belgium, Denmark, Finland, France, Germany, Greece, Ireland, Italy, Luxembourg, The Netherlands, Norway, Portugal, Spain, Sweden, Switzerland and the United Kingdom. Dow Jones Euro STOXX 50 is a subgroup of 50 companies of Dow Euro STOXX index excluding those countries not in the EMU.

The S&P Latin America 40 includes highly liquid securities from major economic sectors of Mexico, Brazil, Argentina, and Chile. Companies represent approximately 70 percent of each country's market cap. The S&P Latin America 40 is maintained by the S&P Index Committee, whose members include Standard & Poor's economists and index analysts. The goal of the Index Committee is to ensure that the S&P Latin America 40 remains an accurate measure of the Latin American markets, reflecting the risk and return characteristics of the broader universe on an ongoing basis.

Table 8-4 provides a sampling of regional index funds. Several new regional funds are in registration with the Securities and Exchange Commission (SEC).

COUNTRY INDEX FUNDS

A majority of country index funds are benchmarked to MSCI country indexes. MSCI constructs an index for each country by listing every security on the market and collects price data, outstanding shares, significant ownership, free float, and monthly trading volume. The stocks are categorized according to industry group, and individual companies are selected from each industry. MSCI methodology requires at least 85 percent representation of each industry group. Therefore, a country index captures at least 85 percent of the market capitalization of that country. Industry replication, more than any other single factor, is a key characteristic of a single country market index.

TABLE 8-4

Regional Market Index Funds

Index	Regional Market Funds	Type	Fee	Symbol	Minimum
Europe					
MSCI EAFE	Vanguard European Stock	Open-End	0.27	VEURX	3,000
MSCI EAFE	Vanguard European ETF	ETF	0.18	VGK	None
S&P Euro-350	iShares S&P Euro-350	ETF	0.60	IEV	None
MSCI EMU Index	iShares EMU Index	ETF	0.59	EZU	None
MSCI United Kingdom	iShares U.K. Index	ETF	0.59	EWU	None
Dow Jones STOXX 50	streetTRACKS DJ STOXX 50	ETF	0.32	FEU	None
Dow Jones Euro STOXX 50	streetTRACKS DJ Euro 50	ETF	0.32	FEZ	None
Pacific Rim					
MSCI Pacific	Vanguard Pacific Stock	Open-End	0.32	VPACX	3,000
MSCI Pacific	Vanguard Pacific ETF	ETF	0.18	VPL	None
MSCI Pacific Free ex-Japan	iShares MSCI ex-Japan	ETF	0.50	EPP	None
Latin America					
S&P Latin America 40	iShares S&P Latin 40 (ADRs)*	ETF	0.50	ILF	None

*The iShares S&P Latin 40 holds ADRs rather than directly holding stocks.
Source: Morningstar Principia.

Table 8-5 illustrates the assortment of country index funds that are currently available.

Once stocks are selected for a MSCI country index, companies with greater than 40 percent float are included at their full market capitalization weight. Companies with less than 40 percent float that are added to an index are included at a fraction of their market capitalization in accordance with the MSCI partial inclusion schedule. This partial inclusion policy facilitates the inclusion of companies with a modest float while taking into consideration potential limited supply.

TABLE 8-5

Country Index Funds

Country Index Fund	Index Provider	Type	Fee	Symbol	Minimum
iShares Australia	MSCI	ETF	0.59	EWA	None
iShares Austria	MSCI	ETF	0.59	EWO	None
iShares Belgium	MSCI	ETF	0.59	EWK	None
iShares Brazil	MSCI	ETF	0.74	EWZ	None
iShares Canada	MSCI	ETF	0.59	EWC	None
iShares FTSE/Xinhua China	FTSE	ETF	0.74	FXI	None
iShares France	MSCI	ETF	0.59	EWQ	None
iShares Germany	MSCI	ETF	0.59	EWG	None
iShares Hong Kong	MSCI	ETF	0.59	EWH	None
iShares Italy	MSCI	ETF	0.59	EWI	None
iShares Japan	MSCI	ETF	0.59	EWJ	None
iShares S&P TOPIX 150	S&P	ETF	0.50	ITF	None
iShares Malaysia	MSCI	ETF	0.59	EWM	None
iShares Mexico	MSCI	ETF	0.59	EWW	None
iShares Netherlands	MSCI	ETF	0.59	EWN	None
iShares MSCI South Africa	MSCI	ETF	0.74	EZA	None
iShares South Korea	MSCI	ETF	0.74	EWY	None
iShares Singapore	MSCI	ETF	0.59	EWS	None
iShares Spain	MSCI	ETF	0.59	EWP	None
iShares Sweden	MSCI	ETF	0.59	EWD	None
iShares Switzerland	MSCI	ETF	0.59	EWL	None
iShares Taiwan	MSCI	ETF	0.74	EWT	None

Source: Morningstar Principia.

The S&P/TOPIX 150 index includes 150 highly liquid securities selected from each major sector of the Tokyo market. The S&P/TOPIX 150 is designed specifically to give portfolio managers and derivative traders an index that is broad enough to provide representation of the market but narrow enough to ensure liquidity.

The FTSE/Xinhua China A50 index is free-float-adjusted and consists of the top 50 Chinese companies by total market capitalization. The index was launched in July 2003. A quarterly review of the index takes place in January, April, July, and October.

GLOBAL INDUSTRY SECTORS

In 2000 MSCI, in collaboration with Standard & Poor's, introduced the Global Industry Classification Standard (GICS). MSCI and S&P categorize the stocks in each of its indexes according to the GICS structure of 10 sectors, 23 industry groups, 59 industries, and 123 subindustries. MSCI offers industry indexes based on GICS covering all global, regional, and country indexes.

The next step for index fund providers was to create a broad range of global industry sector funds. Some of those funds are highlighted in Table 8-6. Global industry funds allow investors the ability

TABLE 8-6

Global Sector Index Funds

Index	Global Sector Funds	Type	Fee	Symbol	Minimum
S&P Global Energy	iShares S&P Global Energy	ETF	0.48	IXC	None
S&P Global Financial	iShares S&P Global Financial	ETF	0.48	IXG	None
S&P Global Health	iShares S&P Global Health	ETF	0.48	IXJ	None
S&P Global Technology	iShares S&P Global Technology	ETF	0.48	IXN	None
S&P Global Telecommunications	iShares S&P Global Telecom	ETF	0.48	IXP	None

Source: Morningstar Principia.

to build exposure to the global marketplace industry classification rather than by geographical regions.

CHAPTER SUMMARY

The global stock market is becoming more diverse and easier to access. A little international stock exposure makes a lot of sense for today's investors because of its diversification benefits. Although there are no hard and fast rules for the amount of international equity exposure placed in a portfolio, historically a 30 percent exposure has helped reduce the risk of an all-U.S. stock portfolio and adds slightly to the return.

One of the best ways to gain exposure to the global markets is through a diversified global or international index fund. Make sure you check the fees in a fund before you buy. They can vary widely in the international index fund marketplace. Ensure that you know which index the fund follows so you will not have redundant country exposure in your portfolio. I do not recommend trying to trade in and out of individual country funds due to the high risk involved. A good idea is to stick with regional funds and multiregional funds when making your selection.

CHAPTER 9

Alternative U.S. Equity Funds

Key Concepts

- Enhanced funds attempt to beat the market by making small adjustments.
- Leveraged funds try to beat the market by using borrowed money.
- Inverse index funds profit when the market moves down.
- Modified-weight and equal-weighted index funds are value funds.

There are ways to beat the market using unconventional and often gimmicky strategies but not without taking more risk. The goal of this chapter is to introduce a special group of mutual funds that are a spin-off of indexing. Some of the funds mentioned make minor deviations from an index to potentially enhance returns, whereas others are completely out of the index fund realm. Minor variations to indexes will not do much harm to your portfolio if the strategies do not work. To the contrary, the radical funds can dissolve your capital in a hurry.

There are several types of special funds discussed in this chapter. Enhanced index funds are one type of special fund that is relatively benign. Enhanced funds attempt to beat the market by making slight adjustments to an index and potentially harvesting an extra one-half percent. A more aggressive type of fund uses leverage to try and beat the markets. Generally, leveraged funds move up more than the market when the market goes up and down more when the market goes down. Your timing had better be right. Inverse funds are quirky characters that move in the opposite direction of the market. If you have God-like foresight, you can enhance your return with a leveraged fund when stocks go up and switch to an inverse fund when stocks go down.

The newest characters in index fund innovations are modified-weight funds. The idea is to weigh the stocks in a portfolio using "other than market weight" index. Simply explained, modified-weight funds reduce the amount invested in large-cap growth stocks, thereby trying to capture the premium the market has historically paid for small stock and value stocks.

The sad part about modified-weight funds is that the issues claim to have found a new indexing nirvana when in fact all they have done is create more funds titled toward value stocks. I call these modified-weight funds *spindexes* for the marketing spin the creators place on their products. Indexing is a hot-selling idea, but spindexes are not indexes.

Whether or not any of these funds work remains to be seen. However, you can guarantee one thing: the expenses of those funds will be higher than almost all traditional index funds discussed in this book.

Before investing in one of the funds listed in this chapter, it is important to know what the risks are. That way, you will not be surprised when a fund is not acting in line with the rest of the market. Just remember one thing: regardless of how great the sellers of these funds claim their products are, there is no such thing as a free lunch on Wall Street.

ENHANCED INDEX FUNDS

Enhanced Index Funds

The basic idea of indexing is to eliminate the risk of underperforming a market by tracking the returns of a market. Nevertheless, enhanced index fund managers believe they can make a few minor adjustments to an otherwise good index and beat the benchmark by a small amount. That means in the event the portfolio manager fails to beat the market, at least the fund should not have very large tracking error against the benchmark. There are two basic methods of index enhancement: security-based strategies and synthetic strategies.

Security-Based Enhancements

Security-based enhancements start from the assumption that an index is almost perfect. It just needs the manager's touch to make it perfect. With a little tinkering, the fund manager believes he or she can achieve a better return than the index without creating large tracking error or inducing extra risk.

One way to tinker with an index is to manage industry sectors. A manager may reduce or eliminate stocks in sectors that he or she thinks are overvalued and increase stocks in a sector he or she thinks are undervalued. For example, in the late 1990s technology stocks were at a historically high valuation. An enhanced index fund manager could have reduced technology holdings or capped the weighting of technology stocks in the fund. The gap would be filled with stocks from an industry group considered to be below its historically normal valuations, such as energy stocks. The rest of the enhanced index fund would remain the same.

Security-based methods of enhancement involve more trading than a straight index fund, and that means higher transaction costs. In addition, the funds in general have higher management fees due to the research needed to manage the fund. Consequently, the fund manager must add significant value through security or sector selection if the fund is going to beat the index after expenses. That is not easy to do.

Enhancements can occur in bond funds as well as in stock funds. A common benchmark for investment-grade bond funds is the Lehman Brothers Aggregate Bond index (see Chapter 10). The index maintains a percentage of bonds in different categories and different maturities. A bond fund manager may try to enhance returns by making slight adjustments to the bond categories or the maturities in the portfolio. If the manager is correct, the bond fund will outperform the LB Aggregate Bond index before fees.

Synthetic Enhancements

Can you imagine a stock index fund that owns no stocks? or a bond index fund that owns no bonds? That is exactly what synthetic index funds are. Managers create an index fund by combining a cash position with a highly leveraged investment called a derivative. Derivatives are manufactured investments such as futures, options, and swaps. The price of a derivative fluctuates based on the price of something else. If the price of the S&P 500 index went up, the price of S&P 500 futures contracts and S&P 500 call options would also go up. In addition, a derivative is typically leveraged, so that a slight move in an index will cause a large move in the derivative.

Derivatives may sound risky, however if a portfolio of cash and derivatives is managed correctly, a derivatives-based index fund will track its benchmark very closely. Mutual fund managers use derivatives to re-create synthetic index funds. Once a fund is created, a variety of strategies can be used in an attempt to capture the small differences that can occur between the value of a derivatives-based index and the actual underlying stock or bond market. If enough anomalies are captured, the synthetic fund will beat the market by a small margin. The strategy is called index arbitrage, and it is very popular with large institutional investment management companies.

Below are a couple of other synthetic indexing strategies used by portfolio managers to enhance returns. Don't be concerned if you do not understand these ideas right away. This is not a book on derivatives trading, and these strategies are complicated even for professionals.

- *Cash plus:* In this strategy, an index fund is created using futures contracts. Because buying futures contracts only requires a small downpayment called *margin*, the rest of the cash in an account can be invested in other securities. One basic assumption about stock future pricing is that the return on the cash portion of an index fund not used for margin is expected to earn the Fed funds rate (the overnight lending rate banks charge each other). If the cash portion earns more than the Fed funds rate, there is an extra return for shareholders of the fund.

- *Option overwrite:* Managers can create and sell (write) options against the actual securities in the fund. Writing options generates extra cash flow to the fund but can also limit the upside profit potential if the market moves up.

Managers typically try to write options against underlying stock or futures positions when they perceive the options are overpriced.

These strategies expose the synthetic index funds to many risks above and beyond the risks of the market, but we will not go into the risks because they are beyond the scope of this book. You will have to take my word for the fact that funny things happen in synthetic index fund accounts, and most are not good for you. Also, synthetic index funds are not designed for taxable accounts. Derivative strategies generate a lot of cash flow, much of which is taxable at ordinary income tax rates.

There are several mutual funds that use securities-based and synthetic enhancement strategies. Table 9-1 lists a few funds that use one or more of the strategies in this section. The table lists examples of enhanced funds and is not an endorsement of those funds. Carefully read the prospectus of any mutual fund before investing.

TABLE 9-1

Enhanced Index Funds

Benchmark	Enhanced Index Funds	Type	Fee	Symbol	Minimum
Security Selection					
S&P 500	Vanguard Growth & Income	Open-End	0.40	VQNPX	3,000
S&P 500	DWA Enhanced S&P AARP*	Open-End	0.98	SSLFX	1,000
S&P MidCap 400	ING DIRECT IdxPlus Md C	Open-End	0.99	IDMOX	1,000
LB Aggregate Bond	TIAA-CREF Bond Plus	Open-End	0.30	TIPBX	2,500
Synthetic Index					
S&P 500	DFA Enhance Large Co†	Open-End	0.34	DFELX	NA
S&P 500	PIMCO Stock Plus A (3% load)	Open-End	1.05	PSPAX	5,000

*Purchase is restricted to AARP members.
†Available only through registered investment advisers.
Source: Morningstar.

LEVERAGED AND INVERSE INDEX FUNDS

Leveraged Index Funds

A leveraged index fund borrows extra money and invests that cash in more stocks or bonds. Depending on the fund, the borrowing may represent 50 percent of the value of the fund. If the return of the leveraged portion is higher than the cost to borrow the money, the fund makes an extra return above the market, albeit with significantly more inherent risk. If the fund does not make up the borrowing costs, it will perform below the market, sometimes significantly below.

The best case for a leveraged fund is when interest rates drop and the stock market goes up. Borrowing costs are reduced, and the fund makes an extra return from the extra market position. The worst-case scenario for a leveraged fund is that the market goes down and interest rates go up. In that, case interest costs increase while the fund sustains excessive losses due to a drop in the market. As you can see, leveraged funds are very risky. You can make or lose a lot of money quickly.

Inverse Index Funds

Want to know a good way to make money if the stock market goes down? The answer is to short the market. This means selling stocks that you do not own and buying them back at a lower price some time in the future. The difference between your initial sell price and buy-back price is a profit, less commissions.

Another way to make money in a bad market is through the use of derivatives. You make money in a declining market by selling futures on the S&P 500 index, buy put options on the index, or do an equity swap. This is not a book on derivatives, but you can be certain that inverse index funds use all the methods listed in this book and more to try making money in a falling market.

A third way to make money in a declining market is by purchasing inverse index funds. They use derivatives and other means to go in the opposite direction of a market. If you are bearish on stocks or bearish on bonds, an inverse index fund may be for you.

Leveraged Inverse Index Funds

Leveraged inverse index funds have to be some of the most esoteric funds on the market and the riskiest. Leveraged inverse index funds basically act the same as a leveraged stock fund but in reverse. If the S&P 500 index goes down by 10 percent, then an inverse S&P 500 index fund with 200 percent leverage should go up 20 percent. Of course there are fees and commissions to pay, so the actual result will be less than the theoretical estimate.

TABLE 9-2

Leveraged and Inverse Index Funds

Index	Leverage	Leveraged and Inverse Funds	Type	Fee	Symbol
Leveraged Long					
Dow Industrials	2×	ProShares Ultra Dow30	ETF	0.95	DDM
NASDAQ 100	2×	ProShares Ultrat QQQ	ETF	0.95	QLD
S&P 500	2×	ProShares Ultra S&P 500	ETF	0.95	SSO
S&P MidCap 400	2×	ProShares Ultra MidCap400	ETF	0.95	MVV
Inverse & Leveraged Inverse					
Dow Industrials	1×short	ProShares Short Dow30	ETF	0.95	DOG
NASDAQ 100	1×short	ProShares Short QQQ	ETF	0.95	PSQ
S&P 500	1×short	ProShares Short S&P 500	ETF	0.95	SH
S&P MidCap 400	1×short	ProShares Short MidCap400	ETF	0.95	MYY
Dow Industrials	2×short	ProShares Ultrashort Dow30	ETF	0.95	DDM
NASDAQ 100	2×short	ProShares Ultrashort QQQ	ETF	0.95	QID
S&P 500	2×short	ProShares Ultrashort S&P 500	ETF	0.95	SDS
S&P MidCap 400	2×short	ProShares Ultrashort MidCap400	ETF	0.95	MZZ

Source: ProShares.com.

There are several mutual funds that use leveraged and inverse index strategies, and there is more to come. Table 9-2 lists a few funds that are currently available. All the funds are expensive. The table is not an endorsement. Carefully read the prospectus of any mutual fund before investing.

MODIFIED STOCK WEIGHTING METHODS

Index funds are capitalization weighted. Stocks are selected for an index based in part on their market capitalization, and those stocks take precedence in an index according to their market value (or free float).

Any weighting scheme other than a market-cap method is consider a modified stock weighting scheme. Modified methods include, but are not limited to, fundamental weights, factor weights, and equal weight. Fundamental weighting is based on a ranking of financial statement numbers such as sales, cash flow, or dividends. Factor weighting is similar to fundamental only it is based on a ranking of financial ratios such as price-to-book, price-to-cash flow, and return-on-equity. Equal weighting is allocation of the same percentage of capital to each stock in an index. Table 9-3 site a sampling of funds that weigh stocks using methods other than market cap.

TABLE 9-3

A Sample of Equal Weight Funds

Index	Equal Weight Funds	Type	Fee	Symbol	Minimum
S&P 500 Equal Weight	Rydex S&P Equal Weight	ETF	0.40	RSP	None
NASDAQ 100 Equal Weight	First Trust NASDAQ 100 Equal Weight	ETF	0.60	QQEW	None
NASDAQ 100 Technology	First Trust NASDAQ 100 Technology	ETF	0.60	QTEC	None
Amex Biotechnology Index	First Trust Amex Biotechnology	ETF	0.60	FBT	None
Source: Morningstar, First Trust Portfolios L.P.					

FIGURE 9-1

Changes in Funds with Modified Stock Weightings

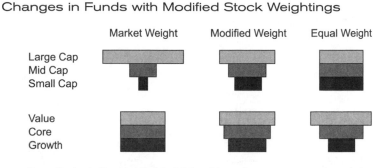

Souce: Morningstar X-ray Tool, Portfolio Solutions data.

When the stocks in the portfolio are the same as those in an index, but the weights of those stocks have been manipulated, the portfolio itself is technically no longer following an index, nor is the portfolio a new or novel way to index as some proponents claim. If a portfolio has the same stocks as a market-weighted index, but with a different weighting scheme than the index, it is simply a portfolio of stocks.

When a market-weighted index is manipulated so that the stocks are weighted in a portfolio using a modified method, it changes the dynamics of that portfolio. Figure 9-1 illustrates how a portfolio changes on two dimensions. First, the market capitalization of the portfolio is reduced as money is taken from large-cap stocks and dispersed among mid- and small-cap stock. Second, the portfolio takes on a value tilt as holdings in growth stocks are reduced and a greater amount is dispersed among value stocks.

Some proponents of modified stock weight methods claim that that cap-weighted indexes are inefficient and that their methodology creates a better index. On their Web site, WisdomTree Investments claim they are "moving the indexing universe in a new direction by creating the first family of fundamentally-weighted dividend indexes." Spokesmen point to hypothetical, historical performance of WisdomTree dividend weighting methods from 1964 to 2005 to show that their strategy had annualized total returns that exceeded the return of the S&P 500 index for the same period.

FIGURE 9-2

S&P 500 Return 1964 to 2005 Relative to
Fama/French Indexes

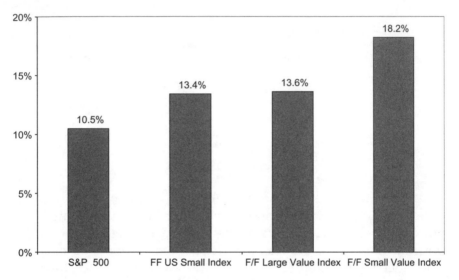

Source: S&P, Dimensional Fund Advisors.

The idea that a modified weighting scheme is superior to cap weighing is marketing malarkey. First, these new methods of weighting stocks do not make new indexes. Second, any modified-weighting method over the past 40 years would have resulted in the same apparent outperformance of the S&P 500. That was due to a premium paid to value stocks and small-cap stocks during the period. The weighting method could be as silly as weighting stocks by the number of letters the companies have in their names (i.e., stocks with lots of letters received more weight than stocks with a few letters). It does not matter on the technique, the results were the same.

Figure 9-2 illustrates the large disparity that occurred during the 1964 to 2005 period between the S&P 500, small stocks, large-value stocks, and small-value stocks. Clearly, any portfolio that was weighted toward small and value stocks using any methodology would have "beat" the market cap–weighted S&P, and that is all the modified weighting scheme discussed in this chapter will do.

Equal-Weight Funds

The easiest modified-weighting scheme to understand is the equal-weighted portfolio. The mutual fund companies start with all the stocks in a cap-weighted index. Then those stocks are given an equal weight in a portfolio. For example, ExxonMobil has approximately a 5 percent position in a cap-weighted S&P 500 portfolio and a 0.2 percent position in an equal-weight S&P 500 portfolio (each stock has 0.2 percent weight in a 500 stock portfolio). Equal weighting thins the allocation to large stocks and places significantly more capital in mid- and small-cap stocks in an index.

Dividend-Weighting Schemes

The first type of fundamental weighting scheme to be developed was the dividend-weighted portfolio. Investors turned to the perceived safety of dividend-paying stocks and mutual funds after the collapse of the tech stock market in 2000–2002. Most tech companies do not pay dividends. The thinking was that companies that paid consistent dividends were more stable than those companies that do not.

Dividend funds are based on so-called dividend indexes that differ from market-weighted indexes in two important ways. First, stocks are screened for a consistency of dividend payments over a period of time; and second, the stocks in the dividend index are weighted according to their dividend yield, not market capitalization.

Choosing stocks by dividend characteristics and weighting those stocks in a portfolio based on dividend yield stretches the definition of a stock market index to the very limit. An index measures something. Either it measures market value of stocks in a predefined portfolio or it measures the average price of a stock in that sector. Dividend indexes measure nothing of value. They cannot be used as a benchmark for a market or for comparing active managers against. The only thing a dividend-weighted index is useful for is licensing to a mutual fund company to create a mutual fund.

Morningstar typically categorizes all dividend-weighted funds as value stocks, and for good reason. Most companies that pay a consistent or increasing dividend are in a mature stage of development. Relative to the stock market, a dividend payer's earnings growth is below average, its price-to-earning ratio is lower, book value and cash flow is higher, and the company is a leader in its industry. There are a lot of financial and utility stocks, energy stocks, health care stocks, and industrial stocks in dividend indexes. To the contrary, there is little exposure to technology, communications, and media stocks.

There is no argument among investment professionals that dividend-paying funds are value funds. The question is which fund should you own? That depends on the type of dividend fund you are seeking. Due to different methodologies, the dividend indexes carry varying industry weights. Some invest heavily in one or two sectors. Others have caps on industry exposure to spread the risk across multiple sectors at the expense of lower overall dividend yields.

The Dow Jones Dividend index reflects the performance of 100 leading U.S. dividend-paying companies. Stocks are selected for the index based on their dividend yield. Index constituents are dividend-weighted rather than market capitalization–weighted. Each stock is given a weight in the index based on the size and strength of its dividend. The weights of individual securities are capped to prevent one or several components from dominating the indexes. The Dow Jones Dividend index is the most diverse of all dividend indexes.

The S&P High Yield Dividend Aristocrat index is designed to measure the performance of the 50 highest dividend-yielding stocks in the S&P SuperComposite 1500 that have followed a dividend policy of consistent annual increases for at least 25 consecutive years. Unlike most dividend-oriented portfolios, the S&P High Yield Dividend Aristocrat index is broadly diversified across sectors. This contrasts with other dividend indexes, which are concentrated in financials and utilities and therefore are more vulnerable to sector-specific and interest-rate risk. The Dividend Aristocrat index is weighted by indicated yield.

The Morningstar Dividend Leaders index captures the performance of the 100 highest yielding stocks that have a consistent record of dividend payment and have the ability to sustain their dividend payments. Stocks in the index are weighted in proportion to the total pool of dividends available to investors. A company's current dividend must be equal to or greater than the dividend paid five years ago. A company's dividend coverage ratio must be greater than or equal to 1 providing a margin of safety. The index currently has a very high 46 percent allocation to financial stocks.

The Dividend Achievers Select index tracks U.S. common stocks with a record of increasing dividends for at least 10 consecutive years but excludes REITs and companies that might have low potential for dividend growth. The index is administered exclusively for Vanguard by Mergent, Inc. Like all other dividend index providers, Mergent uses a yield-driven weighting methodology rather than a market-cap method. The Dividend Achievers Select index is currently allocated across several industry groups and is one of the more diverse dividend indexes.

Table 9-4 is a comparison of the Morningstar industry allocation in each dividend index as of June 2006.

Table 9-5 represents four low-cost funds benchmarked to the indexes described above.

Noticeably absent from Table 9-4 are WisdomTree funds. WisdomTree is a relatively new mutual fund provider that currently has 20 separate dividend-weighted ETFs benchmarked to its own

TABLE 9-4

Morningstar Industry Weights of Dividend Indexes

Morningstar Sector	Dow Jones Dividend	S&P High Yield Dividend Aristocrat	Morningstar Dividend Leaders	Dividend Achievers Select
Software	0	0	0	4
Hardware	0	1	0	8
Media	0	0	0	7
Telecommunications	4	2	17	3
Health Care Services	6	12	17	12
Consumer Services	1	2	0	7
Business Services	2	1	0	2
Financial Services	40	26	38	15
Consumer Goods	12	20	12	11
Industrial Materials	7	12	4	21
Energy	6	3	1	7
Utilities	22	20	12	2

Source: Morningstar.com.

TABLE 9-5

Dividend Index Funds

Dividend Index	Low-Cost Dividend Funds	Type	Fee	Symbol	Minimum
Dividend Achievers Select	Vanguard Dividend Appreciation	ETF	0.28	VIG	None
FTSE High Dividend Yield	Vanguard High Dividend Yield Index	Open-End	0.40	VHDYX	3,000
FTSE High Dividend Yield	Vanguard High Dividend Yield Index	ETF	0.25	VYM	None
S&P High Yield Dividend Aristocrat	SPDR Dividends	ETF	0.30	SDY	None
DJ Select Dividend	iShares DJ Select Dividend	ETF	0.40	DVY	None
Morningstar Dividend Leaders	Morningstar Dividend Leaders	ETF	0.45	FDL	None

Source: Morningstar Principia, S&P, Vanguard.

U.S. and international stock indexes. WisdomTree weights the securities in each index based on either the amount of cash dividends paid by companies in each index or the dividend yield of the companies in each index.

Index fund companies typically license their indexes from an independent index provider so there is no conflict of interest when investors compare fund results to the index. That is not true for WisdomTree. They run the indexes that their funds are benchmarked to. I suppose that is one way to ensure low tracking error.

Table 9-6 is a laundry list of WisdomTree dividend-weighted exchange-traded funds.

TABLE 9-6

WisdomTree Dividend ETFs

WisdomTree ETFs	Fee	Symbol
Domestic		
Dividend Top 100	0.38	DTN
High-Yielding Equity	0.38	DHS
LargeCap Dividend	0.28	DLN
MidCap Dividend	0.38	DON
SmallCap Dividend	0.38	DES
Total Dividend	0.28	DTD
International		
DIEFA Fund	0.48	DWM
DIEFA High-Yielding Equity	0.58	DTH
Europe High-Yielding Equity	0.58	DEW
Europe SmallCap Dividend	0.58	DFE
Europe Total Dividend	0.48	DEB
International Dividend Top 100	0.58	DOO
International LargeCap Dividend	0.48	DOL
International MidCap Dividend	0.58	DIM
International SmallCap Dividend	0.58	DLS
Japan High-Yielding Equity	0.58	DNL
Japan SmallCap Dividend	0.58	DFJ
Japan Total Dividend	0.48	DXJ
Pacific ex-Japan High-Yielding Equity	0.58	DNH
Pacific ex-Japan Total Dividend	0.48	DND

Source: WisdomTree.com.

Fundamental Weighting and Factor Weights

Fundamental weights and factor weights are similar. Stocks are still selected from a cap-weighted benchmark, however the weights in a portfolio shift as the fundamentals behind the company shift, not the price of the stock. For example, when a company makes an announcement, the weighting of that company in a market-cap index may not change, but its weighting in a fundamental-weight or factor-weight portfolio may change as the company reports good or bad sales, earnings, or cash flow.

S&P/Citigroup Pure Style Index Series uses seven fundamental factors to identify approximately a third of the market capitalization of the market as pure growth and a third as pure value. There is no overlapping of stocks in style selection. The seven factors are listed in Chapter 6 in the section "Standard & Poor's U.S. Equity Indexes." There are three financial ratios that consider a companies growth, three the look at valuation, and one divided factor.

S&P/Citigroup Pure Style indexes are not market weighted. They are weighted based on the combined fundamental attractiveness score of the stock. Six ETFs benchmarked to the Pure Style indexes are listed in Table 9-7.

T A B L E   9–7

S&P Pure Style Index Funds

Index	Fund Name	Class	Fee	Symbol	Minimum
S&P/Citi 500 Pure Value	Rydex S&P 500 Pure Value	ETF	0.35	RPV	None
S&P/Citi 500 Pure Growth	Rydex S&P 500 Pure Growth	ETF	0.35	RPG	None
S&P/Citi 400 Pure Value	Rydex S&P Midcap 400 Pure Value	ETF	0.35	RFV	None
S&P/Citi 400 Pure Growth	Rydex S&P Midcap 400 Pure Growth	ETF	0.35	RFG	None
S&P/Citi 600 Pure Value	Rydex S&P Midcap 600 Pure Value	ETF	0.35	RZV	None
S&P/Citi 600 Pure Growth	Rydex S&P Midcap 600 Pure Growth	ETF	0.35	RZG	None

Source: Morningstar Principia.

FTSE RAFI US 1000 (Research Affiliates Fundamental Index) is a good example of a fundamental weighting process. Using a stock universe comprising all stocks of the FTSE USA All Cap and FTSE Developed indexes, Research Affiliates calculates the percentage representation of each stock using sales figures, cash-flow figures, book value, and dividends. Next, stocks are ranked in descending order based on their RAFI score, and the largest 1,000 U.S. companies become the FTSE RAFI US 1000 index constituents. Weights in the portfolio are set proportional to their fundamental values. The RAFI fundamental value of each company is divided by its free-float-adjusted market capitalization, and that is the weighting factor for use in the index calculation.

PowerShares FTSE RAFI US 1000 portfolio (symbol PRF; fee 0.75) is benchmarked to the RAFI US 1000 strategy. As long as value stocks outperform growth stocks, PowerShares may be able to make up the hefty fee and "beat" the broad market. You will have to decide if paying five times the cost of the iShares R1000 index is worth the money.

Modified Weight and a Value Premium

It should be no surprise that RAFI, like WisdomTree, claims its modified-weight fundamental indexes have produced consistently higher returns, at modestly lower risk, when compared with market capitalization–weighted indexes. It is no great feat. All modified-weight schemes the titled a portfolio to value stocks would have hypnotically beat the market over the past 40 years due to a value premium in the market.

The big question is will value premiums occur in the future? I do not have the answer to that question, and neither do the spin-dexers selling modified-weighted funds. I use the term *spindexing* to define the tendency of some promoters to market their modified-weight funds as following a better index methodology than capitalization weighted funds. It is unfortunate that they do so because it confuses the public. The methods used to tilt modified-weight portfolios to value stocks are not indexing methods, they are active-management decisions. A value fund created by modified index weighting is a value fund, not a better index fund.

CHAPTER SUMMARY

There is no such thing as a free lunch.

A fundamental axiom of economics

In this chapter, we reviewed various special index funds whose aim is to beat the stock and bond markets. The funds are divided into three categories: enhanced, leveraged and inverse, and modified market weights.

Are these special products worthy of your money? That depends on who you are. An index purist would say that these funds are more expensive actively managed funds and do belong in a portfolio. Mutual fund firms claim their new methods can be used to enhance your portfolio so they are worth the higher fee. Academics say none of those arguments matter because the higher costs of the enhanced funds will likely wipe out any potential benefit.

I believe former Federal Reserve Chairman Alan Greenspan said it best in 1998 after the startling collapse of Long Term Capital Management, a Connecticut-based hedge fund:

> This decade is strewn with examples of bright people who thought they built a better mousetrap that could consistently extract abnormal returns from the financial markets. Some succeed for a time. But while there may occasionally be misconfigurations among market prices that allow abnormal returns, they do not persist.

If you are interested in any of the funds mentioned in this chapter, please order a prospectus and read it carefully before you invest.

CHAPTER 10

Investing in Bond Index Funds

Key Concepts

- Bond index funds add diversification to a portfolio.
- Bond funds are categorized by maturity and credit risk.
- Bond index funds are difficult to manage, and sampling is often used.
- Choose a low-cost active fund in markets without index funds.

A well-diversified investment portfolio always contains a fixed-income component. Adding bonds to a portfolio of stock index funds lowers investment risk without significantly lowering returns. The best way to build a bond portfolio is through fixed-income index funds that charge minimal fees. In the absence of index funds, low-cost actively managed bond funds also work well.

Although bond funds play a crucial role in portfolio management, a majority of investors do not pay nearly as much attention to selecting their bond investments as they do to their stock investments. By gaining an understanding of the dynamics and structure of the bond market, you will be better equipped to select an appropriate bond fund for your needs.

A SHORTAGE OF BOND INDEX FUNDS

If this book were to recommend only low-cost bond index funds, it would be a very short book because there are not many bond index funds available. Although dozens of mutual fund companies offer hundreds of stock index funds, only a handful offer bond index funds, and many of those funds charge more than 0.5 percent in fees. Those funds do not make the list.

The Vanguard Group currently manages four open-end bond index fund with ETF shares available. BarclaysGlobal Investors manages five exchange-traded funds benchmarked to the Lehman Brothers indexes and one benchmarked to the Goldman Sachs GS $InvesTop index of investment-grade corporate bonds.

Despite the efforts of Vanguard and Barclays, a lack of funds leaves many holes in the fixed-income market where no index funds exist. To fill the gaps, this chapter also includes a section on "almost" index funds. These funds are low-cost, actively managed bond funds that are the next best thing to indexing.

Over the next few years, mutual funds companies are committed to expanding their offerings of fixed income funds. As of this writing, new products in registration with the SEC include the first preferred stock ETF and more corporate bond ETFs. Visit www .indexuniverse.com for new fund offerings.

SAMPLING STRATEGIES OF BOND MANAGERS

One reason for the lack of bond index funds is that it is actually more difficult for mutual fund companies to manage a bond index fund than a stock index fund. Most of the popular bond indexes are not designed with the underlying objective of being used as a benchmark for index funds. Rather, the indexes have historically been used as a theoretical guide to measure the movement of the broad bond market. This is evidenced by the fact that most of the indexes hold thousands of bonds, many of which are illiquid. For example, the Lehman Aggregate Bond index tracks more than 6,000 bonds, most of which do not trade on a regular basis. Index funds need access to all bonds in the index to fully replicate an index.

Because full replication is not possible, index fund managers resort to using a technique called *sampling*. The term describes a portfolio management method to make up for a lack of liquidity in a bond index. Bond fund managers try to combine the liquid, investable bonds in the index to form a portfolio that has the same characteristics and return as the illiquid index. This strategy is similar to a total stock market index fund approach that samples about 3,500 stocks in the Wilshire 5000 rather than trying to buy all the stocks.

Sampling is a complex mathematical system that requires index fund managers to categorize each bond in an index into different quadrants. Factors such as industry, issue size, credit rating, maturity, and bond coupon are used to determine the quadrant a bond belongs in. The manager then selects a few liquid bonds from each quadrant to represent all bonds in that quadrant. The portfolio is then run through an optimizer program to see if there was a significant difference in past returns of the model and the index. If there is a difference, it is called tracking error. If the tracking error of a model is too high, different bonds are selected. This procedure continues until the tracking error of the model is within acceptable limits.

Sampling may appear to take a lot of time; however, once the data are entered and the programming is complete, computers do most of the heavy number crunching. Portfolio managers spend a lot of time testing models and tweaking the program before actual trading takes place. A successful model will require only a few hundred bonds be purchased in the index fund to bring the tracking error between the fund and the index within tolerance.

BOND MARKET STRUCTURE

The fixed-income market is divided into two general types of bond funds: taxable and tax-free. We will cover tax-free municipal bonds later in the chapter. Taxable bond funds can be categorized on two axes. On the horizontal axis is the average maturity of the bonds in a fund, and on the vertical axis is the average creditworthiness of the portfolio.

The average maturity of a bond fund is illustrated on the horizontal axis in Figure 10-1.

Bond maturities can be divided into three ranges. Short-term funds hold bonds that have an average maturity of three years or less, intermediate bond funds have an average maturity of four to nine years, and long-term funds have an average maturity of 10 years or longer. If a bond mutual fund has an average maturity of

FIGURE 10-1

Bond Maturity and Creditworthiness

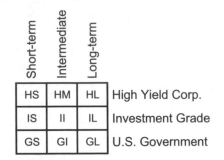

five years, it does not mean all bonds in the fund mature in five years, although that may be the case. The bonds could mature from one year through 10 years or any combination thereof. Read the prospectus of a bond fund so you know how the fund is being managed.

Under normal economic conditions, you should expect long-term bond funds to generate a higher total return because there is more interest rate risk. Interest rate risk is the amount a bond fund fluctuates with changes in general interest rates. Because a long-term bond portfolio moves around more than a short-term fund, you should get paid for taking that risk by earning a higher yield on the fund.

The credit risk on the vertical axis in Figure 10-1 is more complex. On the bottom of the chart are the least risky government bonds. These bond funds hold direct obligations of the U.S. government or indirect obligations of quasi-government agencies such as the Federal National Mortgage Association (FNMA). The middle credit level includes investment-grade U.S. corporate bonds and foreign "Yankee" bonds that trade in U.S. dollars on a U.S. exchange. U.S. corporations with sound fundamental characteristics receive an investment-grade rating from credit rating agencies such as Standard & Poor's. At the top of the risk level are high-yield bond funds. These funds invest in below-investment-grade corporate bonds. Companies with below-investment-grade debt ratings have a questionable ability to repay their obligations. Below-investment-grade bonds are also referred to as "junk" bonds. Historically, more than 90 percent of junk bonds are paid off without defaulting. However, the risk of default certainly justifies a higher return.

FIGURE 10-2

Term Risk, Credit Risk, and Expected Yield

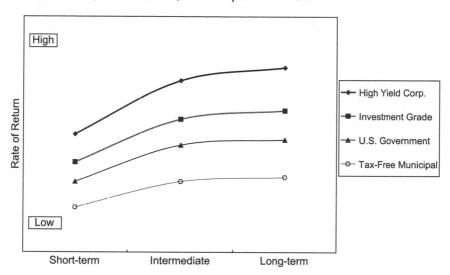

By putting the two factors of term risk and credit risk in Figure 10-2 together, you can see the expected return of a bond fund is a function of its average maturity and average credit rating. The greater the overall risk in a bond fund, the higher the expected long-term return. Figure 10-2 illustrates the spread that occurs between the various types of bond funds based on these two factors. Short-term government funds have the lowest interest rate risk and the lowest credit risk; therefore, they are expected to produce the lowest long-term return. High-yield (junk) bond funds have the highest interest rate risk and highest credit risk; therefore, they pay investors the highest yield.

FIXED-INCOME INDEXES

The three most widely recognized providers of fixed-income indexes are Lehman Brothers, Merrill Lynch, and Citigroup. All three companies construct hundreds of fixed-income indexes covering all the global bond markets. Because all of the indexes are constructed from the same universe of bonds, they look very much alike. A short-term corporate bond index of one provider holds nearly the same bonds as the short-term corporate bond index of another provider. The liquidity of bonds in an index is not a problem for the provider of the index because the indexes are theoretical. The liquidity problem is only an issue for the index fund managers who attempt to buy the bonds in the index.

The typical structure of a U.S. investment-grade market index is structured as follows:

1. Government and credit markets
   a. Government bills, notes, and bonds
      (1). Treasury, including inflation-protected securities
      (2). Agency (FNMA and FHLMC bonds, etc.)
   b. Corporate (investment grade, BBB, or better)
      (1). Industrial
      (2). Finance
      (3). Utility
      (4). Yankee bonds (foreign bonds trading in U.S. dollars)
2. Mortgage market
   a. Government National Mortgage Association (GNMA)
   b. Federal Home Loan Mortgage Corporation (FHLMC)
   c. Federal National Mortgage Association (FNMA)
3. Asset-backed securities
   a. Credit card receivables
   b. Auto loans
   c. Home equity loans

The structure used by all three providers is basically the same as above, although there are a few subtle differences among the indexes. The first difference is how interest payments are reinvested. The Lehman Brothers indexes assume that interest paid during the month is not reinvested until the end of the month. Citigroup and Merrill Lynch assume interest paid during the month is reinvested during the month. The difference in accounting for interest does not affect the makeup of bonds in an index, only the performance results.

Naturally, the Citigroup and Merrill Lynch method should generate slightly higher returns due to the assumed automatic reinvestment of interest payments at the bond market rate during the month. However, it is an unrealistic assumption for index fund managers to follow the reinvestment method in their "live" portfolios because there are delays between payment dates and cash received and reinvested.

The minimum size of a bond issue also differs among providers. Lehman requires a bond to have an issue size of at least $100 million, whereas Merrill Lynch only requires a float of $25 million, and Citigroup has a minimum size for each market to include only those bonds that are "reasonably available" for institutional investors under normal market circumstances. The size issue is a moot point for index fund managers because they are not able to buy most of the smaller issues. Managers typically sample the largest and most liquid bonds from the indexes.

Of the three main fixed-income index providers, Lehman Brothers is clearly the most popular with index fund managers. Currently, all index funds except one are benchmarked to Lehman indexes. Only one index fund is benchmarked to a Goldman Sachs index, and no index funds are benchmarked to the Merrill Lynch or Citigroup indexes, not even the Merrill Lynch Aggregate Bond Index Fund (symbol MDABX; fee 0.64)

Lehman Aggregate Bond Index

The broadest and most popular index in the Lehman Brothers (LB) fixed-income series is the Lehman Aggregate Bond index. The index tracks more than 6,600 U.S. Treasury securities, government agency bonds, mortgages, corporate bonds, and international dollar-denominated bonds (Yankee bonds). The index measures the performance of the U.S. investment-grade bond market, which includes investment-grade U.S. Treasury bonds, government-related bonds, investment-grade corporate bonds, mortgage passthrough securities, commercial mortgage–backed securities, and asset-backed securities that are publicly offered for sale in the United States.

The securities in the Lehman Aggregate Bond index must have $250 million or more of outstanding face value and must have at least one year remaining to maturity. In addition, the securities must be denominated in U.S. dollars and must be fixed rate and non-convertible. Certain types of securities, such as state and local government series bonds, structured notes with embedded swaps or other special features, private placements, floating-rate securities, and Eurobonds are excluded from the index. The index is market capitalization–weighted, and the securities in the index are updated on the last calendar day of each month.

Bonds in the Lehman Aggregate Bond index have an average maturity of about seven years, which places the index in the intermediate-term category. Bonds in the index also have a high average rating of AA by Standard & Poor's. More than 70 percent of the Lehman Aggregate Bond index holdings are in U.S. Treasuries and agency- and government-backed mortgages. The rest are investment-grade corporate and about 3 percent Yankee bonds. At any time there may be a handful of non-investment-grade bonds in the index due to credit downgrades. However, those bonds will eventually be deleted from the index. As of July 2006, the assets held in the Lehman Aggregate Bond index were as shown in Table 10-1.

Several index funds track the Lehman Aggregate Bond index. The lowest cost funds are included in Table 10-2. All the fund

TABLE 10–1

Characteristics of the Lehman Aggregate Bond Index

Distribution by Issuer	
Mortgage Backed	39%
Treasury & Agency	36%
Corporate: Finance	11%
Corporate: Industrial	9%
Corporate: Utility	2%
Foreign (Yankee bonds)	3%
Distribution by Quality	
AAA	79%
AA	6%
A	8%
BBB	7%
BB (non-investment grade)	0%
B (non-investment grade)	0%

Source: Lehman Brothers.

T A B L E 10−2

Low-Cost Funds Benchmarked to Lehman Bond Indexes

LB Bond Index	Fund Name	Class	Fee	Symbol	Minimum
Aggregate Bond	Dreyfus Bond Market Index Basic	Open-End	0.15	DBIRX	10,000
Aggregate Bond	Vanguard Total Bond Index	Open-End	0.20	VBMFX	3,000
Aggregate Bond	iShares Lehman Aggregate	ETF	0.20	AGG	None
Aggregate Bond	TIAA-CREF Bond Plus	Open-End	0.30	TIPBX	2,500
Aggregate Bond	T. Rowe Price US Bond	Open-End	0.30	PBDIX	2,500
1−3 Treasury Index	iShares Lehman 1−3 Treasury	ETF	0.15	SHY	None
7−10 Treasury Index	iShares Lehman 7−10 Treasury	ETF	0.15	IEF	None
20+ Treasury Index	iShares Lehman 20+ Treasury	ETF	0.15	TLT	None
1−5 Year Gov/Credit	Vanguard Short-Term Bond Index	Open-End	0.18	VBISX	3,000
5−10 Year Gov/Credit	Vanguard Intermediate-Term Bond Index	Open-End	0.18	VBIIX	3,000
Long Year Gov/Credit	Vanguard Long-Term Bond Index	Open-End	0.18	VBLTX	3,000
LB TIPS Index	iShares Lehman TIPS	ETF	0.20	TIP	None

Source: Morningstar, iShares.com.

managers use a sampling technique to replicate the index. The difference in performance between one fund and another is based on the manager's ability to sample the index effectively and the fee charged to the fund.

The Lehman Aggregate Bond index is the starting point for the creation of smaller subsets. The bonds in the aggregate index are sorted by maturity into various categories. These categories become subindexes.

Lehman Treasury Indexes

The securities in Lehman Treasury indexes must be publicly issued U.S. Treasury securities denominated in U.S. dollars and must be fixed rate and nonconvertible. In addition, the securities must be rated investment-grade and have $250 million or more of outstanding face value. Excluded from the index are state and local government series bonds and coupon issues that have been stripped from bonds included in the index. The indexes are market capitalization–weighted, and the securities in the index are updated on the last calendar day of each month. Index funds benchmarked to Lehman Treasury indexes.

The Lehman Brothers 1–3 Year U.S. Treasury index measures the performance of all publicly issued U.S. Treasury securities that have a remaining maturity of greater than or equal to one year and less than three. As of May 31, 2006, there were 36 issues included in the index.

The Lehman Brothers 7–10 Year U.S. Treasury index measures the performance of public obligations of the U.S. Treasury that have a remaining maturity of greater than or equal to 7 years and less than 10 years. As of May 31, 2006, there were 20 issues included in the index.

The Lehman Brothers 20+ Year U.S. Treasury index measures the performance of public obligations of the U.S. Treasury that have a remaining maturity of 20 or more years. As of May 31, 2006, there were 12 issues included in the index.

Index funds invest in the Lehman Brothers U.S. Treasury index by sampling, meaning a fund holds a range of securities that, in the aggregate, approximates the full index in terms of key risk factors and other characteristics.

Lehman Brothers Investment/Credit Indexes

The securities in the Lehman Brothers Investment/Credit indexes have $250 million or more of outstanding face value and must have at least one year remaining to maturity. In addition, the securities must be denominated in U.S. dollars and must be fixed rate and nonconvertible. The indexes are market capitalization–weighted, and the securities in the indexes are updated on the last calendar day of each month.

The Lehman Brothers 1–5 Year Government/Credit index includes all medium and larger issues of U.S. government, investment-grade corporate, and Yankee bonds that have maturities between one and five years and are publicly issued.

The Lehman Brothers 5–10 Year Government/Credit index includes all medium and larger issues of U.S. government, investment-grade corporate, and investment-grade Yankee bonds that have maturities between five and ten years and are publicly issued.

The Lehman Brothers Long Government/Credit index includes all medium and larger issues of U.S. government, investment-grade corporate, and investment-grade Yankee bonds that have maturities of greater than 10 years and are publicly issued.

Index funds invest in the Lehman Brothers Government/Credit indexes by sampling, meaning a fund holds a range of securities that, in the aggregate, approximates the full index in terms of key risk factors and other characteristics.

Lehman Brothers Treasury Inflation-Protected Securities Index

Unlike a conventional bond, whose issuer makes regular fixed-interest payments and repays the face value of the bond at maturity, an inflation-indexed security provides principal and interest payments that are adjusted over time to reflect a rise (inflation) or a drop (deflation) in the general price level. This adjustment is a key feature, given that the Consumer Price Index (CPI) has risen in each of the past 50 years (source: Bureau of Labor Statistics). Importantly, in the event of deflation, the U.S. Treasury has guaranteed that it will repay at least the face value of a bond issued by the U.S. government.

Inflation-indexed securities are designed to provide a *real rate of return*, or a return after adjusting for the impact of inflation. Inflation erodes the purchasing power of an investor's portfolio. For example, if a conventional bond provides a "nominal" total return of 6 percent in a given year and inflation is 4 percent during that period, the inflation-adjusted, or real, return is just 2 percent.

Interest rates on conventional bonds have two primary components: a "real" yield and an increment that reflects investor expectations of future inflation. By contrast, interest rates on an inflation-indexed security are adjusted for inflation and are not affected meaningfully by inflation expectations. This leaves only real rates to influence the price of an inflation-indexed security.

Inflation-protected public obligations of the U.S. Treasury are commonly known as *TIPS*. The Lehman Brothers U.S. TIPS index measures the performance of the inflation-protected public obligations of the U.S. Treasury. The index includes all publicly issued U.S. Treasury inflation-protected securities that have at least one year remaining to maturity, are rated investment-grade, and have $250 million or more of outstanding face value. As of May 31, 2006, there were 18 issues included in the index.

THE LONE CORPORATE BOND FUND

The Goldman Sachs (GS) $InvesTop Corporate index measures the performance of a fixed number of highly liquid, investment-grade corporate bonds. As of May 31, 2006, there were 100 bonds included in the index. The index consists of highly liquid, investment-grade U.S. dollar–denominated corporate bonds. It seeks to maximize liquidity while maintaining representation of the broader corporate bond market. The index was started in 1999 and is a subset of the GS $ Investment Grade index, an index of more than 500 investment-grade bonds. Bonds in the index are selected from the universe of eligible bonds in the GS $ Investment Grade index using defined rules.

Currently, the bonds eligible for inclusion in the GS $InvesTop index include U.S. dollar–denominated, SEC-registered corporate bonds that (1) are issued by companies domiciled in the United States, Canada, Western Europe, or Japan; (2) are rated investment-grade; (3) have at least $500 million of outstanding face value; and

(4) are less than five years old and have at least three years to maturity. Bonds are automatically disqualified from being included in the index if their average spreads and volatility fall outside of certain defined ranges. The index is equally weighted by par value, and the securities in the index are updated on the last business day of each month.

The iShares GS $ InvesTop Corporate Bond Fund (symbol LQD; fee 0.15) uses a sampling strategy to closely track the GS $InvesTop index. As of July 2006, the fund had 101 securities with an average rating of A2 by Moody's. The average maturity of bonds in the fund was 9.8 years.

LOW-COST ACTIVE BOND FUNDS

There is only one investment-grade corporate bond index fund available and one TIPS index fund. There are no GNMA mortgage index funds, U.S. high-yield corporate bond index funds, or tax-free municipal bond funds. Thus, I have included this section to provide a list of low-cost active bond funds where index fund inventory is lacking. Low cost is less that a 0.5 percent expense ratio and no sales charges or 12b-1 fees. Table 10-3 includes several low-cost active funds in each sector that have the look and feel of an index fund but do not state they are tracking an index in the prospectus.

TIPS Fund

The Vanguard Inflation-Protected Securities Fund seeks to provide investors inflation protection and income consistent with investment in inflation-indexed securities. The fund is not an index fund. However, it included in Table 10-3 because it has very similar yield and maturity characteristics to the Lehman Treasury Inflation Notes index, and the cost of the fund is very low.

GNMA Fund

The Government National Mortgage Association (GNMA, or "Ginnie Mae") passthrough certificates are fixed-income securities representing part ownership in a pool of mortgage loans supported by the full faith and credit of the U.S. government. Securities issued

TABLE 10-3

Almost Bond Index Funds

Index	Fund Name	Class	Fee	Symbol	Minimum
LB TIPS Index	Vanguard Inflation-Protected Sec.	Open-End	0.20	VIPSX	3,000
Lehman GNMA Index	Vanguard GNMA	Open-End	0.21	VFIIX	3,000
Lehman 1–5 Year Credit	Vanguard Short-Term Investment-Grade	Open-End	0.21	VFSTX	3,000
Lehman 5–10 Year Credit	Vanguard Intermediate-Term Investment-Grade	Open-End	0.21	VFICX	3,000
Lehman Long Credit A/Better	Vanguard Long-Term Investment-Grade	Open-End	0.25	VWESX	3,000
Merrill B-BB High Yield Corp	Vanguard High-Yield Corporate	Open-End	0.25	VWEHX	3,000
Merrill B-BB High Yield Corp	TIAA-CREF High Yield Bond	Open-End	0.34	TCHYX	2,500

Source: Morningstar, Vanguard.

by most U.S. government agencies, other than the U.S. Treasury and GNMA, are neither guaranteed by the U.S. Treasury nor supported by the full faith and credit of the U.S. government. A GNMA fund's dollar-weighted average maturity depends on homeowner prepayments of the underlying mortgages.

GNMA funds have higher yields than other government bond funds, but that is due to prepayment risk, which is the chance that during periods of falling interest rates, homeowners will refinance their mortgages before their maturity dates, resulting in prepayment of mortgages. A GNMA fund would then lose potential price appreciation and would be forced to reinvest the unanticipated proceeds at lower interest rates, resulting in a decline in the fund's income.

The Vanguard GNMA Fund invests at least 80 percent of its assets in GNMA passthrough certificates. The remainder is invested in other U.S. government obligations. It is a low-cost fund that holds GNMA securities that are very close to the same average yield and maturity as the Lehman GNMA index.

Corporate Bond Active Funds

There are no index funds that track the Lehman Brothers corporate bond indexes directly; however, Vanguard manages three investment bond funds that come close. There are between 250 and 700 bonds in each fund, so they are well diversified. Vanguard used to title all three funds as corporate bond funds. The names were changed a few years ago to investment-grade funds when the SEC enacted rules on naming mutual funds so that a name reflects the underlying objective of a fund. It became questionable whether some quasi-government agency bonds and asset-backed securities were corporate bonds or something else. Better safe than sorry.

High-Yield Bond Funds

Below-investment-grade, high-yield "junk" bonds reflect the speculative bard of fixed-income investing. Most of the companies who issue junk bonds, or whose ratings have been degraded to junk status, have only a fair chance of paying off their debts. Because there is a higher risk, there must be a potentially high return to investors in this sector. As a group, junk bonds achieve almost the same return as the broad stock market. However, I do not recommend investing in the most speculative junk bond issues. If you venture into this area, buy a well-diversified mutual fund that invests in higher quality high-yield bonds.

There are no index funds that track the high-yield bond market. Some high-yield bonds in the high-yield indexes are extremely illiquid and rarely trade. Therefore, it makes no sense for a fund manager to attempt to replicate an index. There are a couple of index funds that invest in the higher quality issues and have delivered long-term results consistent with the indexes. Vanguard's High-Yield Corporate Fund is a good fund to look at. It has very low fees and invests in B or better quality bonds. The TIAA-CREF High-Yield Bond Fund also invests in B or better bonds and tracks the Lehman Brothers High-Yield index fairly closely.

Municipal Bond Funds

Investors in a high income tax bracket may be wise to invest in tax-free municipal bond funds in place of taxable bond funds. Generally, the interest from a municipal bond issued in the state you live in is free from all federal, state, and city income taxes. Because the interest is free of tax, municipal bonds have lower returns than taxable government bonds or corporate bonds. There is a rough rule of thumb you can use to determine if you should own tax-free bonds. Generally, if your combined state and federal income tax rate is 30 percent or more, then municipal bonds may be an appropriate choice for taxable accounts.

All of the low-cost tax-free bond funds listed in Table 10-4 are national series funds. That means the funds select bonds from all 50 states, Guam, Puerto Rico, and the U.S. Virgin Islands. Most states tax the interest on municipal bonds issued from other states. If you are in a state that has an income tax, then some or all of the interest from a national bond fund may be subject to state income tax.

The funds in Table 10-4 may invest a small portion of the portfolio in Alternative Minimum Tax (AMT) bonds. If you are subject to AMT tax, call the fund company to check the level of AMT in each fund before investing. The federal government expects you to pay

TABLE 10-4

Almost Tax-Free Bond Index Funds

Lehman Benchmark	Fund Name	Class	Fee	Symbol	Minimum
1 Year Municipal Index	Vanguard Short-Term Tax-Exempt	Open-End	0.18	VWSTX	3,000
1–5 Year Municipal Blend	Vanguard Limited-Term Tax-Exempt	Open-End	0.18	VMLTX	3,000
7 Year Municipal Index	Vanguard Intermediate Tax-Exempt	Open-End	0.18	VWITX	3,000
20 Year Municipal Index	Vanguard Long-Term Tax-Exempt	Open-End	0.18	VWLTX	3,000
20 Year Municipal Index	TIAA-CREF Tax-Exempt Bond	Open-End	0.30	TCTEX	2,500

Source: Morningstar, Vanguard.

a tax on that portion of the interest paid from AMT bonds, and that may reduce your overall after-tax return.

CHAPTER SUMMARY

The easiest way to capture the broad taxable bond market is to invest in a bond index fund. Unfortunately, the fixed-income index fund market is minuscule when compared with the burgeoning equity index fund market. Investors may have to be creative when building a portfolio of mutual funds.

The easiest way to get started is to invest in a total bond market index fund that samples the Lehman Brothers Aggregate Bond index. A total bond market fund has exposure to the government markets, the mortgage market, and the investment-grade corporate markets, including some foreign debt. The average maturity of a total bond fund is about 9 years.

Once the core of your portfolio is formed, you can piece the rest of the portfolio using a combination of index fund and low-cost almost index funds. As in past chapters, the funds mentioned in this chapter are not meant to be a recommended investment list. They are a sample of the low-cost fund marketplace. For a complete list of bond index funds, visit www.IndexUnvierse.com. For a more complete list of bond funds in general, visit www.Morningstar.com.

CHAPTER 11

Commodity and Currency Funds

Key Concepts

- Diversification benefits are the allure of commodity investing.
- Commodity indexes vary considerably between providers.
- Commodities funds have grown in number and scope.
- Invest in currencies using index funds.

Index funds have been expanded well beyond stock and bond funds over the past few years. Low-cost index funds are now available in several alternative asset classes including individual commodities, commodity indexes, and currencies. This new aspect of investing is playing an expanded role in portfolio management as the cost is driven down by competition.

The advantage of adding an alternative asset class such as commodities to your portfolio is that they tend to exhibit low correlation with traditional stock and bond investments. In addition, individual commodity sectors tend to have low correlation with each other. The benefit of low correlation between investments is that it lowers overall portfolio risk, and lower portfolio risk may also increase in the long-term return (see Chapter 13).

The disadvantages include the cost of investing in an alternative asset class such as commodities is the higher cost over stock and bond index funds; the lack of a real expected return over fees and

inflation; and low tax-efficiency. For many years, the cost of investing in commodities and currencies exceeded any diversification
benefit. However, that may be changing as competition continues to
increase investment options and drive down investment costs. If
the cost cuts continue and commodity prices recede from their lofty
levels, I may even recommend this asset class someday, but not today.

COMMODITIES BASICS

Commodities are common products such as food, basic materials,
and energy-related items that are used every day. Food products
include items such as sugar, corn, and oats; basic materials include
items such as steel and aluminum; energy is traded in the form of
crude oil, natural gas, and electricity. Another category includes precious metals such as gold and silver. All together, these resources
make up the global commodities market.

- Energy: crude oil, heating oil, natural gas, electricity
- Industrials: copper, steel, cotton
- Precious metals: gold, platinum, silver, aluminum
- Livestock: live cattle, lean hogs
- Grains and oilseeds: corn, soybeans, wheat
- Softs: cocoa, coffee, orange juice, sugar

The global market for commodities is as wide as it is deep. Because
commodities are dug up, manufactured, or grown in almost every
nation in the world, there are hundreds of global commodities
markets. Trading in commodities is going on someplace 24 hours a
day, 7 days a week. If you want to buy an ounce of gold at 10 p.m.,
it can be arranged through any large commodities broker. If you
want to sell oil at 3 a.m., that can also be arranged.

By definition, commodities mean abundance. There is a lot
around and more to be grown, dug up, or manufactured. Although
there are occasional shortages in a sector that create a temporary
jump in prices, those shortages tend to be marginalized over time.
If wheat prices rise due to greater demand, farmers will grow more
wheat next season and beyond until supply exceeds demand and
prices fall. If a shortage of steel causes prices to rise, producers will
dig more ore, and new producers will come on line all over the

world. If oil is scarce, companies will explore for more oil. Whenever a commodity is priced high enough to make a profit, more is produced by current suppliers and new competitors bring even more supply to the market.

It make take several years for new supply to meet demand because of start-up costs and build-outs, but it does eventually happen. That typically leads to oversupply, which leads to a rapid decline in prices. Hence, the commodities markets are characterized by boom and bust. It is either feast or famine for the producers of oil products, metal suppliers, and ranchers.

SPOT PRICES AND FORWARD CONTRACTS

Pick up any issue of the *Wall Street Journal* and turn to the "Money and Investing" section to find a partial list of commodities that trade on U.S. exchanges. The *Wall Street Journal* includes *spot* and *futures* prices. The spot price is what a physical commodity is changing hands for today, and a futures price is a contract for delivery of a set amount of the physical commodity some time in the future.

Before a practical discussion of commodities and currency can take place, we need to cover the differences between physical commodity prices and paper contracts on future commodity prices.

The trading of physical commodities is not an option for most individuals. Unless you own a silo to store 10,000 bushels of corn or a tank to store 1,000 gallons of crude oil, a direct investment in most commodities is not practical. To make investing in commodities practical, most people invest in futures contracts or mutual funds that buy futures and other types of forward contracts.

Commodity futures do not represent direct exposure to actual commodities. Future prices are a based on the expected future spot price of the commodity yet to be delivered. A commodity futures contract is an agreement to buy or sell a specified quantity of a commodity at that future delivery date and at a price agreed upon when the contract expires.

The future spot prices will be different from the value of a futures contract. Because the spot price at a future date is unknown at the time the contract is traded, it must be estimated. It starts with the current spot price and adjustments for interest rates, possible seasonal changes that effect supply and demand, possible storage expenses, and other costs to carrying the contract. If spot prices are expected to be much higher at the maturity of the futures contract than they are today, the current futures price will be set at a high level relative to the current spot price. Lower expected spot prices in the future will be reflected in a low current futures price. Buyers benefit when the spot price at maturity turns out to be higher than expected when they entered into the contract, and they lose when the spot price is lower than anticipated.

By definition, unexpected deviations between expected future spot price and actual future price are unpredictable. Take the randomness out, and over the long-term the performance of spot prices and futures prices should be the same. The 50-year analysis in Figure 11-1 between the equal-weighted Reuters Commodity Research Bureau (CRB) Futures index and the equal-weighted CRB Spot index confirms that expectation. Although two CRB indexes did not track exactly the same commodities, it was close enough to do a comparison.

When the buyers and sellers enter into a futures contract, no cash changes hands between them. However, both parties are required to

FIGURE 11-1

CRB Spot Prices and Reuters CRB Futures (1956–2006)

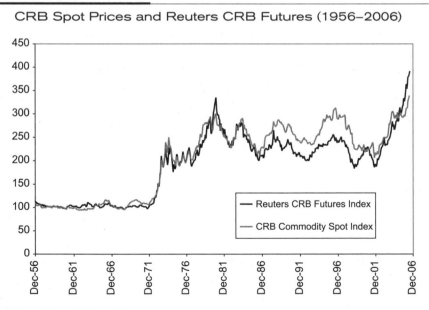

Source: Commodity Research Bureau.

put up a small amount of "margin" to affirm the contract. The contract is settled on expiration date either with cash or with cash delivered on one side and the actual physical commodity delivered on the other in the form of a warehouse receipt. That is where the stories come in about bushels of corn being dumped on investors' lawns.

When you "roll" a futures contract from one month to the next month to avoid having bushels of corn on your lawn, there will be a gain or loss based on the price difference between the expiring contract and the second-month contract. That is the *roll yield*, and it can be positive or negative. In a simplistic sense, if the second-month contract is less expensive than the first month, buyers of futures earn a profit, and if the second-month contract is more expensive than the first month, buyers of futures lose out.

For many years, the roll yield was positive, and that meant futures buyers benefited from excess returns. For example, Deutsche Bank estimates that over a 15-year period ending in 2005, the crude oil component of its commodity index had a compound annualized total return of more than 20 percent even though the spot return was only 6 percent. The other components were roll returns of 9 percent, and collateral returns were less than 5 percent.

In 2005, after a surge in commodity prices, the roll yield turned decidedly negative. That favors sellers of futures contracts over buyers. Mutual fund investors are buyers of futures contracts and will bear the extra expense of a negative roll until it turns positive again. Unfortunately, in the past that has only occurred after a prolonged bear market in commodity prices.

INVESTING IN INDIVIDUAL COMMODITIES

If your timing is perfect, you can make money investing in individual commodities. Over the past 50 years there have been two major runs in commodities prices. One occurred during the high-inflation years in the 1970s, and the second occurred during the first decade of the new millennium. Figure 11-2 illustrates the value of gold and oil adjusted for inflation between 1956 and 2006. The two spikes in prices during the 1970s and 2000s are clearly evident. For the rest of the years, commodity prices were characterized by flat or falling values.

Unless an investor's timing was impeccable, there was little chance of making money in these two commodities. Nonetheless,

FIGURE 11-2

One Dollar in Oil and Gold since 1956, Inflation Adjusted

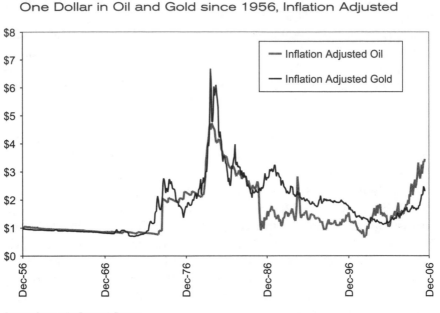

Source: Commodity Research Bureau.

the recent run-up in prices has promoted a huge demand for investment benchmarked to individual commodities, and mutual fund companies complied.

Oil

The United States Oil Fund (USO) investment objective is for the NAV of its units to reflect the performance of the spot price of West Texas Intermediate light, sweet crude oil. USOF invests primarily in oil futures contracts and seeks to have its aggregate NAV approximate at all times the outstanding value of the oil futures contracts.

iPath GSCI Crude Oil Total Return Exchange Traded Note (ETN) symbol (OIL) tracks the performance of a nonleveraged investment in West Texas Intermediate crude futures, plus the return that would be earned by an investment of collateral assets in Treasuries.

ETNs are debt-linked instruments that trade much like traditional exchange-traded funds (ETFs). The chief difference is that

ETNs do not actually hold a stake in the underlying commodity or commodities futures. Instead, ETNs are simply senior debt notes from Barclays PLC, under which Barclays promises to pay you the exact return of the underlying commodity index, minus an expense ratio of 0.75 percent per year.

Gold and Silver

streetTRACKS Gold Shares (GLD) offer investors a way to access the gold market without the necessity of taking physical delivery of gold and to buy and sell that interest through the trading of a security on a regulated stock exchange. The trust holds gold and issues exchange tradeable shares in exchange for deposits of gold and distributes gold in connection with redemptions of those securities. Each ETF share represents one-tenth of an ounce of gold, backed by bullion held in a vault. The investment objective of the trust is for the shares to reflect the performance of the price of gold bullion, less the 0.40 percent expense. There was more than $6 billion investing in the fund as of June 2006. streetTRACKS Gold Shares is the world's largest private owner of bullion.

iShares Comex Gold Trust (IAU) corresponds with one-tenth of a troy ounce of gold. The ETF's trustee, the Bank of New York, will value the trust's gold on the basis of that day's announced Comex settlement price for the spot month gold futures contract. The shares of the trust will reflect the price of the gold owned by the trust, minus expenses and liabilities. The annual management fee is 0.40 percent. There was more than $800 million invested in the fund as of June 2006.

Gold TRAKRS (GLD:CME) are nontraditional futures contracts that trade on the Chicago Mercantile Exchange (CME). They provide investors with an alternative way to gain exposure to the spot price of gold. Unlike traditional futures contract, investors are required to post 100 percent of the TRAKRS market value at the time of purchase. Gold TRAKRS are complicated securities with a varying cost structure. Read the "Disclosure Document" on www.trakrs.com before investing.

iShares Silver Trust (SLV) is backed by silver. Each share is equal to about 10 ounces of silver. The custodian of the trust is JPMorgan Chase, although the silver itself is held in the vault of the Bank of England. The annual management fee is 0.50 percent. There was almost $900 million invested in the fund as of June 2006. The trust will sell silver to pay its expenses, so the amount of the metal represented by the ETF's shares will decline over time. If the price of silver does not increase enough to compensate for those sales, the share price will decline. Those silver sales will be a taxable event for U.S. investors.

Under current law, gains recognized by individuals from the sale of "collectibles," including gold and silver bullion, held for more than one year are taxed at a maximum rate of 28 percent, rather than the 15 percent rate applicable to most other long-term capital gains. Check with your tax advisor before investing.

COMMODITIES INDEXES

Commodities mutual funds invest in derivatives of commodity total return indexes. Therefore, investors in those funds should understand how commodity indexes are constructed. There are several competing commodity total return indexes. As with stock indexes, each commodity index provider has its own methodology for calculating returns and its reasons to believe that its system is superior to everyone else's.

Four popular indexes for measuring commodity futures prices are the Goldman Sachs Commodity Index (GSCI), Dow Jones-AIG Commodity Index (DJ-AIGCI), Commodity Research Bureau index (Reuters/Jefferies CRB index), and the Rogers International Commodity Index (RICI). In addition, Deutsche Bank (DBLCI), Lehman Brothers, and Merrill Lynch have recently entered the commodity index race. The most important difference between the indexes is their approach to weighting the different commodity sectors and the periodic rebalancing of those sectors. Table 11-1 illustrates the weighing differences that can occur between major index providers.

The word *index* is used liberally in this chapter. Most of the commodity indexes listed below are not indexes—they are managed investment strategies. Some index providers change the weightings of the various commodities in the index on an ongoing basis based on the provider's perceived opportunity. Others engage in an annual rebalancing process to take into account changes in the level of global commodity production or consumption. Still others make regular adjustments to the weightings in accordance with certain mechanical rules set in advance. With the exception of the Goldman Sachs and Deutsche Bank, which attempts to weigh each commodity in their index by global market value, most providers manage their index to sector target weights and cap individual commodity allocations to ensure diversification.

Over the past 10 years, many indexes providers have engineered or reengineered their indexes to take advantage of the large spike in energy and metals prices. Manipulating and back-testing strategies to find a mix that puts the index on top of its beaten peer may seem unethical, but it tends to be acceptable among today's product providers. Then again, everyone has to make a living, and mutual fund investors have very short memories. If the allocation to energy and metals was not high in an index over the past few years, the provider of that index would not find one fund company willing to license their product.

Goldman Sachs Commodity Index

The GSCI was created in 1991 and is widely considered to be the most heavily followed commodity index. It is world-production-weighted, which means that the quantity of each commodity in the index is determined by the average value of production in the past five years of available data and then adjusted for a liquidity factor. Weights are adjusted annually and put into effect on January 1.

The GSCI considers the price of 24 commodities based on overall market value; six energy products, five industrial metals, eight agricultural products, three livestock products, and two precious metals. Because the total value of oil produced globally dominates the commodities markets, the GSCI methodology generates an excessively heavy energy weighting. A small rise in the price of crude oil has a significant effect on the GSCI.

Dow Jones-AIG Commodity Index

The DJ-AIGCI was created in 1998 and has a large following among institutional investors. The index is derived from the value of 20 commodities. It is a market during the year, but with a twist. The weighting of the various commodities is based on a combination of average global production and average trading volume over the most recent five-year period. The weightings are adjusted once a year and put into effect in early January. However, the DJ-AIGCI is reweighted and rebalanced annually with restrictions. No commodity sector starts the year with more than 33 percent position (energy), and no single group component may be more than 15 percent of the group or 2 percent of the index (W.T.I. crude oil). Dow Jones claims the rebalancing to fixed weights adds about 4 percent per year to the index return.

Reuters/Jefferies CRB Index

For more than 50 years, the Commodity Research Bureau (CRB) was the only commodities firm that had good records of historic commodity prices. Reuters-CRB index was an equal-weighted benchmark of approximately 20 commodities; equal weighting means the same allocation in the index was given to cotton as it was to crude oil. Unfortunately, the equal-weighting methodology caused problems for Reuters over the past few years. The Reuters-CRB index was left far behind newer commodities indexes during the boom in energy prices that occurred after 2002. That meant no licensing fees for Reuters as mutual fund companies passed up the stodgy Reuters-CRB index for new indexes with high energy exposure.

In 2005, the Reuters Group affiliated with Jefferies Financial Products to produce the Reuters/Jefferies CRB index (RJ-CRB). The new index placed a significant holding in energy. Crude oil was given a 23 percent position, and a 16 percent more was spread between gasoline, heating oil, and natural gas. As expected, Jefferies shows that hypothetical back-testing of the RJ-CRB index handily beat rivals GSCI and DJ-AIGCI.

Deutsche Bank Liquid Commodity Index

The DBLCI was created in 2003 and intended to reflect the performance of a handful of the most liquid, globally traded commodities. Commodities in the index are set weights and comprise crude oil (35 percent), heating oil (20 percent), aluminum (12.5 percent), gold (10 percent), corn (11.25 percent), and wheat (11.25 percent). The percent of each commodity included in the index is broadly in proportion to historic levels of the world's production and stocks.

Deutsche Bank says the limited number of commodities is not important because price movements for commodities in the same sector tend to be highly correlated.

The index has an unusual policy on rebalancing. Positions in energy futures, namely W.T.I. crude oil and heating oil, are rebalanced each month, whereas positions in the other four contracts are rebalanced once a year. The dual rebalancing policy is supposed to increase the roll return, or reduce the negative effect of rolling the futures contracts.

Rogers International Commodity Index

The RICI was created in 1998 and is based on monthly closing prices of a fixed-weight portfolio of the nearby futures and forwards contract month of international commodity markets. There are 35 different contracts represented in the index including obscure commodities such as zinc, nickel, lumber, oats, barley, azuki beans, wool, rubber, and silk. Rebalancing in the RICI is done monthly, and the selection and tactical weighting of the index is reviewed annually in December. Jim Rogers, the founder of the index and author of several books, has a significant degree of discretion with respect to the RICI. On par with the rest of the new indexes, the RICI index had hypothetical back-testing returns superior to GSCI, DJ-AIGCI, and CRB.

Standard & Poor's Commodity Index

The Standard & Poor's Commodity Index (SPCI) was introduced in 2001 and tracks 17 commodities that trade on U.S. exchanges. The weighting is based on liquidity as measured by the level of open interest held by traders. Standard & Poor's uses a geometric methodology to calculate the index rather than an arithmetic methodology used by the other index managers. That leads to lower volatility but higher trading costs. The SPCI also reduces "double counting" in the index by lowering the weighting of commodities that are "upstream" from another commodity in the index. For example, the live cattle component is reduced to take into account the amount of corn used as cattle feed. The SPCI is also the only index that excludes gold, with the reasoning being that the vast majority of gold inventory is held in storage and is not a consumable item like all other commodities.

Merrill Lynch Commodity eXtra Index

The Merrill Lynch Commodity eXtra index (MLCX) was devised in 2006 to present an accurate representation of the value of commodities in the global economy. However, the share of any given subindex has a cap of 60 percent and a floor of 3 percent in the overall index to control for risk.

MLCX also has a different strategy when trading commodities. Commodities index funds hold futures contracts that must be "rolled over" from time to time. The funds typically hold soon-to-expire "front-month" contracts and roll them to the next available "second-month" contracts prior to expiration. The MLCX takes a different approach. It holds the "second-month" contract and rolls it into the "third-month" contract. Merrill claims the second- to third-month roll has been more favorable for investors than the first- to second-month roll.

Lehman Brothers Commodity Index

The Lehman Brothers Commodity Index (LBCI) was created in 2006 to measure the performance of a diversified mix of commodities futures contracts. The LBCI contains 20 commodities that span the four major segments of the market: energy, metals, agriculture, and livestock. Individual commodity indexes are published as well. The weights of the major components of the index as of the beginning of 2006 were energy, 56 percent; metals, 23 percent; agriculture, 18 percent; and livestock, 3 percent.

Total Return Indexes

The commodity indexes described above are futures price indexes. They reflect the change in price of commodity futures. That is not the return investors earn. Total return indexes are designed to replicate the return of fully collateralized commodity futures. The total return is the price return on the commodity futures, plus the difference in price between old futures contracts near expiration and new futures

TABLE 11—1

Approximate Sector Allocation of Commodity Indexes

Commodities Index	Percent Energy	Percent Metals	Percent Agriculture	Percent Livestock
DJ-AIGCI	34	25	30	10
GSCI	74	11	10	4
Reuters/Jefferies CRB	39	20	33	8
Rogers ICI	44	23	31	2
Deutsche Bank LCI	55	23	23	0
S&P CI	49	7	37	7
Merrill Lynch (MLCX)	60	20	15	6
Lehman Brothers	53	27	17	3

Source: Goldman Sachs, Merrill Lynch, RICI, Standard & Poor's, Lehman Brothers.

prices on the day contracts are rolled to the next month, plus the income from the Treasury bills where the collateral sits.

As you recall, margin is required to enter into a futures contract. Assume, for example, that margin is 5 percent of the underlying commodities value that a futures contract represents. A futures contract for $4,000 worth of gold for delivery in one month would require a 5 percent margin of $200. That money goes to a separate account where it earns a small interest rate. The other $3,800 stays in your investment account and earns money market interest. The "total" return on your $4,000 over one month equals the price change on gold futures contract, plus the roll yield, plus the interest on the cash sitting in your margin account and money market account.

Figure 11-3 illustrates the performance of the back-testing Reuters/Jefferies Total Return CRB index (Reuters CRB Total Return Index prior to 1995). With minor differences, the performance of Reuters total return indexes are on par with the back-tested performance of all other commodity total return indexes.

Figure 11-3 has the same characteristics as all other commodity indexes. It is years of poor performance followed by period of wild speculation. Futures prices did not match the inflation rate from 1981 to 2002 and then surged from 2003 to 2006 with energy and metals prices. Performance is represented before fees and expenses.

Figure 11-3

Reuters/Jefferies Total Return CRB Index and Inflation

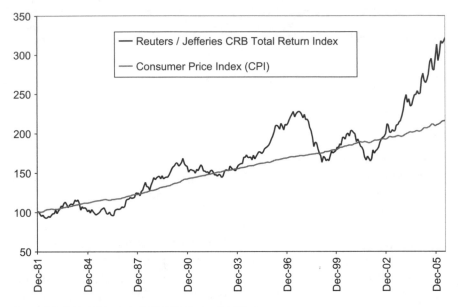

Source: RJCRB Total Return Index 1995–2006, Reuters-CRBTRI prior.

Total Return Commodity Funds

The published returns of the indexes do not reflect the returns of investors in mutual funds that benchmarked those indexes. First, every managed fund of commodities and futures has annual management fees and possibly a sales commission to buy in. The costs can be expensive. Some commodity mutual funds fees reach 2 percent per year in addition to a sales charge reaching 5.75 percent. Second, tracking error in commodities funds is typically higher than with stock or bond funds. Fund managers battle the cost and timing of rolling from one contract date to another in an effort to maintain continuity with the index.

All of the mutual funds listed in Table 11-2 are total return commodities index. You will receive the price change of the commodities price index, the price difference in near-term and one-month futures contracts, plus the return of the interest income earned overall on the cash and margin, less fees and commissions.

TABLE 11-2

Commodity Total Return Funds

Index	Commodity Product	Type	Fee	Symbol	Minimum
GSCI	iShares GSCI Commodity-Indexed Trust	ETF	0.75	GSG	None
GSCI	iPath GSCI Total Return Index	ETN	0.75	GSP	None
GSCI	Oppenheimer Real Asset A (5.75 load)	Open-End	1.40	QRAAX	1,000
GSCI	Merrill Lynch Real Invtmt A (5.25 load)	Open-End	1.87	MDCDX	1,000
DB LCI	PowerShares DB Comm. Index Trkng	ETF	0.83	DBC	None
DJ AIGCI	iPath DJ AIGC Total Return Index	ETN	0.75	DJP	None
DJ AIGCI	Commodity TRAKRS	TRAKRS	†	CCC:CME	None
RICI	Rogers International Commodity TRAKRS	TRAKRS	†	RCI:CME	None
Hybrid*	PIMCO Commodity Real Rtn A (5.5 load)	Open-End	1.24	PCRAX	5,000
Hybrid*	PIMCO Commodity Real Rtn TRAKRS	TRAKRS	†	PCT:CME	None

*PCRAX and PCT(CME) follow a TIPS collateralized DJ AIGCI strategy (see prospectus).
†The overall cost to purchase is typically between 1.5 Percent and 3 Percent.
Source: IndexUniverse.com

SLICING AND DICING COMMODITY INDEXES

A natural progression of commodity index fund offerings was to move from broad-based indexes to sectors and subsectors. Barclays Global Investors (BGI) and Deutsche Bank have filed with the SEC for the right to launch new commodity ETFs that offer investors access to different slices of the commodities market.

The BGI funds track Goldman Sachs–branded commodity indexes and track those indexes by investing in a new type of option called CERFs. CERFs are long-term (five-year expiration) options contracts and are a relatively unproven product on the market. CERFs are tied to the value of the "excess return" versions of the commodity benchmarks, which means that, despite the five-year expiration dates, they are priced as if the underlying futures contracts were being rolled from month to month. The funds also capture interest income from the cash held as collateral.

The iShares GS Commodity Industrial Metals Index Trust is designed to offer investors exposure to the industrial metals market, tracking a production-weighted index of copper, aluminum, zinc, nickel, and lead futures (prospectus). Currently, the index is dominated by copper and aluminum, which have a 43 percent and 33 percent weight, respectively. Many investors are itching for exposure to metals, and especially to copper, which many see as exquisitely leveraged to the rise of the global economy.

iShares GS Commodity Livestock Indexed Trust is designed to provide exposure to the livestock components of the commodities universe. Currently, that includes just three commodities: live cattle at 50.5 percent of the index, live hogs at 45.6 percent of the index, and feeder cattle at 14.9 percent of the index.

iShares GS Commodity Light Energy Indexed Trust attempts to mitigate the chief criticism of the traditional GSCI—that it is too heavily weighted in energy—by reducing energy exposure from 77 percent of the index to just 39 percent. The result is a much more diversified index that could find a strong place in the commodities market.

iShares GS Commodity Non-Energy Indexes Trust takes things one step further and excludes energy altogether, allowing investors to track the performance of the ex-energy component of the commodities boom.

Deutsche Bank has filed with the SEC for a series of commodity subsector funds including energy, agriculture, and base metals funds.

CURRENCIES FUNDS

Institutional investors, such as banks and brokerages, have traditionally dominated the currency markets. Now individual investors can easily invest in this market through ETFs that have the sole objective to reflect the price of the currency held by the fund. Table 11-3 is a list of currency ETFs that are available.

Some interest is paid in the account while money is held in trust, but the main attraction remains the currency exposure. If the currency held by a fund appreciates relative to the U.S. dollar and a shareholder sells shares, the shareholder will earn a profit. If the currency held by a fund depreciates relative to the U.S. dollar and a shareholder sells shares, the shareholder will incur a loss.

Rydex Investments launched the first currency ETF, the Euro Currency Trust, on the New York Stock Exchange in December 2005. In June 2006, Rydex added six more currency-based ETFs to the market when it launched the CurrencyShares series of funds. Each fund holds a different foreign currency with on overseas branch of JPMorgan Chase Bank. The funds track the price of their underlying currency based on the Federal Reserve Noon Buying Rate.

There are a few ways that individuals can use currency funds. First is to speculate on currency movements, which is not advisable; second, as a hedge against currency declines prior to a purchase or sale of land or goods in another country; third, to hedge the currency risk of a large asset owned in another country, such as a large position in a foreign stock with headquarters in Europe.

FUTURE DEVELOPMENTS

Fund providers have just begun to issue new products benchmarked to new and interesting alternative asset class indexes. One key to development is an active derivatives market in the product the fund companies are trying to introduce. Where there is an active derivatives market, there can be mutual funds.

TABLE 11–3

Pure Play Currency Funds

CurrencyShares Trust	Type	Fee	Symbol	Minimum
Australian Dollar	ETF	0.40	FXA	None
British Pound Sterling	ETF	0.40	FXB	None
Canadian Dollar	ETF	0.40	FXC	None
Euro Currency Trust	ETF	0.40	FXE	None
Mexican Peso	ETF	0.40	FXM	None
Swedish Krona	ETF	0.40	FXS	None
Swiss Franc	ETF	0.40	FXF	None

Source: ww.currencyshares.com

What new developments are in the future? How about mutual funds that track the average market price of homes in your city? The Case-Shiller indexes represent movements in housing price values in 10 major metropolitan areas across the country. The 10 cities include Boston, Chicago, Denver, Las Vegas, Los Angeles, Miami, New York, San Diego, San Francisco, and Washington, D.C. Futures contracts launched in the second quarter of 2006 track those indexes. I speculate there will be established index funds benchmarked to the Case-Shiller indexes available shortly. That means homebuyers and sellers will be able to hedge their exposure to rising or falling home prices.

CHAPTER SUMMARY

The growth of index funds in alternative asset classes has exploded in recent years. Low-cost index funds are now available in several alternative asset classes including individual commodities, commodity indexes, and currencies. These new opportunities may play an expanded role in portfolio management in the future as the cost is driven down by competition.

There are advantages and disadvantages to adding an alternative asset class to a portfolio. One advantage is that an investment in commodities tends to exhibit low correlation with traditional stock and bond investments. That lowers the risk of a portfolio overall. However, the disadvantages include the cost of investing, the lack of a real expected return over fees and inflation, and low tax-efficiency.

As innovation continues in the financial markets, more low-cost index fund products will be introduced. Some of those products will enter new markets, such as housing prices and possibly the art market. It is an exciting time for index fund investors who seek a broadly diversified portfolio.

Managing Your Index Fund Portfolio

CHAPTER 12

Forecasting Index
Fund Returns

Key Concepts

- One should understand the potential risks and returns of various markets.
- Past history offers some clues to future market behavior.
- In the long run, economics drives market returns.
- No method of forecasting is perfect. It is better to be conservative.

Effective portfolio management requires an awareness of market history and a framework for fashioning realistic long-term market forecasts. In the short-term, markets are not predictable, but in the long run they follow economic trends. If we conduct business today as we conducted business in the past, and our lawmakers do not impose radical changes to tax laws and the way we conduct business, the future of the financial markets will likely resemble the past in some regards.

This chapter will help you establish a method for allocating your portfolio among different asset classes given a presumed moderate pace of growth in the U.S. economy. The steps are logical but not simple. Projecting the nominal returns of the past 25 years into the future is a simple method of forecasting but a poor one. Stock and bond market returns since the 1980s have been historically high, and is it not economically possible to duplicate them. Adjustments have to be made before arriving at a logical forecast. This chapter reviews a framework to forecasting expected returns into the future.

THE LIMITATIONS OF FORECASTING

There are various methods for predicting market returns, and none of them are accurate. In the absence of a crystal ball, however, this is all we have to work with. One method of forecasting returns projects past performance into the future using mathematical models, with adjustments for today's interest rates, corporate earnings levels, and tax rates. A second method of market prediction starts with economic forecasts. These methods can be more effective than manipulating past return data. However, unpredictable events such as natural disasters, wars, and political instability can derail the most diligent economic prediction. A third method is to combine past market data with a conservative estimate of long-term economic growth.

Combining the technical aspects of past market returns with the fundamental inputs from economic estimates may yield clues to the future of financial market returns. The market forecasts put forth in this chapter are based on that combination. These forecasts are intended to be a guide, not an absolute. No one knows what will actually happen in the marketplace. Consequently, it is always better to err on the side of conservatism. If you are conservative in your estimates and the markets perform better than expected, you will end up with more money, which is always better than planning for higher returns and falling short.

STOCK PRICE HISTORY

Market forecasts should be estimated over the long-term. How long is long-term? A lifetime is an appropriate period, although by the time most people get around to investing, half of their lives is over. Therefore, we will call 30 years long-term.

The reason 30 years seems to be a good forecast goal is because stock prices seem to move in long bull and bear wave. Each wave includes a multiyear bull market followed by a multiyear bear market. The bull markets were characterized by a gradual slow climb that lasted about 20 years, ending in a climax. The bear markets were characterized by a sharper descent that lasted about half as long as the preceding bull market. Those are very rough observations.

Since 1880, there have been four major stock market waves since 1880 (Figure 12-1). Each wave lasted roughly 30 years, which, coincidentally, is the equivalent of one generation. If this secular wave sequence continues over the next few generations, the average person will see two waves during his or her lifetime.

When people experience the first bull market in their lives, they are usually young and do not have a lot of money invested. By the time they experience the second bull market, a person is generally well established in a career and has more assets set aside for retirement. It is during the generational bull market that people make their gains in the stock market.

The most recent wave began in 1982, and that bull market did not belong to the baby boomers. Most boomers were in the beginning of their careers and did not have a lot of money in the market at the time. On the other hand, the bull market of the 1980s and 1990s was a huge benefit to the baby boomers' parents, if they invested early enough. When the first edition of this book was written in 2001, I stated that it may be several years before the baby boomers get to participate in a bull market that helps them directly. That time may be getting closer.

Although the wave theory of forecasting calls for a bull market starting in the next decade or so, there have been periods when the

FIGURE 12–1

The Long Wave of the Stock Market (Inflation Adjusted)

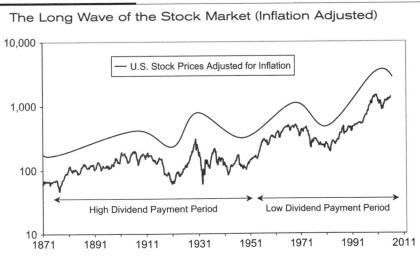

Source: Robert Shiller, Federal Reserve data.

market did not go up in value over a 30-year period. Figure 12-1 shows that during the period from 1881 to 1950, the inflation-adjusted price of stocks did not go up. However, that did not mean that investors made no money in stocks during the period. During the late 1880s and the first half of the 1900s, the average dividend yield on common stock was more than 6 percent. It was a time when companies paid cash dividends to shareholders using about 70 percent of the earnings they made.

As Figure 12-2 illustrates, today companies pay a cash dividend of 1.7 percent, which is less than 35 percent of corporate earnings. The retained earnings are used for internal growth, acquisitions, or stock buybacks. There are lots of reasons for this change, one being different tax treatment of capital gains and dividends. It does not really matter if you are paid by dividends or growth. In the long run, dividends and capital gains are all part of the market "total return."

The purpose of discussing waves is to point out that it may take 30 years or more for an investor to be justly rewarded for taking risks in the stock market. Now you may be thinking, "I don't have 30 years!" and that may be true. But according to new annuity tables

FIGURE 12–2

Dividend Yield of the S&P 500

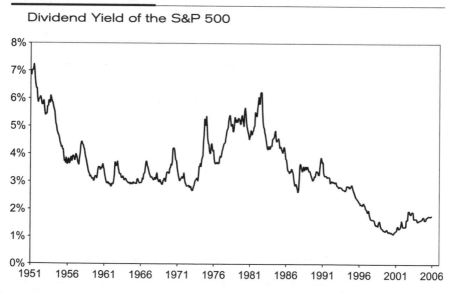

Source: Standard & Poor's.

released by the IRS in 2005, the life expectancy for a 70-year-old is another 16 years, and if both a husband and wife make it to age 70, then one of the two is expected to live another 26 years.

Should you wait for the next bull market to begin before investing? No. No one knows when the next bull market will begin, how long it will last, and when it will end. The best way to take advantage of the fruits of the stock market is through a consistent, long-term investment strategy starting now.

NOMINAL RETURNS AND REAL RETURNS

Over long periods of time, stocks are expected to perform better than bonds because stocks have more risk than bonds. In addition, bonds are expected to perform better than money market funds because bonds have more risk than money market funds. However, even when stocks, bonds, and money market funds make money, do investors really earn a profit? That question cannot be answered by looking at "nominal" market returns; the returns quoted in the press and by every bank and every mutual fund company. The inflation rate must be stripped out of the nominal return to see if you made any "real" money.

Inflation is a hidden income tax that a government places on its people through fiscal and monetary policy. Inflation distorts investment results. Nominal returns may look great on paper, but real returns are what count. If an investment earned 5 percent one year, and that year inflation was also 5 percent, then the "real" rate of return was 0 percent. Actually, it is less than 0 percent because the IRS taxes the full 5 percent nominal gain regardless of the inflation rate, which in effect is a government income tax on a government inflation tax. In the above example, a 30 percent tax on a nominal return of 5 percent leaves you with 3.5 percent, and a real return of negative 1.5 percent. Taxes are a big expense. Lowering taxes will be a subject addressed in upcoming chapters.

THE HISTORY OF MARKET RETURNS

Benjamin Graham once said, "In the short run the market is a voting machine, and in the long run it is a weighing machine." Market prices are the result of an auction that we all participate in. On any

TABLE 12-1

U.S. Financial Market 1950–2005

Asset Class	Compounded Return	Standard Deviation
Large-cap stocks	11.9	14.3
Small-cap stocks	13.6	19.5
Long-term corporate bonds	6.3	8.0
Treasury bills	4.9	0.8
Inflation (CPI)	3.9	0.3
Source: Morningstar.		

given day, millions of people decide the price of individual stocks and bonds by placing buy and sell orders. Those individual prices cumulate into market indexes. In the short term, markets can move erratically as new information is introduced that may conflict with forecasts and opinions. However, in the long run the true economic impact of the news becomes clearer, and that causes stock prices to gradually readjust closer to fair value.

"History may not repeat itself, but it rhymes," as the saying goes. To gain an understanding of the future potential of the stock and bond markets, we need to begin with the past data. Table 12-1 lists the nominal rates of return and historic price volatility of various financial markets. Subtracting the inflation rate from the nominal index return yields the real return. Because different indexes have different starting dates, there are three groups. The year 1950 was chosen for the return of major U.S. indexes.

By focusing on the past 55 years, the returns of "regulated" markets are presented. In the early 1900s, the stock market was only minimally regulated, and that had made a difference in the risk and return characteristics during that period. A start date of 1950 also takes us through two generational waves including two major bull markets and two major bear markets. Two complete market cycles are hardly an adequate statistical sample, but they are all we have to work with.

Risk as a Driver of Market Returns

Markets derive returns from a number of factors. Risk is certainly a major factor in the calculation of expected future returns. The most

TABLE 12-2

Returns and Risks over Independent Periods

Period	Compound Return			Risk (Standard Deviation)		
	S&P 500	5-Year T-Note	T-Bills	S&P 500	5-Year T-Note	T-Bills
1956–1965	11.1	3.1	2.8	11.8	3.1	0.2
1966–1975	3.3	5.7	5.6	15.6	4.8	0.4
1976–1985	14.3	10.3	9.0	14.2	7.7	0.9
1986–1995	14.9	9.0	5.6	15.0	4.8	0.5
1996–2005	9.1	5.8	3.6	15.6	4.5	0.5
Source: Standard & Poor's, Federal Reserve.						

common measure for risk in the financial markets is standard deviation, written as the Greek symbol σ. Standard deviation is a mathematical formula that expresses the average amount of price volatility in a market. Standard deviation does not express the limit of market risk; it simply reports the "average miss" any given year a market has had from its historical average annual return.

The return of stocks and bonds varies from period to period as is evident in Table 12-2. However, the data also show that risk of a market tends to be more consistent and predictable than its return. Notice the risk as measured by standard deviation is more consistent than the period returns.

Because market risk is more consistent than returns, we use that as a starting point to forecast an expected return for taking risk. Using Treasury bills risk and expected return as a starting point, we plot the expected long-term *risk premiums* for each asset class. The actual financial equation used to forecast expected market returns using risk as a factor is called the capital asset pricing model (CAPM).

No knowledgeable investor would commit capital to a risky investment without the prospect of a payoff for taking that risk. Figure 12-3 is based on the logical assumption that the more risk an investment has, the higher the expected return of that investment.

I will spare you the details of the CAPM equation that went into Figure 12-3 and just provide an overview. The figure shows the predicted nominal returns of various markets based on a modified CAPM model and a stable 3 percent inflation rate. It starts with the

F I G U R E   12–3

Expected Risks and Returns of the Capital Markets

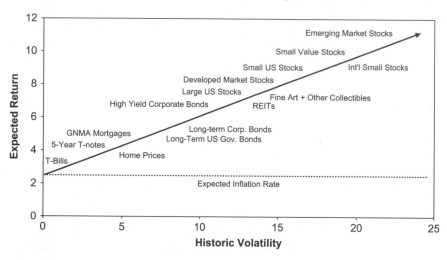

Source: Portfolio Solutions, LLC.

assumption that the safest security you can own is a Treasury bill (T-bill). They are considered a risk-free investment because the federal government has unlimited taxing power and the power to print money. Based on the data in Table 12-1, the return of T-bills has been about 1.0 percent higher than the inflation rate on average over a long period of time. Investors have to earn some return over inflation to pay taxes, so it is logical to forecast that T-bills should earn more than inflation in the future.

Once the real return of T-bills is established, we estimate the real return of other investments by adding an extra risk premium on top of the expected 1 percent real return of T-bills. The extra layer of return is directly related to the extra asset risk in the investment.

You may be wondering why the expected returns are higher than the historical returns for bonds and lower than the historical returns for stocks. Bond prices have become more volatile since the 1950s due to increased volatility in the inflation rate. Because we must get paid more for taking more risk, the projected return of bonds is higher than the previous 50-year average. Stock returns are expected to be lower that the historical average because economic growth is expected to be slightly lower than the historical norm, and

TABLE 12-3

Expected Risk Premiums

Asset Class Premiums over T-Bills	Historic Risk Premium over T-Bills	Forecast Risk	Expected Return
T-Bills	—	—	Inflation + 1.0%
Long Treasury bonds	0.8	1.50%	T-bill rate + 1.5%
Corporate bonds	1.3	2.00%	T-bill rate + 2.0%
Large U.S. stocks	7.0	3.50%	T-bill rate + 3.5%
Small U.S. stocks	8.0	5.00%	T-bill rate + 5.0%
Source: Portfolio Solutions, LLC.			

stocks are currently trading at slightly higher valuations than their historical norm. Recall that our philosophy on forecasts is that is it better to be safe and pleasantly surprised than the other way around.

Risk premiums make sense from a practical standpoint. Greater risk should yield greater returns. Table 12-3 is an example of the expected return premium for several asset classes based on their increased risk. In addition to forecasting individual market returns, the CAPM is useful in determining the relationship of returns that should occur between markets and how mixing asset classes together actually reduces risk and increases return. The subject of asset allocation is explored in Chapter 13.

Economics Is the Driver of Financial Markets

Thus, far, we have only looked at past market risk and returns to create a forecast of future returns. A second method for calculating expected market return is through the use of economic models. We start by using economic growth assumptions to forecast corporate earnings growth, then add the market's dividend yield and adjust for any change in valuations or the price people put on the first. To better understand this model, each part is explained separately.

Economic Growth Becomes Earnings Growth

The primary driver behind stock prices is current earnings and projected earnings growth. The more money companies make, the more money shareholders make, and stocks go up in value. One way to

FIGURE 12–4

GDP and S&P 500 Corporate Earnings Growth

Source: Federal Reserve, Standard & Poor's.

forecast earnings growth is to start with the expected growth in overall economic activity. Gross Domestic Product (GDP) is the single best
measure of economic activity. Real GDP is the sum total of all goods
and services produced in the United States during the year adjusted
for inflation. It is composed of four components: consumer spending,
government spending, business spending, and exports minus im-
ports. There is a direct and consistent relationship between GDP
growth and corporate earnings growth. Figure 12-4 illustrates that
relationship by showing that earnings growth follows GDP growth.

It is the Federal Reserve's job to target GDP growth and "adjust"
the economy by changing short-term interest rates and other means.
The Federal Reserve considers an inflation-adjusted growth rate of 3
percent to be a good target. Any more than 4 percent GDP growth is
considered inflationary because there is too much demand for goods
and services; and less than 2 percent per year means the economy is
not operating at an efficient level. Because corporate earnings growth
seems to follow GDP growth closely over time, we will forecast earnings growth to be about 3 percent per year adjusted for inflation.

Cash Dividends

The second part of the formula covers the cash payment of dividends. U.S. stocks currently pay about 1.7 percent per year in dividend yield as measured by the S&P 500 index. That is historically a very low number. As was illustrated in Figure 12-2, dividend yields have dropped significantly since the 1950s, hitting a low of 1 percent in 2000. Although dividends are not as large a part of the total return equation as they used to be, they are still very important in the long-term.

Speculation (Price-to-Earnings Expansion and Contraction)

The third driver of total return is speculation. If most investors believe that corporate earnings will increase faster and greater than the average, the price of stock will increase in anticipation of the greater earnings forecast. This is exactly the reason Internet stocks kept going higher and higher in the late 1990s. The prices of those stocks were simply adjusting to the lofty earnings forecasts of investors. When real earnings became known, or no earnings in the case of most Internet stocks, the values of the markets fell.

Speculation creates about 10 times more volatility in the market than actual earnings changes and about 100 times more volatility than dividend changes. If you have a crystal ball and can predict the mind of the masses, then you can make a lot of money on changing market valuation. Personally, I have never had any luck at it.

Figure 12-5 clearly illustrates the speculative booms and busts we have experienced in the stock market over the years. The S&P 500 price-to-GDP ratio is derived by dividing the price of the S&P 500 index by GDP (in billions). This ratio is similar to the popular price-to-earnings ratio (P/E), only it is more stable because GDP figures are more stable than reported corporate earnings figures. In September 1981, the S&P 500 price index was trading at only 3.4 percent of GDP; by September 1999, it was at 15.6 percent. That is a speculative increase of almost five times.

In a fair economy with inflation at about 3 percent, I believe the S&P 500 price-to-GDP ratio should be around 10 percent. You can see how speculation radically changed the value of the stock market in the late 1990s, even though the level of economic activity in the United States remained fairly consistent (see Figure 12-4).

FIGURE 12-5

Nominal GDP and S&P 500 Price Ratio

Source: Portfolio Solutions, LLC.

In the short run, speculation creates the volatility in stock prices, but in the long run the speculative noise tends to cancel out and economic growth drives stock prices. Speculation is not predictable, so there is no sense trying to input that variable in a long-term forecast. It is impossible to predict what investors will think about the value of the markets next week, next month, or next year, let alone 30 years from now. For the following forecasts, we assume the price-to-GDP and P/E ratios of the stock market are held constant at current levels, thereby eliminating speculative noise.

Inflation

No sensible investor would go into any investment knowing that the expected return of the investments was below the inflation rate. Consequently, the inflation rate is embedded in the expected return of all investments and is added into the expected equity market return.

Calculating the expected inflation rate has become much easier over the years. The U.S. Treasury now issues Treasury Inflation Protected Securities (TIPS) that pay interest on only a real rate of return. To find the market-anticipated inflation rate over the next 10 years,

FIGURE 12–6

Inflation Expectation Implied from the 10-Year TIPS Spread

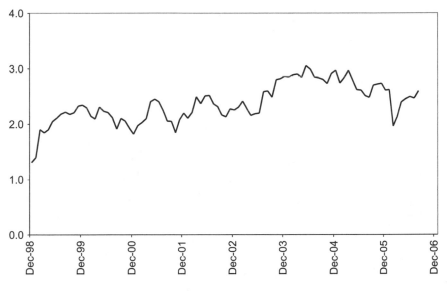

Source: Federal Reserve

simply subtract the yield on a 10-year TIPS from the nominal yield on a traditional 10-year Treasury bond. The result is the inflation rate that market investors expect. See Figure 12-6 for the historical inflation expectation measured by the difference between the 10-year Treasury and 10-year TIPS.

Inflation Drives Bond Returns

The expected return of bonds is much simpler than the expected return for stocks. There is a formula for calculating the expected long-term return of Treasury bonds: expected bond return equals interest payments plus the reinvestment of interest plus or minus changes in the expected inflation. If a nongovernment bond is being evaluated, there is a fourth and a fifth element: the credit quality of the bond and the call option. In the long-term, inflation factors drive the price of all bonds, and the additional credit risk and call features of a nongovernment bonds adds to the formula.

There is a direct and inverse relationship between the inflation rate and the price of all bonds. When inflation is rising, bond prices

FIGURE 12-7

Annual Inflation and Treasury Bond Returns (1976–1987)

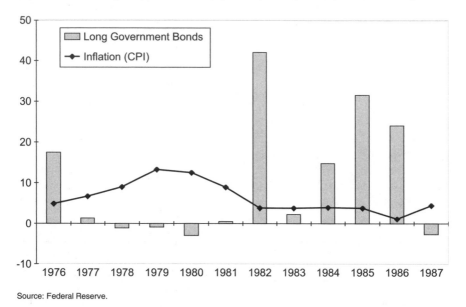

Source: Federal Reserve.

are falling, and when inflation is falling, bond prices are rising. Figure 12-7 highlights the inverse relationship between inflation and traditional bond market returns. The figure highlights one of the most volatile periods in U.S. bond market history. From 1976 through 1980, inflation soared to 15 percent, creating havoc in the Lehman Brothers Long-Term Government Bond index. By 1982, inflation fell back to significantly lower levels, setting the Lehman index up for huge short-term price gains.

It is impossible to forecast the movement of the inflation rate. However, you can limit your risk by purchasing short-term bond index funds and intermediate-term funds. Short-term funds hold bonds that are closer to maturity than long-term funds, so you will not experience the intense volatility of long-term bonds. Although there is extra interest from long-term bonds, the pickup in yield does not justify the added risk in most cases. Historically, there has been less than a 0.5 percent return advantage from long-term bond funds over short-term bond funds while adding over 3 percent per year in extra risk. See Chapter 9 for more information on bond indexes and bond index funds.

CREATING A FORECAST

We have analyzed four primary drivers of market returns: risk, inflation, earnings growth, and cash payments from interest and dividends. These factors are part of every valuation model. It would require a book much thicker than this one to detail all the alternative models used in forecasting expected stock and bond returns. I have drawn from a number of these models and present my best guess for the future. Table 12-4 is my median expected return for all of the major markets. These are 30-year estimates.

TABLE 12-4

Expected Long-Term Financial Market Returns and Risks

Asset Class	Real Return in Percent	With 3% Inflation	Risk* in Percent
Government-Backed Fixed Income			
U.S. Treasury bills (1-year maturity)	1	4	1.5
Intermediate-term U.S. Treasury notes	1.5	4.5	4.8
Long-term U.S. Treasury bonds	2	5	5.3
GNMA mortgages	2	5	8
Intermediate tax-free (AA rated)	1	4	5
Corporate and Emerging Market Fixed			
Intermediate high-grade corporate	2	5	5.5
Long-term investment-grade bonds	2.8	5.8	8.5
Preferred stocks (rated A or better)	3.5	6.5	9
High-yield corporate (B to BB)	4	7	15
Emerging market bonds	4	7	15
U.S. Equity			
U.S. large stocks	5	8	15
U.S. micro-cap stocks	7	10	25
U.S. small-value stocks	7	10	22
REITs (real estate investment trusts)	5	8	14
International Equity			
International developed country stocks	5	8	17
International small country stocks	6	9	22
International emerging country stocks	7	10	25
Gross Domestic Product Growth	3	6	2

*The estimate of risk is the estimate standard deviation of annual returns.

CHAPTER SUMMARY

The market forecasts in this chapter are meant to be a guide for planning portfolios. No one knows what the actual returns of the markets will be over the next 30 years. We do know there are consistent factors that contribute to market returns, and those factors are likely to persist into the future. It is evident that investments with greater price volatility demand higher returns, and a risk-based model for expected return can be created using that data. Small stocks should outperform large stocks, large stocks should outperform corporate bonds, and corporate bonds should outperform Treasury bills, and so forth. In addition, economic growth and inflation drive stock and bond returns. By using government and private forecasts of GDP, it becomes possible to create market forecasts. Of course, the task is never easy and never totally accurate.

A close forecast is the best it gets, so always try to err on the side of a conservative approach. It is wiser to plan for lower returns and be pleasantly surprised in a bull market than to rely on a rosy forecast and possibly run out of money later in life. Simply put, it is better to be safe than sorry.

CHAPTER 13

Asset Allocation Basics

Key Concepts

- Asset allocation reduces risk and increases return.
- Low correlation between asset classes is the key.
- Choose the right types of investments.
- Annual rebalancing of a portfolio is critical.

Asset allocation is a modern way of saying "don't put all your eggs in one basket." The essence of the idea seems to be intuitive to all investors who have had long-term success in the markets. However, prior to the 1970s, the theory behind asset allocation was foreign to all but a few academic researchers. This chapter is an introduction to the basic concepts. For an advanced understanding, read *All About Asset Allocation* by Richard A. Ferri (McGraw-Hill, 2005).

To manage a portfolio of index funds effectively, you must develop a method for choosing among alternative stock and bond markets. The traditional view of diversification was simply to avoid putting all your money in one place. When the financial system collapsed in the 1930s, many banks and brokerage firms became insolvent and investors lost everything. Investors who lived through that period avoided putting all their money in one bank or brokerage house for the rest of their lives.

Government regulation and insurance have made our financial institutions more secure, and there is little risk of a repeat of the problem of insolvency that occurred during the Depression. However, proper diversification is still needed inside an account to make the portfolio more secure and to avoid the possibility of a large loss. Asset allocation is the cornerstone of a solid, long-term investment plan.

MODERN PORTFOLIO THEORY

In 1952 Harry Markowitz, a 25-year-old graduate student at the University of Chicago, wrote a revolutionary research paper entitled "Portfolio Selection." In short, the paper discussed the idea that financial risk is necessary in a portfolio to achieve a higher rate of return and that portfolio risk can be reduced through proper diversification. The idea of using diversification to reduce risk was not revolutionary thinking, and for that reason Markowitz's paper was not viewed as original research by many of his primary instructors. However, he did do something unique. Markowitz mathematically quantified the risk and return relationship in a stock portfolio and for the first time explained why combining large numbers of stocks in a portfolio lowered risk and increased return. Markowitz argued that the risk of an individual investment is not as important as how the entire portfolio fit together to achieve a positive result. After much deliberation in the economics department at the university, Markowitz's paper was submitted for publication in the *Journal of Finance*.

Initially, Markowitz "Portfolio Selection" paper had little readership. The research began to be taken seriously in 1959, when Markowitz published a book on the subjet entitled *Portfolio Selection: Efficient Diversification of Investments*. That book earned Markowitz wide recognition and even a Nobel Prize in Economics in 1990. Certainly, no one anticipated the small 14-page paper would eventually become the backbone of portfolio management for the next 50 years.

In the 1970s, portfolio management research expanded at institutions such as universities, banks, and private money management companies. The computing power needed to do the long calculations was finally becoming available at a reasonable cost. Using historical return data, stock and bond allocations were mixed together and back-tested. The idea was to find the right allocation of assets from each asset class that achieved a *portfolio effect* of higher returns with less risk. This strategy of portfolio management became known as modern portfolio theory (MPT). Harry Markowitz is often referred to as the father of MPT.

Today, nearly every institutional investor uses some form of MPT to invest in the financial markets. Abundant computing power crunches reams of market data at light speed in an attempt to find the most effective asset allocation mix at any given moment.

An Example of MPT

The best way to explain the benefits of MPT is through an example using two asset classes. By combining stocks and bonds in one portfolio, you will see how they can work together to increase the expected return of the portfolio and reduce the risk. Figures 13-1 and 13-2 illustrate the benefit of diversification using the S&P 500 index and the Lehman Brothers Aggregate Bond index from 1976 to 2005. Various mixes of the two investments are combined at 10 percent intervals, creating different points on Figure 13-1. Point 1 is 100 percent bonds, Point 2 is 100 percent stocks, and Point 3 is 70 percent bonds and 30 percent stocks.

The 100 percent stock portfolio has the highest return and the highest risk. The 100 percent bond portfolio has the lowest return and the lowest risk. A 70 percent bond and 30 percent stock mix would expect to have a return of 9.9 percent and a risk of 8.6 percent (Point 4). This risk and return figure is based on a simple weighted average of market returns using 70 percent of the return and risk of the bond index and adding it to 30 percent of the return and risk of the S&P 500 index. It is marked as a star on Figure 13-1. The actual result of the 70 percent bond and 30 percent stock mix was better than expected. The return during the period was 10.2 percent (Point 3), higher than the 9.6 percent expected (Point 4). The risk was only 6.8 percent, lower than the 8.6 percent expected.

Figure 13-2 illustrates the return advantage of diversification in a different way. As we begin to add stocks to an all-bond portfolio, there was a large return advantage at first. By 30 percent allocation to stocks, the advantage was 0.23 percent annualized. Then the advantage of adding more stocks slowed. At the peak, 50 in stocks and 50 percent in bonds had an advantage of 0.27 percent annualized.

FIGURE 13 - 1

S&P 500 and LB Aggregate Portfolio Mixes (1976–2005)

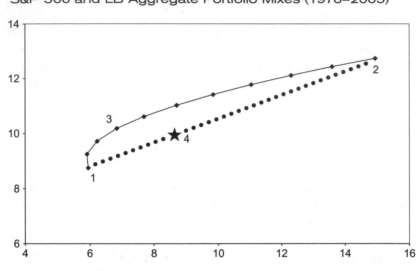

Source: Standard & Poor's, Lehman Brothers.

FIGURE 13 - 2

Diversification Advantage of Various Allocations (1976–2005)

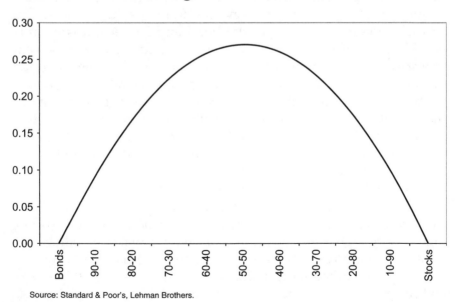

Source: Standard & Poor's, Lehman Brothers.

T A B L E   13–1

Figure 13-1 Data

Index Returns from 1976 to 2005	Annualized Return Percent	Risk as a Percent
100% bonds (LB Aggregate Bond index)	8.7	5.9
100% stocks (S&P 500 index)	12.3	14.9
Expected 70% bond and 30% stock mix	9.9	8.6
Actual 70% bond and 30% stock mix	10.2	6.8
MPT advantage	0.3	–1.8
Source: Standard & Poor's, Lehman Brothers.		

This does not mean that you should not own more than 50 percent stocks; only that portfolio effect of owning more stocks begin to diminish per extra unit of portfolio risk after that allocation.

The MPT example assumes that the portfolio is rebalanced every year to its original 70 percent bond and 30 percent stock mix. If the stock portion went down one year while the bond portion increased in value, the model assumes you sold bonds and bought stocks to bring the portfolio back to a 70 percent bond and 30 percent stock mix. Rebalancing often feels counterintuitive and does not always produce immediate gratification. However, applying a consistent rebalancing strategy over several years increases portfolio returns and significantly reduces risk.

Table 13-1 quantifies the portfolio advantage in the example, and Table 13-2 offers a mathematical explanation of why rebalancing works. Two hypothetical asset classes are created and tracked

T A B L E   13–2

Why Rebalancing Works

	Year 1	Year 2	Total Return
Asset class no. 1	20%	–10%	$1.20 \times 0.90 = 1.08$ $1.08 - 1 = 8.0\%$
Asset class no. 2	–10%	20%	$0.90 \times 1.20 = 1.08$ $1.08 - 1 = 8.0\%$
50%/50% mix rebalanced after one year	5%	5%	$1.05 \times 1.05 = 1.1025$ $1.1025 - 1 = 10.25\%$

over a two-year period. The risk and return of each asset class are identical, but an equally weighted portfolio holding 50 percent of each behaves very differently than the asset classes themselves.

Each asset class individually earned 8.0 percent over the two-year period. A portfolio that held 50 percent in each asset class, with rebalancing after one year, eliminated all the volatility in the portfolio and resulted in a 2.25 percent higher return than either asset class measured separately. If you diversify across different investments and rebalance at regular intervals, you actually increase the return of the portfolio over time. The "free lunch" from asset allocation and rebalancing is the essence of modern portfolio theory, and the proof of this theory earned Harry Markowitz a Nobel.

CORRELATION EXPLAINED

The challenge of investment management is to lower the risk in a portfolio while not lowering the return. This goal can be accomplished by mixing asset classes together that have a low correlation with each other. If one asset class moves in perfect harmony with another, they have a perfect positive correlation. There is no benefit to diversifying into an index fund that has a near perfect positive correlation with an index fund you already own. For example, it makes no sense to buy an index fund benchmarked to the Russell 3000 index if you already own a fund benchmarked to the Wilshire 5000 index. The funds are almost perfectly correlated, and buying both does not add diversification to your portfolio.

Many investors make the mistake of thinking they are diversified because they own several mutual funds. That may be the case. In the 1990s, investors diversified their retirement holdings by purchasing two or three aggressive growth funds, but there was no diversification in those funds because the funds all invested in the same market sectors and likely the same stocks. The bear market of 2000–2002 clearly pointed out their mistake.

Figure 13-3 illustrates a portfolio that is invested in two separate investments but is not diversified. Investment A and Investment B have a perfect positive correlation with each other, so there is no risk reduction in a portfolio that invests 50 percent in Fund A and 50 percent in Fund B.

It is much better to invest in two mutual funds that are expected to have negative correlation, no correlation, or a low correlation over

F I G U R E   1 3–3

Positive Correlation

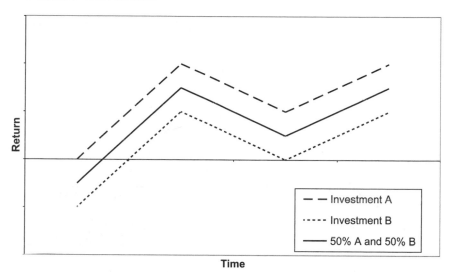

the long-term. Figure 13-4 shows that Fund C and Fund D frequently move in the opposite direction of each other. These investments have perfect negative correlation. A portfolio of 50 percent Fund C and 50 percent Fund D, rebalanced at each interval, will result in a return that is much smoother than either of the two investments individually. This reduction in risk will increase the portfolio return in the long run.

When two investments move randomly with each other and the performance of one has no effect on the performance of the other, they have zero correlation. Figure 13-4 is an example of two asset classes that have had zero correlation. The pair creates an ideal mix in a portfolio, if you can find them.

A correlation matrix is used to show the correlation among multiple investments. The matrix in Table 13-3 shows the correlation among four asset classes from 1978 to 2005. The matrix compares large U.S. stocks (S&P 500), international stocks (EAFE index), real estate investment trusts (Wilshire REIT), and bonds (Lehman Brothers Intermediate Term Government/Corporate Bond index).

I will caution you not to take the correlation numbers in Table 13-3 too seriously. The table represents past correlations, not the future. Like asset-class returns, asset-class correlations are not consistent. They move around a lot. Past correlations are only a

FIGURE   13–4

Negative Correlation

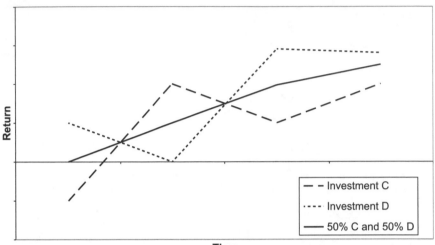

TABLE   13–3

Multi-Asset-Class Correlation Matrix

	S&P 500	LB Aggregate	REITs	EAFE
S&P 500 index	1.00	0.22	0.48	0.57
Lehman Brothers Aggregate index	0.22	1.00	0.18	0.15
Wilshire REIT index	0.48	0.18	1.00	0.33
MSCI EAFE index	0.57	0.15	0.33	1.00
Source: Morningstar.				

hint of the future. For more information on correlations and their tendencies, see Richard A. Ferri's book *All About Asset Allocation* (McGraw-Hill, 2005).

MULTI-ASSET-CLASS PORTFOLIOS

If portfolios are put together where the index funds have low correlation with each other in the future, then there is a greater benefit to the portfolio. Earlier you learned that adding an S&P 500 index fund to an intermediate-term bond index fund decreased the risk of a portfolio and increased the return in the past. We can now go a step further. Adding a position in international stocks and REITs to the S&P 500/bond index portfolio has also increased the portfolio return and reduced risk. An asset allocation mix using four asset classes is more efficient than a portfolio consisting of only two if the correlations are low. If a fifth asset class is added, the risk is reduced more and the return increases slightly above the old *efficient frontier* (Figure 13-5). That is the theory. The trick is to add asset classes that will have a low correlation with each other in the future.

Here are a few guidelines to selecting asset classes:

1. It is very difficult to find major asset classes that have expected low, negative, or constantly inconsistent correlates with each other.

2. Past correlation should be viewed as a guide, not as an absolute. The correlation between asset classes is constently changing. Investments that once had good diversification benefits may not have those benefits in the future.

FIGURE 13–5

Multi-Asset Class Investing as Positive Portfolio Effects

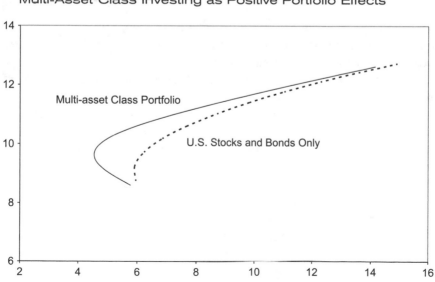

3. During a time of crisis, the correlation among like asset classes increases. This is exactly the opposite of what you would like to see happen. When the World Trade Center was destroyed in September 2001, all stock markets around the world fell by more than 5 percent. Global diversification did not help during that horrific period.

4. Finally, don't expect absolute answers from any asset allocation model. The data used to create efficient frontiers and optimal portfolios are based on historical relationships and expected relationships. History is only a loose guide. The future is not known to anyone.

Asset allocation in the real world requires just as much common sense as it does quantitative number crunching. Investors can become fixated on unimportant factors while missing the big picture. The topic asset allocation is not as clear cut as it seems. Further study is required to effectively implement a lifelong asset allocation strategy.

CHAPTER SUMMARY

> My ventures are not in one bottom trusted, nor to one place; Nor is my whole estate upon the fortune of this present year; Therefore, my merchandise makes me not sad.
>
> *Antonio in The Merchant of Venice*

To manage a portfolio of index funds effectively, you should create a forecast of expected risks and returns for each asset class and then study how those investments acted in relation to each other in the past. That will offer some clues about the returns and correlation relationship in the future.

Asset allocation is the cornerstone of every long-term investment plan and is the science of blending index funds together in hope of reducing risk and increasing return. You do not need to be a Nobel laureate to benefit from the reduction in risk and increase in return that proper asset allocation and rebalancing are expected to deliver. Every long-term investor knows that buying, holding, and rebalancing a well-diversified portfolio is a much better strategy than putting all your eggs in one basket.

CHAPTER 14

Defining Your Financial Goals

Key Concepts

- Estimate your future cash flow and income needs.
- Calculate a required return to meet your needs.
- Create a low-risk allocation that is expected to match the return.
- Stress-test the allocation to ensure you can handle the risk.

We save and invest for many reasons: to buy a home, a car, vacation property; pay for a child's education; retirement; and if there is any money left, to pass it on to heirs or charity. Saving and investing effectively means understanding when the major cash flows in life will occur and having a general idea of how much money you will need to pay for those events, especially retirement. This chapter is all about calculating your financial needs so you can design an effective portfolio of index funds to meet those needs. Specifically, we address the biggest financial hurdle in everyone's life: investing for retirement.

Financial security is the most sought-after financial goal in everyone's life. No one wants to be burdened wondering if they have enough money to survive at the lifestyle they have grown accustomed to.

Attaining financial security typically takes years of hard work and sacrifice. If you are still working and saving, this chapter will help answer questions revolving around how much money is enough to retire. If you are already retired, this chapter will help answer questions concerning the amount of money you can spend each year during retirement. We will also discuss changes to your index fund portfolio as you transition from working and saving to preretirement and full retirement.

Attaining financial security means first recognizing what that is to you. That requires an understanding of your current financial situation and accurately forecasting your future expenses. You need to address issues such as estate planning, health insurance, long-term care, and a multitude of other related subjects.

Once you have a good handle on your financial situation and have a vision of the future, you will be ready to put together a sensible portfolio of index funds that matches those needs. Unfortunately, there is only limited space in this book, and we cannot go into details on subjects not directly related to investing.

There are informative books in bookstores that can help you with many of the financial planning issues not addressed here. I wrote a book on the subject, titled *Protecting Your Wealth in Good Times and Bad*. It is a great fact-filled book about retirement planning that was assigned a poor title. As a result, the book is currently out of print. However, the book may be resurrected in the future under a different title. In the meantime, a little searching will turn up used copies that are for sale.

Later in this chapter, we will look at an abreacted technique for analyzing financial needs as they relate to managing an investment portfolio. That analysis will assist in selecting a simple stock and bond asset allocation, which will be expanded on in Chapter 15. Before beginning the analysis, there are a couple of points that need to be considered.

UNDERSTANDING RISK

Faithfully saving a percentage of your income each year is an important part of a secure retirement. Equally as important is the way you invest the money in your retirement accounts. Investing effectively means holding realistic expectations about market returns and having a solid understanding of the amount of risk you can personally handle.

Some risk in a portfolio is good, but too much risk in a portfolio leads to lower long-term returns. If you assume too much risk in a portfolio, there is a high probability that you will abandon your investment strategy prematurely, and that puts your financial plan off track. During severe market downturns, investors who are not emotionally prepared for the risks they have taken in a portfolio tend to reduce the risk after the markets have sold down to low market levels. In sense, too much risk causes an investor to buy high and sell low.

It is always better to have a lower amount of risk in a portfolio than too much risk. If you have less risk, there is a strong probability that you will hold onto the stocks in your portfolio during a bear market. By investing in a well-balanced portfolio and maintaining a level of risk at or below your pain threshold, you and your portfolio will be well prepared to face the uncertainties in the markets.

RISK TOLERANCE AND RISK AVOIDANCE

Risk tolerance means having an understanding of the maximum level of risk you can handle and not investing above that mark. Investment questionnaires are a popular method used by financial advisors to assess a person's tolerance for risk. Unfortunately, many risk questionnaires tend to be inadequate, and some financial firms use questionnaires that push investors into taking more risk than they can handle. That is because those firms make higher commissions and fees if people pursue aggressive investments than if they bought low-risk investments. The Vanguard Group has a good risk tolerance questionnaire that you can start with. It is on their Web site at www.Vanguard.com.

Risk avoidance is a conscious decision to invest below your risk-tolerance level. There is nothing wrong with avoiding risk if you do not need to take it. At some point during your life, the financial freedom you are seeking will be realized. The money you need will be "in the bank," or at least you know you can get there by investing in a lower risk portfolio. You have made the money; don't lose it. There is no longer a need to take a lot of financial risk to maintain your goals. At that point, your portfolio should change from growth orientation to wealth preservation. That does not mean getting out of the stock market entirely. If you have always been 60 percent in stocks and a secure retirement is now in sight, it is probably wise to reduce your exposure to 30 or 40 percent stocks. If you avoid risk when it is no longer necessary, it will reduce your anxiety during the next bear market.

If there is one lesson I hope you take from this section of the book, it is that your portfolio should reflect a combination of investments based on what you need and what you are comfortable with, not what your maximum risk-tolerance level is. I believe people should invest below their maximum tolerance for risk if they do not have a good reason for taking maximum risk.

CONTROL WHAT YOU CAN

There are many items in an investment plan that we can control, but much more that we cannot control. There are three areas where investors have control: costs, risk, and taxes.

Costs are the easiest item you can control in a portfolio. Cost control is making a conscious decision to be aware of all fees and expenses surrounding your portfolio and purchasing only those investments that have the lowest cost. There is no advantage to purchasing a high-cost mutual fund that has the same investment objective and invests in the same securities as a low-cost index fund. There is no reason to buy a mutual fund that has a front-end commission, back-end load, or a 12b-1 fee when pure no-load funds are available. There is no reason to buy ETFs from a full-service broker that charges high commissions when you can buy them from a discount broker for pennies per share.

Portfolio risk (volatility) can be controlled by allocating money between stock and bond index funds. The more short-term bond index funds you have in a portfolio, the lower the risk. Although your tolerance for risk may be high, when you reach financial security, it may make sense to reduce risk for the sake of maintaining financial security.

We can control taxes in an account through various portfolio management techniques and estate planning. One way to control taxes is to place tax-friendly investments in taxable accounts and tax-inefficient investments in tax-sheltered retirement accounts. Tax-control items are discussed in Chapters 5 and 15.

There are many more items that affect portfolio returns that we cannot control. We cannot control the economy, the markets, the political situation, laws passed by government, the tax code, the weather, and so forth. Because there is much we have no control over, and so little that we can control, it makes sense to take full advantage of controlling portfolio costs, taxes, and risk. Control what you can control and you have done the most you can to ensure your long-term plan will be successful.

INVESTING FOR RETIREMENT

> I would rather be certain of a good return than hopeful of a great one.
>
> *Warren Buffett*

This book uses a simple planning tool to help you make a very important investment decision. In fact, that investment decision is probably the most important one you will make in your lifetime. Once you make the decision, you should be prepared to stick by it for many years. In a sense, you become married to your decision. If you break away from it prematurely, it will cost you more than any divorce. The investment decision is, How much money should you invest in the safety of bonds and how much should you risk in the stock market? Making an asset allocation decision will be very difficult unless you approach it using a simple, sensible model.

A planning model should help you assess your current financial situation and project future needs. The model in this book includes a financial needs analysis and risk-tolerance test, and it results in a simple asset allocation mix between stocks and bonds. The simple stock and bond mix will be expanded using more advanced portfolio management techniques in Chapter 15.

The amount of savings one person needs at retirement is always different from another. Once people have been retired a few years, they find they need about 85 percent of their preretirement income. One reason the amount needed is less in retirement is due to lower income taxes. There is no tax on retirement income in many states, and the federal government does not collect a Social Security or Medicare payment from pension checks. This chapter builds a model that attempts to quantify the amount you may need at retirement and begins to develop an investment plan to achieve that level of wealth.

A STARTING POINT

Investment planning starts by asking yourself: What do I want my money to do for me when I am alive, and what do I want my money to do for my heirs when I am dead? When asked these questions, most people have three common answers. First, we want financial security, which means we don't want to worry about running out of money while we are alive. Second, we want to live comfortably in retirement, which basically means living at a lifestyle that we have grown accustomed to. Third, we want to help our children, grand-children, or other heirs get ahead in life and possibly help a favorite charity or two along the way.

If you agree with those answers, ask yourself: Is my investment portfolio set up to achieve these goals? Most people have never thought of a portfolio in those terms. Having reviewed thousands of portfolios over the years, I am saddened to report that most retire-ment accounts are a poorly constructed collection of unrelated stocks, bonds, and mutual funds gathered over the years from various sources. There were few well-constructed portfolios and certainly no "investment policy statement" to guide in the management of the portfolio. I strongly recommend setting up a simple, workable investment plan and committing that plan to writing. An annual review of that document does wonders for keeping your ship on course.

The process of building an investment plan begins by putting dollar figures on subjective goals like how much money do you need to feel financially secure? How much money will you be spending each year in retirement? What is the maximum you should spend in retirement so that the money will last longer than you do? How much do you intend to gift to heirs or charity now, and how much would you like to leave them when you die? These important questions relate directly to the amount of money you will need to attain financial independence.

A FIVE-STEP METHOD

When large corporations invest money in a company pension plan, they use a process called liability matching. This process matches the investments in a portfolio with the expected cash outflows of the pension plan over the years. If the cash flows are needed in the short-term, a company invests in short-term investments with low risk. If cash flows are not needed for several years, a company can take more risk with a portion of the portfolio and potentially earn a higher reward. Under no circumstances should a pension committee allocate more to risky assets than is needed. The committee has a fiduciary responsibility to act prudently and control the risk in the pension fund.

Personal retirement accounts are not very different from large pension funds. You have a fiduciary responsibility to yourself to act prudently and control the risk in your retirement account. If you design a portfolio to achieve a long-term investment objective based on future cash needs and the portfolio is within your risk tolerance, there is a strong likelihood that you will meet your retirement liabilities when they come due. In other words, you will gain financial independence. The idea is to design a portfolio that fits your needs and follow the plan closely, without being swayed by market volatility, media hype, and the madness of the markets.

The five-step method is designed to help you decide your overall asset allocation between stocks and bonds. Before you buy any index funds for your account, you will need to know how much you are going to invest in stock index funds and how much in bond index funds.

1. Setting Goals

The largest financial liability we have in life is to build and maintain an adequate retirement fund. The size of the retirement fund will determine the quality of life you will live during the golden years and how much your heirs will receive when you are gone. So the obvious question is, How large of a nest egg do you need at retirement? The minimum amount you will need at retirement depends in part on how much you spend each month prior to retirement. Most people do not increase the amount they spend after they retire, especially if all the children are out of the house. In fact, you may not need as much income because your taxes will be less. So, if you are still working toward retirement, calculate the amount you will need by analyzing your current monthly budget.

An example: A 45-year-old couple has one 18-year-old child who is a freshman in college. The couple runs a small business. They plan to sell the business and retire in 20 years at age 65. The couple has accumulated $350,000 in a company profit-sharing plan and contributes $25,000 per year to their personal profit-sharing accounts. They spend about $5,500 per month on living expenses, excluding college costs.

The $5,500 per month budget is an after-tax figure, which means the couple needs about $8,000 per month pretax to cover all federal, state, and social security taxes. When they retire, the couple will likely need the same amount to live comfortably, adjusted for inflation. If Social Security survives in some form, that would generate about $1,500 per month in income at age 65. To get the pretax income back to $8,000, the remaining $6,500 per month would have to come from retirement savings. However, we will reduce the amount of monthly pretax income needed from the profit-sharing plan by $1,000 because the couple will no longer pay Social Security tax and will pay less in federal and state tax. The bottom line is, the couple needs a distribution of $5,500 per month ($66,000 per year) from the profit-sharing plan to maintain the lifestyle they have grown accustomed to.

Now that we know the profit-sharing distribution at retirement, we can work backward to determine the minimum value of the plan at retirement. I recommend people withdraw no more than 5 percent off of their retirement savings each year. That way you should not run out of money during retirement. This assumes that the financial markets cooperate and do not give us multiyear negative returns in both the stock and bond markets. The figure also assumes plowing back into the account any excess return over 5 percent for an inflation hedge.

For this couple to draw $66,000 per year out of their retirement fund, they would need a nest egg of $1,320,000 at retirement in today's dollars. To calculate that number, simply multiply the income needed by 20. The calculation is $66,000 times 20 equal $1,320,000. To double-check that figure, multiply the nest egg amount by 5 percent. The calculation is $1,320,000 times 0.05 equals $66,000.

The couple needs $1,320,000 at retirement in today's dollars to retire at a lifestyle they have grown accustomed to. Obviously, there are going to be other considerations that go into the nest egg figure, such as special needs of family members, health care concerns, future tax law changes, gifts made or received, inheritance, proceeds from the sale of a house, the sale of a business, or other assets, and so forth. These extra events could have major positive or negative effects on cash flow and should be considered when formulating a lump-sum retirement amount. Unfortunately, there is not enough space in this book to cover all the contingencies, so I'll assume there are no other considerations in our example.

2. Inflation Adjustment

A nest egg of $1,320,000 would suffice if our couple were to retire today; however, they are not going to retire for a number of years, so the figure needs to be adjusted for expected inflation. Assuming a 3 percent annual inflation rate over the next 20 years, the couple will need to withdraw $119,000 per year from the profit-sharing plan, which is $66,000 adjusted for inflation. Multiplying $119,000 by 20 equals a new nest egg target of $2,384,000, adjusted for inflation.

3. Required Investment Return

Now that we know how much the couple needs at retirement, we can create a savings plan to get there. We have all the facts and figures, except a required investment return. What rate of return does the couple need on their retirement savings to reach $2,384,000 in 20 years?

There are four parts to this equation, and we already know three of the inputs:

1. The amount needed at retirement is $2,384,000.
2. The amount the couple has saved is $350,000.
3. What rate of return is needed to achieve their retirement goal?

Using a financial calculator or Microsoft Excel, you can calculate a required rate of return for the couple. Using an Excel spreadsheet, the commands are as follows:

1. Select the Function Key (fx) and find the RATE function.
2. Enter 20 in the NPER box. This is the number of years to retirement.
3. Enter the expected annual savings in PMT. Type −25,000, a negative number.

4. Enter the amount the couple has saved under Pv. Type –350,000, a negative number.

5. Enter the amount needed at retirement under Fv. Type 2,384,000, a positive number.

6. Press the OK button, and you should get a return of 7.0 percent. This is the required return that the couple needs to reach $2,384,000 in 20 years.

A 7.0 percent return is a reasonable expected return for a diversified investment portfolio. A mix of stock and bond index funds can be created that has a high probability of achieving a 7 percent return, but there is never a guarantee. Had the couple calculated a higher required return, such as 10 percent, then something would need to change in their retirement plan. A 10 percent return is simply not a realistic rate of return to use, and the probability of attaining that number is very low, especially after investment expenses. Consequently, the couple would need to either save more money each year, spend less in retirement, work longer, or leave a smaller inheritance to their child (my favorite option). For planning purposes, do not use more than 7.5 percent in any model.

4. The Asset Allocation Decision

Now we finally get to the fun stuff: selecting a stock and bond mix. We know our couple needs a minimum return of 7.0 percent compounded over 20 years to meet the target goal of $2,384,000. Using forecasted returns from Chapter 12, we can create an asset allocation between stocks and bonds that is expected to deliver a 7 percent return (see Table 14-1).

Using the estimates, a logical asset allocation for this portfolio would be 60 percent in a large U.S. stock index fund and 40 percent in an intermediate-term corporate bond index fund. This allocation is expected to earn about a 7.2 percent rate of return, which is slightly higher than the required return of 7.0 percent (see Table 14-2).

From a purely mathematical point of view, a 60 percent stock and 40 percent bond allocation is the correct answer. Most investors would accept this mix because the popular notion is that a 60 percent stock and 40 percent bond mix is "normal" or even "prudent." However, a more detailed analysis is warranted. There may be problems lurking beneath the surface. One problem that emerges is the cost of implementation. The forecasted return of the markets is not the forecasted return of index funds. A small management fee must be paid to the index fund provider. That fee can vary based on the index fund you choose. A downward adjustment of 0.2 percent to 0.5 percent needs to be made to put the portfolio forecast in line. The cost of investing reduces the expected return of the 60/40 mix from 7.2 percent to about 7.0 percent. That return is right on top of what the couple requires.

Fees are one concern, but there is a deeper concern with the suggested allocation. Does the asset mix truly fit the personality of the investors? Is the portfolio within their risk tolerance?

5. Assessing Portfolio Risk

Up to this point, we have taken a purely mathematical approach to discovering the best asset allocation for the couple. Now comes the hard part. Can the couple accept the risk in a 60 percent stock and 40 percent bond allocation that was determined to be technically correct or will they feel the need to reduce their allocation of stocks during stressful times in the market? In other words, is the portfolio above the couple's risk-tolerance level? To find out, we need to switch hats from financial engineer to behavioral psychologist.

We live in a capitalistic country, and taking financial risk is part of our national heritage. As a result, when people are asked how much risk they can handle, most tend to exaggerate. However, a look back in history shows that many people do not handle stock market declines very well. In fact, many self-proclaimed long-term investors duck out during and after bear markets. Individual investors were net sellers of stock after the crash of 1929, the deep bear market of 1973–1974, the "crash" of 1987, and during the bear market of 2000–2002. Despite a lot of brave talk, Joe and Jane average investor cannot handle a lot of market risk. All investors must do serious soul searching before deciding what level of risk is appropriate.

How can we determine if the mathematically correct 60 percent stock and 40 percent bond mix is at or below our couple's risk tolerance? Many financial advisers believe the answer to that question can be found by using a simple risk-tolerance questionnaire. These forms inquire about your age, time horizon, and ask a few "if-then" questions. The answers are fed into a computer, which spits out a risk profile and investment portfolio designed just for you. I believe this method of determining risk is nearly useless. Most of the questionnaires are too short, the questions are too vague, and there is little chance of capturing the essence of someone's risk tolerance.

One of the best methods to determine if an allocation of stock and bond index funds is acceptable is to run the portfolio through a stress test. This method of risk testing helps clients understand how they will react to losses in the portfolio during particularly difficult periods in the market. Most people react differently than anticipated when they start losing money month after month and year after year while getting closer and closer to retirement. The objective of a stress test is to simulate dollar losses from a chosen asset mix. If someone makes it through the test without saying "uncle," then the mix may be acceptable.

To conduct a stress test, it helps to use a recent period in market history. Prior to the 2000–2002 bear market, the stress test period I used was 1973–1974. That period was also particularly painful for stock investors. Most people who took the 1973–1974 stress test prior to year 2000 reduced their exposure to stocks by 20 to 40 percent. This reduction in stocks was not in anticipation of the upcoming 2000–2002 bear market. People reduced their allocation to stocks simply because they realized they had a lower tolerance for risk than they originally thought.

A 2000–2002 STRESS TEST

The next example follows Tables 14-1 and 14-2. The first part of the example follows Table 14-1, and the second part follows Table 14-2.

The Aggressive Allocation

Assume a retired couple in their sixties would like to draw $3,000 per month from their portfolio of $300,000. That is a withdrawal rate of 4 percent based on starting capital. The couple has determined that in order to achieve their long-term objectives, they need a portfolio that is 70 percent in a total stock index fund portfolio and 30 percent in a total bond market index fund. The time is January 2000.

TABLE 14-1

Stress Test for a 70 Percent Stock and 30 Percent Bond Portfolio with a $300,000 Investment

Quarter End	Vanguard Total Stock	Vanguard Total Bond	Portfolio Return	Before Withdrawal	Withdraw per Quarter	Ending Value	Withdrawal Cumulative	Cumulative Investment Gain / Loss
Mar-00	3.84%	2.42%	3.41%	$310,242	($3,000)	$307,242	($3,000)	$10,242
Jun-00	-4.39%	1.48%	-2.63%	$299,165	($3,000)	$296,165	($6,000)	$2,165
Sep-00	0.27%	3.07%	1.11%	$299,452	($3,000)	$296,452	($9,000)	$5,452
Dec-00	-10.17%	3.98%	-5.93%	$278,887	($3,000)	$275,887	($12,000)	($12,113)
Mar-01	-12.27%	3.24%	-7.62%	$254,873	($3,000)	$251,873	($15,000)	($33,127)
Jun-01	7.47%	0.79%	5.47%	$265,640	($3,000)	$262,640	($18,000)	($19,360)
Sep-01	-15.93%	4.29%	-9.86%	$236,733	($3,000)	$233,733	($21,000)	($45,267)
Dec-01	12.32%	-0.08%	8.60%	$253,835	($3,000)	$250,835	($24,000)	($25,165)
Mar-02	0.97%	0.06%	0.70%	$252,583	($3,000)	$249,583	($27,000)	($23,417)
Jun-02	-12.69%	2.80%	-8.04%	$229,509	($3,000)	$226,509	($30,000)	($43,491)
Sep-02	-16.84%	3.71%	-10.68%	$202,329	($3,000)	$199,329	($33,000)	($67,671)

In 2000, the stock market had a bad year and the bond market a decent year. The value of the portfolio after market losses and withdrawals stood at $275,887. The couple lost $12,113 to the market and withdrew another $12,000. Is the couple able to hold on? Let's assume they are.

The year 2001 proved to be another bad year in the markets. The portfolio lost more than $13,000 in the markets, and another $12,000 was withdrawn. By the end of 2001, the value of the portfolio was only $250,835. Is the couple able to hold on? Again, let's assume they are.

The year 2002 was another very bad year for the financial markets. Consequently, by September the couple's portfolio hovered at $199,000. Is the couple able to hold on? They have lost more than $67,000 in value in a little over two years and have withdrawn another $33,000. They are retired and do not have any other means of income. Chances are, the couple will not be able to maintain their allocation at the high loss rate. Most couples will sell out.

Investing above one's tolerance for risk will cause an emotional "market-timing" reaction during a bear market. Investors who are over their heads will sell out close to the bottom of the stock and bond markets.

The Conservative Allocation

Let's go back and rerun the 2000–2002 stress again test using a more conservative portfolio. A portfolio of $300,000 is created with 50 percent in the total stock market and 50 percent in the total bond market. The forecasted return on this portfolio is slightly less than the 70 percent stock portfolio but still achieves the individual's financial objectives. Data for the scenario is in Table 14-2.

At the end of 2000, the portfolio was worth $288,611. That is a gain of $611 after withdrawals of $12,000. Considering the tough market for stocks, the couple is probably going to stay with the strategy.

By the end of 2001, the portfolio was worth $274,496. Considering more than $24,000 in cumulative withdrawals, the account has suffered only a minor market loss totaling $1,504 since inception. Chances are the couple is going to stay put.

The year 2002 was a very difficult year in the market. However, by September of that year the couple's portfolio was still worth

TABLE 14–2

Stress Test for a 50 Percent Stock and 50 Percent Bond Portfolio with a $300,000 Investment

Quarter End	Vanguard Total Stock	Vanguard Total Bond	Portfolio Return	Before Withdrawal	Withdraw per Quarter	Ending Value	Withdrawal Cumulative	Cumulative Investment Gain / Loss
Mar-00	3.84%	2.42%	3.13%	$309,390	($3,000)	$306,390	($3,000)	$9,390
Jun-00	−4.39%	1.48%	−1.46%	$301,932	($3,000)	$298,932	($6,000)	$4,932
Sep-00	0.27%	3.07%	1.67%	$303,924	($3,000)	$300,924	($9,000)	$9,924
Dec-00	−10.17%	3.98%	−3.10%	$291,611	($3,000)	$288,611	($12,000)	$611
Mar-01	−12.27%	3.24%	−4.52%	$275,580	($3,000)	$272,580	($15,000)	($12,420)
Jun-01	7.47%	0.79%	4.13%	$283,837	($3,000)	$280,837	($18,000)	($1,163)
Sep-01	−15.93%	4.29%	−5.82%	$264,493	($3,000)	$261,493	($21,000)	($17,507)
Dec-01	12.32%	−0.08%	6.12%	$277,496	($3,000)	$274,496	($24,000)	($1,504)
Mar-02	0.97%	0.06%	0.52%	$275,910	($3,000)	$272,910	($27,000)	($90)
Jun-02	−12.69%	2.80%	−4.95%	$259,414	($3,000)	$256,414	($30,000)	($13,586)
Sep-02	−16.84%	3.71%	−6.57%	$239,581	($3,000)	$236,581	($33,000)	($30,419)

$236,581. The couple had withdrawn $33,000 to date, and invest ment losses totaled $30,419. The loss was less than half the $67,000 loss that would have occurred with just 20 percent more stocks in the portfolio.

The period 2000–2002 was a very difficult period for stock investors. However, the couple would be much more likely to stick with a 50 percent stock and 50 percent bond allocation during the period than a 70 percent stock and 30 percent bond allocation. As a result of the stress test, an allocation of 50 percent stocks and 50 percent bonds would be considered appropriate and within the couple's tolerance for risk.

IMPORTANT POINTS TO REMEMBER

The 70 percent stock and 30 percent bond allocation may have been a mathematically correct asset mix for the couple in the example. However, it would have proved too volatile during a steep downturn in the stock market, and the couple would have likely sold most of their stocks at the bottom of the next bear market. The stress test revealed that the couple needed a more conservative asset mix.

Once the changes were in place, we ran the stress test again. This time the couple stayed with the allocation during the entire 2000–2002 period and rebalanced the account at the end of each year. This put them in an ideal position to benefit from a strong rally of more than 30 percent in the stock that occurred in 2003. The moral of the story is that the best asset allocation is the one that you can maintain during all market conditions.

MORE IDEAS ABOUT INVESTMENT PLANNING

Should you always reduce your exposure to risk once you have met your investment goal, as we discussed at the beginning of the chapter? For most people the answer is "yes" if you saved only enough to retire. On the other hand, the answer is "no" if you have accumulated significantly more wealth beyond your needs. People who have accumulated more wealth than they need to live on for the rest of their lives are actually investing for the benefit of their heirs. The portion of wealth that will not be needed by the investor has a different time horizon; therefore, it warrants a different asset mix than the rest of the portfolio. This chapter was written with the first level of wealth in mind: retirement money. However, the model can be adapted to different levels of wealth, including multigeneration estate plans.

CHAPTER SUMMARY

> You can't always get what you want. But if you try sometimes, you just might find you get what you need.
>
> *The Rolling Stones*

Understanding your financial needs is not a one-minute subject, and there are many items to think about. When constructing an investment plan, the asset allocation mix is the most important decision you will make because it determines the level of risk in a portfolio. The true essence of investment planning is to develop a mix of stocks and bonds that satisfies your return objectives while keeping the risk at or below your risk-tolerance level. Investors who maintain a comfortable and consistent asset allocation to stocks during all market conditions will perform better than investors who take too much risk and ultimately sell stocks at the wrong time.

Risk tolerance is an understanding of the maximum level of loss you can handle in a portfolio before changing your allocation. Risk avoidance is a conscious decision to invest below your risk-tolerance level. Risk avoidance is a well-planned decision that is made with no emotion. At some point during your life, you financial goals will be realized. At that time, you should reduce the risk you are taking in a portfolio and concentrate on conserving wealth.

CHAPTER 15

Designing Your Index Fund Portfolio

Key Concepts

- An index fund can complete a portfolio or be used as a base to build on.
- A complex portfolio may not be more advantageous than a simple one.
- Taxable portfolios are managed differently than nontaxable portfolios.
- The right mix of index funds is the one you are comfortable with.

If you have followed along in Part III of this book, it should be clear that building and maintaining a portfolio of index funds involves a multistage process. It starts with an inventory of your financial goals and risk tolerance, builds on realistic market expectations, and results in a well-balanced portfolio of stock and bond index funds that matches your needs. In addition, tax planning plays an important role in the selection and management of a taxable account. In this chapter, we finally start to consider actual index funds and how a portfolio of index funds fits together.

Developing an appropriate index fund portfolio requires time. It is unlikely that your first mix of funds will be correct because you probably have not gathered enough information. That is fine because you have to start someplace. The model portfolios presented in this chapter are a good place to start. As you learn more about index funds and the markets, you can adjust the portfolio to your specific needs. At some point, you will become satisfied with the portfolio and stop tinkering with it, even during poor market conditions. That will be the ideal index fund portfolio for you. This chapter cannot tell you what the best portfolio should be. It can only guide you in a direction of self-discovery.

Your ideal portfolio will be unique. It can be a simple two-fund mix or a complex multi-asset-class portfolio. A complex portfolio is not better than a simple one, especially if it is not fully understood by you. Warren Buffett's philosophy is that if you invest within your sphere of competence, you will be much happier with your investments and will accumulate more wealth. There is no guarantee that a complex portfolio will generate higher returns than a simple two-fund portfolio. However, it is a risk-reduction technique. The idea is to have several different types of investments to reduce the risk of a large loss in one of them.

THE STOCK AND BOND DECISION

The most important decision you will make in a portfolio is the overall mix between stock and bond index funds. This decision accounts for more than 90 percent of the portfolio's performance over time.[1] The asset allocation studies assume that an investor maintains the same weight in both the stock and bond index funds for a very long time. Thus, it is very important to select a good one right from the start and rebalance those investments annually.

First, here is a quick review of where we have been and a snapshot of where we are going. Several details of the portfolio management process have been discussed in earlier chapters. Those chapter numbers are indicated in parentheses.

1. Understand the historical relationship between risk and return and have realistic expectations of what the financial markets can achieve in the future (Chapter 12).
2. Analyze your current financial situation and determine the amount needed to achieve your financial goals. Calculate a minimum return needed on an investment portfolio to attain your goals (Chapter 14).

3. Create a simple asset allocation using forecast stock and bond returns that match your required return. Use a stress test to ensure that the selected mix is not above your risk-tolerance level. Make adjustments to the stock and bond mix as needed (Chapter 14).

4. Using information from this chapter, enhance the initial asset allocation with additional asset classes based on your income needs and personal convictions. Select index funds that are benchmarked to those asset classes. For a review of individual index funds in each category, see Part II of this book.

LIFE-CYCLE INDEX FUND MODELS

People of different ages have different financial needs and different perceptions on investing. One of my previous books, *Protecting Your Wealth in Good Times and Bad* (McGraw-Hill, 2003), categorizes investors into four general groups based on age. Those groups are Early Savers, Mid-Life Accumulators, Preretirees and Active Retirees, and Mature Retirees. The material in this chapter is a summary of the four stages with an example of an index fund portfolio for each. Many of the index funds in the portfolios are similar. What is different is the amount in each one.

The four life phases of investing are

- ◆ Early Savers: Investors who are in the beginning stages of their careers and families. They start with few assets and a lot of ambition. The group generally spans ages 20 to 39.
- ◆ Mid-Life Accumulators: Investors who are established in their careers and family life. They are accumulators of many things from cars to homes to appliances to children. Between ages 40 to 59, accumulators know where they stand on career and family and have a good idea about what to expect in the future.
- ◆ Preretirees and Active Retirees: The stage covers people near retirement, the transition into retirement, and active retires enjoying the fruits of their labors. The stage generally covers people from ages 60 to 79.

- ◆ Mature Retirees: These fully retired investors are not as active as they used to be. They have different needs ranging from long-term care to estate planning issues. At this stage, financial matters are often jointly decided with children and/or other family members.

Investors in all stages have some similar financial goals and similar concerns. Similar goals include a desire for financial security and the desire to pay less income tax. Similar concerns include the fear of running out of money and the fear of not having adequate health care coverage when needed. These common goals and concerns are considered in every asset allocation regardless of stage.

In addition to similarities, investors have a range of differences. They include personal investment experiences, career challenges, health issues, family situations, risk tolerance differences, personality strengths, and personality weaknesses.

When all the pieces of the puzzle are put together, portfolio design is a balance between a technical solution and a behavioral solution. The right asset allocation should have a high mathematical probability of achieving your financial goal while at the same time being compatible with your emotional makeup.

An Index Fund Portfolio for Each Stage

Each index fund model offers a good base on which to build. Start with the index fund portfolio as a core and add or take away to suit your personal needs and desires. No portfolios include commodity or currency funds, although all equity index funds have a healthy allocation to companies that are in a commodity business (i.e., ExxonMobil is 5 percent of a U.S. total market index fund).

The mutual funds recommended in this chapter are the lowest cost funds in each category or style in each fund that are open to all investors. Funds were screened for a minimum initial investment of $3,000 or less. It did not matter if the funds are available as open-end or ETFs. Substitutes are available in many investment categories and from several different mutual fund companies.

The sample portfolios provided should help guide you on your portfolio design decisions but cannot solve the puzzle completely. Other issues that need to be considered include taxes, fund access, investment acquisition costs, and your tolerance for investment risk. Several of those topics are addressed other chapters. More information on portfolio design including detailed model portfolios for each life stage can be found in my fourth book, *All About Asset Allocation* (McGraw-Hill, 2005).

Phase 1 : Early Savers

Three key components for accumulating wealth are savings consistency, time horizon, and cost control. For early savers, the rate of return on an investment portfolio is important but not nearly as important as a consistent savings plan. Savings and investing regularly in a prudently selected mix of mutual funds will build wealth faster than any other strategy. Young investors certainly have the advantage of time and can make some horrendous investment mistakes without doing too much long-term damage. However, the biggest mistake they can make is not to save. Ideally, a young person will start saving at the same time they land their first full-time job.

Young investors have many years ahead of them and can be aggressive. On the other hand, they have the least amount of investment experience and do not know their personal tolerance for financial risk. Being macho and going for 100 percent in stocks does not typically work. Rarely can a person stand to be 100 percent in stocks 100 percent of the time. Consequently, youthful vigor must be tempered with a bit of humbleness when investing.

I recommend that Early Savers place about 70 percent of their long-term investment capital in stocks. A 70 percent allocation to equity and 30 percent to fixed income has almost the same long-term return as 100 percent equity but with considerably less volatility. A 70 percent position in equity also allows for rebalancing when the stock market sours. As discusses in Chapter 13, there is a diversification bonus available to investors who rebalance between stocks and bonds on an annual basis. The bonus is a reduction in portfolio risk that leads to an increase in long-term returns.

Table 15-1 highlights a core index portfolio, with one exception. A 10 percent position was added in the Vanguard High-Yield Corporate Bond index, which is almost an index fund of better quality

TABLE 15-1

Core Index Fund Portfolio for Early Savers

Asset Class	Percent	Fund Name	Fee	Symbol
U.S. Stocks and REITs	45			
Total U.S. market	15	Vanguard Total Market ETF	0.07	VTI
Small value	15	iShares S&P 600 Small Value	0.25	IJS
Micro-cap	5	First Trust DJ Select MicroCap	0.50	FDM
REITs	10	Vanguard REIT ETF	0.12	VNQ
International Stocks	25			
Pacific Rim	10	Vanguard Pacific ETF	0.18	VPL
Europe	10	Vanguard European ETF	0.18	VGK
Emerging markets	5	Vanguard Emerging Market ETF	0.30	VWO
Fixed Income	30			
Total U.S. bond	20	Vanguard Total Bond Index	0.20	VBMFX
Inflation protected	5	iShares Lehman TIPS	0.20	TIP
High-yield corporate	5	Vanguard High-Yield Corporate	0.25	VWEHX
		Weighted Average Fee	0.20	

Source: Portfolio Solutions, LLC.

non-investment-grade bonds. Overall, this broadly diversified portfolio had a weighted average cost of only 0.20 percent!

Phase 2: Mid-Life Accumulators

As we progress through life, most people mature physically, emotionally, professionally, and financially. Accordingly, during mid-life, people develop a different attitude about their money and thus need different financial tools to help them tailor an asset allocation that is correct for them.

Sometime during mid-life, most people concede that they are mortal, that there are ceilings to their careers, and that a conservative lifestyle is probably more rewarding than an extravagant one. In addition, people in mid-life have seen a recession or two, they have jumped out of good investments and held onto bad ones, and have watched consumer prices and interest rates flip-flop over the years. As a result of these experiences, Mid-Life Accumulators are better equipped to commit to a long-term investment plan that fits their long-term needs.

At mid-life, each person reaches the halfway mark in their careers. It is a period when salaries are increasing and that means the amount allocated to savings should be increasing. It is a point in life when investors can see the future with more clarity and can use that vision to develop a strategic asset allocation that matches future retirement needs.

Investors form a vision of what retirement will look like for them and begin to calculate how much they will need to get there. Once those estimates are made, it is time for the Mid-Life Accumulator to refine his or her investment allocation so that the portfolio is in line with that vision of retirement. The time for speculation is over. It is time to treat retirement savings as serious business. Table 15-2 offers an example of a core index fund portfolio for a Mid-Life accumulator.

Taxes can play a considerable role in asset allocation during this phase. If a person's total taxable income places them in a tax

TABLE 15-2

Core Index Fund Portfolio for Mid-Life Accumulators

Asset Class	Percent	Fund Name	Fee	Symbol
U.S. Stocks and REITs	40			
Total U.S. market	15	Vanguard Total Market ETF	0.07	VTI
Small value	10	iShares S&P 600 Small Value	0.25	IJS
Micro-cap	5	First Trust DJ Select MicroCap	0.50	FDM
REITs	10	Vanguard REIT ETF	0.12	VNQ
International Stocks	20			
Pacific Rim	8	Vanguard Pacific ETF	0.18	VPL
Europe	8	Vanguard European ETF	0.18	VGK
Emerging markets	4	Vanguard Emerging Market ETF	0.30	VWO
Fixed Income	40			
Total U.S. bond	26	Vanguard Total Bond Index	0.20	VBMFX
Inflation protected	7	iShares Lehman TIPS	0.20	TIP
High-yield corporate	7	Vanguard High-Yield Corporate	0.25	VWEHX
		Weighted Average Fee	0.20	

Source: Portfolio Solutions, LLC.

bracket of 30 percent or more, they should consider municipal bonds for their taxable fixed income account rather than taxable bonds. A selection of municipal bond funds is given in Chapter 10.

Phase 3: Preretirees and Active Retirees

A person typically enters the preretirement phase three to five years before leaving full-time employment. Preretirement is not a formal announcement of impending retirement; rather, it is an attitude. During this period, many people become perplexed with questions such as when to retire, will they have enough to retire, and what amount of money they can safely withdraw from savings so that they do not outlive their money. This phase is the most conservative period in a person's life.

As investors close in on a retirement date, they should shift their portfolios to an asset allocation that they will use during retirement. The shift does not need to be all at once. The allocation can gradually take place during the transition.

Some people tend to go too far and eliminate all risks from their portfolio. That is not necessary. There is little reason to be overly conservative during the transition phase. Although some extra cash may be appropriate, normally the jitters go away after about a year or two, and people become very comfortable with a moderate allocation to stocks.

One question asked by most people in preretirement is how much they can safely withdraw from their portfolios without touching the principal. There have been several in-depth studies on this question, and they all point to about a 4 percent withdrawal rate.

Cash for withdrawals can be produced in a portfolio in many ways. Interest and dividend income are two sources. There is also annual rebalancing in a portfolio. You can easily calculate the amount of income the investments will give you and then take any shortfall during a rebalancing.

The transition from full-time work to retirement signals a new investment phase in a portfolio. The portfolio will convert from accumulation to distribution. That means investors will soon stop putting money in and soon start taking some out. Accordingly, new retirees will probably want to reduce their allocation to riskier assets and play it safe, at least at first. Table 15-3 highlights a core index

TABLE 15–3

Core Index Fund Portfolio for Preretirees and Active Retirees

Asset Class	Percent	Fund Name	Fee	Symbol
U.S. Stocks and REITs	35			
Total U.S. market	22	Vanguard Total Market ETF	0.07	VTI
Small value	8	iShares S&P 600 Small Value	0.25	IJS
REITs	5	Vanguard REIT ETF	0.12	VNQ
International Stocks	15			
Pacific Rim	6	Vanguard Pacific ETF	0.18	VPL
Europe	6	Vanguard European ETF	0.18	VGK
Emerging markets	3	Vanguard Emerging Market ETF	0.30	VWO
Fixed Income	50			
Total U.S. bond	34	Vanguard Total Bond Index	0.20	VBMFX
Inflation protected	8	iShares Lehman TIPS	0.20	TIP
High-yield corporate	8	Vanguard High-Yield Corporate	0.25	VWEHX
		Weighted Average Fee	0.18	

Source: Portfolio Solutions, LLC.

fund model that is an appropriate asset allocation for people entering an early retirement.

Phase 4: Mature Retirees

The good news is that Americans are living longer; the bad news is we do not live forever. The Fountain of Youth has still not been discovered. At some point, we all need to get our financial house in order and prepare for the afterlife. Plan to appoint someone else to handle your financial affairs when you are no longer capable.

I highly recommend that if you choose a son or daughter to handle your finances that you do it far in advance, while you're still capable of managing your own affairs. Once a helper has been chosen, they will need to become fully informed of your financial situation, and the earlier the better. That includes an understanding of your estate plan, investment accounts, insurance documents, and knowledge of where everything is.

The asset allocation of a mature retiree's portfolio can vary depending on who is going to use the money. On one hand, a portfolio should be conservatively managed to carry a retiree through the remainder of his or her life. On the other hand, if a retiree is not going to need all of his or her money, the allocation could favor the needs and ages of the beneficiaries. Generally, a portfolio is managed based on a combination of both scenarios. Table 15-4 highlights a suggested core index fund portfolio for a Mature Retiree.

Cash is not included in the portfolio although it is assumed that an allocation to cash is created as needed. Many people in the Mature Retiree stage of life make annual gifts to charities and family members. An increase in cash allocation is recommended if a person is inclined to gift.

The appropriate portfolio asset allocation for a Mature Retiree may be a combination of two asset allocations. One portion of the portfolio can be based on the needs of the retiree and the other portion can be based on the needs of the heirs. Splitting the allocation has become a popular idea for families who want to take care of both the current owner of the assets and the future owners.

Assume an 80-year-old widow has named her two children as her heirs. Their ages are 40 and 43. An appropriate asset allocation

TABLE 15-4

Core Index Fund Portfolio for Mature Retirees

Asset Class	Percent	Fund Name	Fee	Symbol
U.S. Stocks and REITs	30			
Total U.S. Market	20	Vanguard Total Market ETF	0.07	VTI
Small value	5	iShares S&P 600 Small Value	0.25	IJS
REITs	5	Vanguard REIT ETF	0.12	VNQ
International Stocks	10			
Pacific Rim	4	Vanguard Pacific ETF	0.18	VPL
Europe	4	Vanguard European ETF	0.18	VGK
Emerging markets	2	Vanguard Emerging Market ETF	0.30	VWO
Fixed Income	60			
Total U.S. bond	44	Vanguard Total Bond Index	0.20	VBMFX
Inflation protected	8	iShares Lehman TIPS	0.20	TIP
High-yield corporate	8	Vanguard High-Yield Corporate	0.25	VWEHX
		Weighted Average Fee	0.18	

Source: Portfolio Solutions, LLC

for her may be 30 percent in stocks and 70 percent in bonds and cash. An appropriate allocation for the children may be 60 percent in stocks and 40 percent in bonds. Assume the widow withdraws little from the portfolio each year. Because she does not need the money and will not use the money in her lifetime, a joint allocation may be the most appropriate. Instead of using 30 percent stocks or 70 percent stocks, an appropriate asset allocation may be 50 percent in stocks and 50 percent in bonds. That is a good balance between the minimum income needs of the woman retiree and the long-term needs of the two children.

ASSET LOCATION

Asset allocation and asset location are two different parts of the same equation. *Asset allocation* is how your overall investment assets are allocated between stocks, bonds, cash, and other investments regardless of the type of accounts those investments are held in. *Asset location* is the term used in the investment industry to define the proper type of account to put an investment in for tax reasons. Some investments are best held in a taxable account, whereas others are better held in a tax-deferred account. Asset allocation and asset location work together to achieve a desired level of risk with the highest expected tax-efficient return.

Taxable Accounts

There are important differences between managing taxable accounts and tax-sheltered accounts. For that reason, this section is divided into two parts: one for managing taxable accounts (personal, joint, trusts, and Uniform Gift to Minor Accounts) and the other for managing tax-sheltered accounts [IRA, Roth, 401(k), and charitable accounts].

The overall asset allocation between stocks and bonds is the most important determinant of portfolio performance. However, in a taxable account, the second most important determinant of performance is tax efficiency. If you can defer taxable gains and reduce taxable dividends and interest, then the performance of your account on an after-tax basis is increased. By creating a low tax portfolio, you will pay less in taxes, which automatically increases your wealth.

There are several strategies you can use to reduce taxes in a portfolio. First, select only investments that are tax efficient. Check the prospectus of an index fund for its tax efficiency. The SEC mandates that all mutual funds report after-tax performance as well as pretax performance. In addition, Morningstar gives each mutual fund a tax-efficiency rating, which is also useful. Morningstar mutual fund reports are free from most public libraries or can be obtained from the company for an annual fee. There is also an inexpensive online subscription to Morningstar's mutual fund database.

Most broad market equity index funds are tax efficient. Turnover of securities is low and trading is minimum, which means few taxable capital gains are distributed. Exchange-traded funds by their design are more tax efficient than most open-end index funds. The redemption and creation feature of ETFs allows fund managers to pass most capital gains onto the institutional investors who redeem shares, thus helping individual investors save on taxes (see Chapter 4).

If an investment is in a portfolio at a loss, a strategy individual investors can use to reduce taxes is *tax swapping*. This strategy involves harvesting tax losses as they occur in your index fund portfolio and simultaneously rolling into a similar index fund; thus, you are never out of the market. The tax losses can then be used to offset realized capital gains and can offset up to $3,000 per year in ordinary income. An explanation of tax-swap strategies is given in Chapter 5.

Bonds in a Taxable Account

The question of bonds in a taxable account is always a tricky one. There is no one-size-fits-all solution. One school of thought is to put equity investments in taxable accounts and fixed-income investments in nontaxable accounts. Whereas that is a wise strategy for some people, it may not be practical for others. There are three reasons. First, an investor may not have much money in tax-deferred accounts, thus by default the bonds go in the taxable account. Second, the after-tax return of bonds may be higher in a taxable account than in a tax-deferred account. This occurs when a person is retired and living off taxable savings currently but will start making large distributions from an IRA account some years in the future. Third, a person may not have the physiologic makeup to divide their investments by account type. Those people focus on and react to the return of one account rather than viewing their portfolio as all accounts taken together.

Assuming bonds are going in your taxable account, deciding which type of bond fund to use in a taxable account is a tax question. To find the answer, dig out your most recent tax return and look for the line on your 1040 Form labeled "Taxable income." Generally, if you are single with taxable income under $75,000 or married with taxable income under $125,000, then you should invest in a taxable bond index fund and pay the taxes on the interest. This will give you the highest after-tax return because your income tax rate is below 30 percent. On the other hand, if you are single with taxable income over $75,000 or married with taxable income over $125,000, you may be better off investing in a tax-exempt bond fund.

Although the interest rate is lower in a tax-exempt bond fund than a taxable one, the interest income is free from all federal tax. That, however, is not the final answer. State taxes will also be part of the decision. If you live in a high-tax state, you may be better off in state municipal bonds even though from a federal standpoint you are better off in taxable bonds. If you do not know which way to go, ask the person who prepares your tax returns.

The Stock Portion of a Taxable Account

Developing a simple index fund strategy on the stock portion of your account can be reduced to one or two index funds. A total U.S. stock market index fund covers the entire U.S. stock market. Some people believe this is the only stock fund you will ever need. John Bogle, founder of the Vanguard Group, is one of those who believe in the one-fund concept. If you take Bogle's advice, you will buy one bond index fund and one total U.S. stock market index fund. There is absolutely nothing wrong with this approach.

Personally, I like to place three different total stock market funds in a taxable portfolio. I start with about 70 percent of the equity money in a U.S. stock market index fund and add about 30 percent in an international developed markets index funds. Rather than using one international fund, for an added long-term portfolio management benefit place 15 percent in a Pacific Rim index fund and 15 percent in a European index fund. All three funds are tax efficient due to low turnover in the indexes.

When you are finished choosing a bond index fund, a total U.S. stock market index fund, and international index funds for your taxable account, you will have a simple yet complete global portfolio. The approach offers broad diversification, low fees, tax efficiency, and ease of maintenance.

Tax-Managed Funds

One way some investors have reduced their tax burden in a portfolio is to use tax-managed index funds offered through Vanguard and other index fund providers. Tax-managed funds use several internal trading mechanisms that reduce year-end taxable distributions to shareholders.

Should you invest in a tax-managed fund? It is no longer necessary, in my opinion. First, most total stock market index funds are extremely tax efficient due to their low turnover of stocks each year. Second, several tax-managed funds have redemption fees attached to them, which makes tax swapping more expensive. Third, ETFs are very tax efficient by design due to their unique operating structure (see Chapter 4). If you use ETFs, the long-term capital gain distributions will be minimal.

Nontaxable Accounts

Management of a nontaxable account builds on the ideas presented in the taxable account section. In many ways, developing and managing a nontaxable index fund portfolio is much easier than a taxable portfolio because taxes do not get in the way of decision making. This gives you the freedom to add many different asset classes to an account and allows rebalancing to take place when needed. In addition, mutual fund dividends can and should be automatically reinvested in the fund that paid the distribution. There is no benefit to accumulating cash and then purchasing different tax lots.

Although you have more freedom to choose between different types of index funds in a nontaxable portfolio because taxes are not a consideration, a simple index fund portfolio is still preferred over complicated strategies. For example, if an IRA account holds only a total bond market index fund, a total U.S. stock market index fund, and total international index funds, it is a good portfolio.

Bonds in a Nontaxable Account

Managing the bond portion of a nontaxable account is very similar to a taxable account, except that you do not have to consider the effects of federal and state income tax. You should start with a well-diversified total bond market index fund and then add other funds to it if you desire. Two of those add-ons may be a high-yield corporate bond fund and a TIPS fund. An appropriate mix between an investment-grade bond index fund and a high-yield corporate bond fund is about 80 and 20 percent, respectively. The same allocation used for high yield can be used for TIPS. The risks in each tend to offset each other slightly. I do not recommend investing more than 10 percent of your total portfolio value in a high-yield bond fund.

The Stock Portion of a Nontaxable Account

Managing the stock side of a nontaxable account can be as simple or as complex as you would like it to be. You can maintain one or two stock index funds in a portfolio, similar to a taxable account, or you can divide the stock portfolio into several pieces and allocate across market sectors. Whichever method you choose, there are no guarantees that a complex stock portfolio will produce better returns than a simple stock portfolio.

There are three major stock asset classes that I use in an advanced allocation of stock index funds. They are the U.S. stock portion, international stock portion, and REIT index funds. In general, the allocation to a REIT index fund is ideal for a nontaxable account. REITs are tax inefficient because of the large amount of taxable income they distribute each year. If you place 10 percent of the total value of a portfolio in REIT index funds, try to do it in a nontaxable account.

Buying a total U.S. stock market index fund based on the broad market index is the easiest and simplest way to participate in the U.S. stock market. You literally own thousands of stocks in one index fund, and it will perform right in line with the broad U.S. index. A small-cap value index fund adds diversification to an otherwise large-cap total market portfolio. Research by Eugene Fama, Kenneth French, and other academics finds that over the long-term, investors earned extra returns by investing in small-value stocks but at potentially higher risk.[2] Small-value index funds have high turnover and are not tax efficient. Therefore, small-value funds are ideal suited for nontaxable accounts.

Allocation between Stocks and Bonds in Different Types of Accounts

A question that is always asked by investors is whether one should own only stock index funds in a taxable account and bond index funds in a nontaxable account or use the same balance in both accounts? There are many opinions on this issue, and I have mine. I believe a majority of people should hold the same mix of stock and bond index funds in all their portfolios regardless of the type of account or tax status. The reason has nothing to do with taxes and everything to do with investor behavior. More often than not, if the stocks are in one account and bonds are in another, investors will start comparing the two rather than focusing on the performance of the overall portfolio.

Focusing on the performance of one account over another can have major consequences. It is very difficult for most people to hold an all-stock account in a very bad market, even though it may be part of an overall balanced portfolio involving bonds in another account. Chances are high among segregated asset investors that they will reduce their equity position in the all-stock account during a bear market. The result of emotionally selling stocks in a stock-heavy account will reduce the chances of meeting a financial goal. Unless you are extremely disciplined and always focused on your entire portfolio, it is recommended that you use the same asset allocation across all accounts.

Rebalancing Accounts

As markets go up and down, the values of asset classes in your portfolio shift around. Inevitably, a portfolio will get so far out of kilter that it will need to be adjusted back to its original target asset allocation. This process is called rebalancing. It is a good idea to rebalance at least annually, especially if the mix between stocks and bonds is off by 5 percent or more. For example, rebalance when market forces cause a 50 percent stock and 50 percent bond portfolio to be a 53 percent stock and 47 percent bond portfolio.

Rebalancing a Nontaxable Account

There are no tax consequences to rebalancing a nontaxable account. The only disadvantages are your time and any commission cost. If there are commissions to trade your index funds, you will have to weigh the cost of the commission against the advantage of rebalancing.

Rebalancing a Taxable Account

Rebalancing a taxable account is a trick because of tax issues. Rebalancing by definition means the selling of some index funds that are up and the purchase of funds that are lagging. Unfortunately, selling a portion of the index fund that went up and buying a fund that went down does not always make sense because it creates a taxable gain. There are better ways to rebalance a taxable account to minimize taxable events. Consider the following methods:

1. Do not automatically reinvest mutual fund income. Let all income distributions flow into your cash account rather than automatically buying more shares of an index fund. Once cash has accumulated in your account, manually invest it in the index fund where it is needed. Taking dividends and interest in cash also allows you to maintain control over the cost basis of your index funds, whereas automatically reinvesting mutual fund distributions can create a tax accounting nightmare.

2. When adding new money to a taxable account, use the opportunity to rebalance the portfolio.

3. If you have a tax loss carry forward or can offset a capital gain through tax swapping (Chapter 5), use the loss to offset the gain from selling the index fund that went up in value. Then use the cash from the sale to rebalance your account.

4. If one asset class moves significantly higher than another and your asset allocation is off by a wide margin, sell only those shares that have been in your account for more than one year. It is better to pay a lower long-term capital gain tax rate than to pay the higher short-term capital gain rate. If no shares have been held for more than one year, then wait until they have been held for more than one year before selling.

Rebalancing in a taxable portfolio does not have to take place on a regular basis to be effective. It is better to wait for an appropriate time and circumstance than to pay the tax bill. If it is possible to srebalance a nontaxable account instead, then you should proceed in that direction.

CHAPTER SUMMARY

After deciding the appropriate amount to invest in stock and bond index funds based on your objective, the rest is tailoring the index fund portfolio to fit your preferences and tax situation.

Your taxable accounts and nontaxable accounts may hold different index funds because of tax considerations. The tax status of a portfolio will affect rebalancing decisions. It is wise to place tax-inefficient index funds in a tax-sheltered account and tax-efficient index funds in a taxable account. This would mean placing most REIT funds, junk bond funds, and U.S. value funds in a tax-sheltered account and placing total market funds and tax-managed funds in a taxable account. Common sense needs to be applied when deciding which account should hold a particular fund.

You are a unique person and your index fund portfolio will also be unique. Developing an appropriate allocation requires time and an occasional tweaking. It is likely that your first index fund portfolio will not be ideal because you have not considered all the options. However, as you continue to read, study, and understand, the right portfolio will reveal itself.

NOTES

1. Gary P. Brinson, L. Randolph Hood, and Gilbert L. Beebower, "Determinants of Portfolio Performance," *Financial Analysts Journal*, Vol. 51, No. 1 (January/February 1995): 133–138.
2. James L. Davis, Eugene F. Fama, and Kenneth R. French, "Characteristics, Covariances, and Average Returns: 1929–1997" (February 1999). Center for Research in Security Prices (CRSP) Working Paper No. 471.

CHAPTER 16

Managing an Index Fund Account

Key Concepts

- Decide which accounts are to be indexed.
- Choose a custodian for your index funds.
- Trading tips reduce commissions and fees.
- Hiring an investment adviser may make sense.

Congratulations! You have decided to join the rational and savvy investors of the world and convert to an index fund strategy. Sound logic has convinced you that index funds make sense from all aspects. You have spent time formulating an investment plan and have designed an index fund portfolio that fits your needs. Now it is time to open an account and put the plan into action. So, what do you do?

This chapter discusses the mechanics of opening and managing an index fund account. It highlights the advantages and disadvantages of working directly with a mutual fund company or purchasing index funds through a brokerage firm. Tips for transferring assets into an account are also discussed. Although the topic of opening an account and transferring assets may seem dull, a delay in processing your paperwork can cost you time and money.

The topic of professional management is also introduced. If you are not inclined to do your own planning, paperwork, and portfolio management, an investment manager can be hired to do it all for you at a nominal fee. Hiring a manager saves you time and keeps you on track.

STEPS TO OPENING AN ACCOUNT

Before you can buy index funds, you need to open an account someplace that is index fund–friendly and then fund that account with cash or securities. Five basic steps are involved in opening and funding an account. These steps are listed here and then discussed in more detail.

1. Decide which account or accounts will use an index fund strategy (i.e., IRA, personal, custodial). Not all accounts have that option.
2. Select a custodian for your account. You can either invest directly with a mutual fund company or buy index funds through a brokerage firm.
3. Request a new account application for the type of account you are opening (IRA, personal). Also request a transfer form if you are moving stocks, bonds, or mutual funds from a different custodian.
4. Complete and return the forms to the mutual fund company or brokerage firm.
5. Track the process of paperwork to ensure the account is opened correctly and the transfer takes place.

Step 1: Deciding Which Accounts to Index

The first step toward managing an index fund portfolio is to decide which account or accounts you are going to commit to an indexing strategy. You may be looking at several accounts, which is good because it is my sincere belief that 100 percent of your money should be in index funds. Within that mix of accounts, an IRA will likely be under consideration. In fact, the easiest account to convert to indexing is an IRA because there are no tax consequences when selling the investments you already own.

Some of your accounts may not be eligible for indexing. For example, you may work at a company that has a 401(k) plan managed by a bank, insurance company, or brokerage firm. Many of these turnkey programs have large embedded fees attached to their mutual funds, so they do not offer low-cost index fund options. If that is the case at your company, you need to talk to the plan administrator at your firm about adding a few index funds to the 401(k) selection.

Variable annuity accounts may also be nontransferable. Many variable annuities have a back-end sales charge that can linger for up to 10 years. If you recently purchased a variable annuity through a brokerage firm or insurance salesperson, there is a good chance you are subject to a horrendous back-end fee. There is no way of getting around this fee unless you die, which is not an option. On the other hand, if the back-end load period is over, I recommend contacting the Vanguard Group and inquiring about their Variable Annuity Plan. Vanguard offers a very-low-cost annuity that has many index fund options. There is no cost or tax consequence to do a 1035 transfer into the Vanguard plan.

Step 2: Select a Custodian

The next step in the process is to decide which investment firm will hold your index fund account. You can go directly to a mutual fund company, such as The Vanguard Group, herein referred to as Vanguard, or you can operate through a brokerage firm that has access to all major index fund companies. There are advantages and disadvantages to each, and there is not a perfect solution.

Going directly to a mutual fund company has the advantage of low cost and the disadvantage of limited flexibility. A likely choice using the direct method is Vanguard. They have the largest variety of index funds on the market. There is no cost to buy index funds directly through Vanguard, but there is a $10 per year charge on accounts below $10,000, and some funds have redemption fees. Another disadvantage of using one mutual fund provider as custodian is limited access. Most fund companies do not allow you to buy the funds of competitors unless you open an additional brokerage account, and there is always a commission and market spread to buy mutual funds through the brokerage side.

Discount brokerage firms such as Charles Schwab, TD Ameritrade, and Scottrade offer access to thousands of mutual funds and all stocks and bonds. In fact, Schwab originated the concept of the mutual fund supermarket in the early 1990s. This made managing a portfolio of index funds from different fund companies very convenient. The disadvantage is cost. Every time you buy a non-Schwab or non-Fidelity mutual fund, there is a commission cost or embedded 12b-1 fee (higher internal fund expense). In addition, not all index funds are available through all mutual fund supermarkets.

If you are considering using one of the full-service brokerage firms, you will pay higher commissions and have limited access to open-end index funds. Exchange-traded funds may be your only avenue to indexing if you decide to use a full-service broker.

Step 3: Dealing with Paperwork

After deciding on a custodian for your account, call that company or visit their Web site and request a new account application and transfer form. If you are simply wiring a check to the account, there is no need to ask for a transfer form. Make sure you get the right application. If you are opening an IRA account, ask for an IRA application. Many accounts are held up because the wrong paperwork was sent in. If you are not sure, it is best to call and ask.

People who live near a major city may have a brokerage office nearby. If that is your situation, make a face-to-face appointment with a customer representative, and they will be happy to help you. They will also provide all the necessary paperwork and help complete it. Opening accounts and transferring money is a free service for all customers. I have not heard of a broker yet that charges for bringing money to them.

Step 4: Complete and Return Forms

The fourth step is completing the new account application and transfer form and putting them in the mail. Make sure you fill in all the blanks on the forms. Many times people leave off important information like Social Security numbers and IRA beneficiaries. Most brokerage companies now have Web sites that allow you to complete most information online and then print a signature page, sign, and send.

You should not be worried about providing personal financial information to the custodian. These firms are required by law to have that information, and they are legally bound to hold the information confidential. Each year, firms are required to send out a Privacy Act statement that explains exactly what the information can be used for and what it cannot be used for.

If you are transferring assets from one custodian to another, you have to make some investment decisions when completing the transfer form. If you are transferring to a brokerage firm, such as VBS, Schwab, or Fidelity, you can transfer cash or securities. That means you need to decide if you will liquidate current investments at your old firm and transfer cash or transfer securities to the new firm and liquidate the securities when they get there. If you are investing directly with a mutual fund company (not a broker), only cash is allowed.

There are two items to consider when making the decision to transfer cash or securities: commissions and taxes. Calculate the commission cost to sell at the old firm and compare it with the cost of selling at the new custodian. It usually makes economic sense to transfer the stocks and ETFs "in kind" and pay a lower commission rate if you are moving stocks from a full-service broker to a discount broker. If you are moving mutual fund shares, it usually makes economic sense to liquidate the funds at the old firm and transfer cash. Full-service brokerage firms do not charge a commission to liquidate most open-end mutual funds when sold, with the exception of "B" shares that have back-end sales loads. The second consideration is taxes. This only applies to a taxable account. If you will realize a capital gain by selling a security, and that security is getting close to the 12-month minimum hold period for the lower long-term capital gains tax rate, then it may be best to wait until 12 months before liquidating.

Step 5: Track the Paperwork

Watch your transfer. The electronic transfer systems used by most financial companies allow for most securities to move flawlessly. However, big problems do arise, mostly from inaccurate paperwork or a lack of oversight. Make sure you monitor the opening of the account and the transfer of assets. After mailing in the new account forms, it takes about one week to get an account number and then another three weeks before the transfer is complete. If you are selling stocks or mutual funds at the old firm, make sure you initiate those trades before submitting a transfer request to the new firm.

Feel free to call the new custodian at any time for an update on your account. Do not trade in an account after sending in the paperwork to transfer it to another firm. Trading during transfer will create big problems that will take a lot of time to correct.

When your assets arrive at the new firm, either do an audit online or contact the company directly to ensure everything arrived. If securities or cash are missing, ask the broker to "status" the account, and they will run a broker-to-broker check. Sometimes a small amount of cash gets stuck at the old firm, and the new custodian can request a "residual sweep." That should take care of the problem. When the entire transfer is complete, you will be well prepared to enter index fund nirvana!

The Enemy within Us

Completing and returning the new account application are the most difficult steps in the account opening process, and it is not because the paperwork is difficult to understand. It is because the paperwork does not get done. A hidden enemy lurks in paperwork piles, and that enemy has a name. It is called *procrastination*. Despite good intentions to get going with an indexing strategy, a very large number of new believers procrastinate for years. The longer your money sits in high-cost investments, the more money you waste. Millions of dollars have been lost because of procrastination. Just do it!

HIRING AN INVESTMENT ADVISER

Some people are better off hiring a fee-only investment adviser to do the work for them. Advisers are not for everyone. If you are too busy, too lazy, or not in a position to keep up with your portfolio, then hiring an adviser may make sense, and you should explore that option.

Investment advisers are paid a management fee for designing, implementing, maintaining, tax-managing, and reporting the progress of an investment portfolio. The right hired help will get the job done in an efficient and cost-saving manner. A second advantage to hiring an adviser is access to institutional index fund shares. These are low-cost mutual funds that only clients of advisers have access to. It is not necessary to have institutional funds in a portfolio, however if you are going to hire an adviser, you might as well take advantage of that access. An example of an institutional fund company is Dimensional Fund Advisors (DFA). That firm offers unique small-cap value funds and international funds.

The problem with hiring an investment adviser is that they come in all shapes, sizes, fees, and levels of competence. You will need to do a lot of homework. I suggest contacting the Vanguard Group and asking for a free copy of "How to Select a Financial Adviser." The booklet is available online at www.Vanguard.com, or it can be obtained by mail by calling 1-800-662-7447. Another place to ask for references to a knowledgeable investment adviser is through the www.Diehards.org Web site. The Diehards site is linked to a Morningstar.com discussion board called Vanguard Diehards. It is used by like-minded investors who are interested in keeping their costs low. Not all participants are index fund investors, but most are extremely knowledgeable about the subject, and they can pass along the name of index-oriented advisers if you ask.

When you find an adviser you like, hiring one may make good economic sense as long as the fee is reasonable. What is reasonable? An annual management fee equaling 1 percent of the account size is normal, but that may not be reasonable if you have a sizable account. With minimum research on the Internet, you can find advisers who charge a fraction of that amount, and most advisers are willing to negotiate.

Services of Advisers

Here is a partial list of services most advisers provide:

1. *Helps tailor an investment plan:* Many people need help formulating an investment plan and developing the correct asset allocation for their needs. They may already have a general idea of where they want to go financially but do not have the tools or expertise to put a complete plan together. An adviser will help clients understand how their needs can be met through low-cost index fund investing and then design, implement, and manage the complete investment plan.

2. *Offers consistency of strategy:* People switch investment strategies about every three years on average (as measured

by the Investment Company Institute mutual fund turnover statistics). In the 1990s, growth stocks were hot. A few years later, investors switched to value stocks, and then international stocks, and then commodity-driven stocks. Good advisers do not chase markets. The consistency of management style will help achieve higher lifetime returns.

3. *Creates a human circuit-breaker:* Sometimes, when investors wake up in the middle of the night because they dreamed the markets collapsed, advisers are there to act as a psychologist. This usually means calming investors' nerves and talking them out of making emotional investment decisions.

4. *Places someone on duty 24/7/365:* There will come a time in your life when you just do not want to deal with investing issues anymore or cannot deal with it for job-, family-, or health-related reasons. Advisers do your investment chores for you day in and day out, especially when you are not able to.

As the founder of a successful low-cost adviser firm, I believe good advisers serve clients best by acting in a consulting and administrative function, not in a guru function. It is our job to understand the risks of the markets and help clients design the right mix of investments for their needs and tolerance for risk and then to implement the plan and keep the portfolio and the client focused. It is not an adviser's job to try to time markets or pick the next Google. Those functions are best left to high-cost brokerage firms who are in the business of trading, not long-term investing.

CHAPTER SUMMARY

Index fund investing is a rewarding strategy. Choose the right index funds for your needs, and choose the right custodian to hold those funds. Compare the advantages and disadvantages of each custodian to ensure they should offer access to a wide variety of index funds at a reasonable cost. If needed, find an adviser to help you manage the process. Make sure you choose an experienced fee-only adviser who is knowledgeable about index funds and wholeheartedly believes in the religion.

Appendixes

◆ Appendix A: Low-Cost Index Fund Providers
◆ Appendix B: Recommended Resources

Selected Low-Cost
Index Fund Providers

Index Fund Providers	Phone Numbers	Web Site
Barclays Global Investors	800-474-2737	iShares.com
Barclays Bank, PLC	877-764-7284	iPathETN.com
Bridgeway Funds	800-661-3550	Bridgeway.com
Dimensional Fund Advisors*	310-395-8005	DFAfunds.com
Dreyfus	800-373-9387	Dreyfus.com
Fidelity Group	800-544-9797	Fidelity.com
First Trust	800-621-1675	ftPortfolios.com
Rydex Funds	800-820-0888	RydexFunds.com
Schwab Funds	800-435-4000	Schwab.com
State Street Global Advisors	800-843-2639	SSGAfunds.com
T. Rowe Price Funds	800-638-5660	TRowePrice.com
TIAA-CREF Mutual Funds	800-223-1200	TIAA-CREF.org
Vanguard Group	800-662-7447	Vanguard.com

*DFA funds are available only through authorized investment advisers and certain qualified retirement plans.

Recommended Resources

INVESTMENT ADVICE WEB SITES

Morningstar.com
Providers of news and analyses on markets, stocks, and mutual funds for the individual investor. The VANGUARD DIEHARDS conversation board is a great place to find information and ask questions.

IndexUniverse.com
An independent index investing and index commentary that provides comprehensive returns, definitions, and tracking of worldwide indexes and index funds, including ETFs; a clearinghouse of information about index funds.

IndexInvestor.com
Provides comprehensive analysis and research on indexes, index funds, and investment strategy. The site is one of the best for hard-core index aficionados. There is a small annual subscription fee that is well worth the price of admission.

EfficientFrontier.com
William J. Bernstein and Susan F. Sharin edit Efficient Frontier: An Online Journal of Practical Asset Allocation. Bernstein's journal is a must read for all serious index fund investors.

ETFguide.com
ETFguide is a leader in exchange-traded fund information and news. Features include an ETF bookstore, a monthly e-mail newsletter, and subscription-based ETF portfolios.

PortfolioSolutions.com
The Web site of Portfolio Solutions, LLC, a leading investment adviser specializing in low-cost index fund management.

LOW-COST INDEX FUND PROVIDER WEB SITES

Vanguard.com
Besides one of the best places to shop for index funds, Vanguard's "Education, Planning, and Advice" section is one of the best on the Web. There is lots of good information in the "Plain Talk® Library."

iShares.com
Barclay's Global Investors (BGI) is the largest holder of ETF assets. The easy to use Web site guides investors to the right iShares for their needs. Use the helpful portfolio management tools on the site.

SSGAfunds.com
State Street Global Advisers fund page. SSGA manages many exchange-traded funds around the world including street-TRACKS and SPDRs.

Fidelity.com
Fidelity offers a full lineup of low-cost equity and bond index funds.

DFAfunds.com
Dimensional Fund Advisors offers unique index funds through investment advisers. Their three-factor approach to portfolio construction is gaining acceptance worldwide.

INDEX PROVIDER WEB SITES

StandardandPoors.com
Standard & Poor's offers comprehensive analyses and commentary on all their global indexes. S&P provides a wealth of data on S&P indexes that can be downloaded and analyzed.

MSCIbarra.com
Morgan Stanley Capital International (MSCI)/Barra is a leading provider of index data on global markets. Many Vanguard index funds are benchmarked to MSCI indexes.

DowJones.com
Dow Jones offers a wealth of information on the markets and a wonderful historical section featuring charts that include major economic and world events.

Russell.com
Comprehensive information about all the Russell indexes and methodology.

Wilshire.com
Wilshire indexes are considered the most complete U.S. equity benchmarks covering more than 5,000 U.S. companies. There is a lot of data available on the site.

FTSE.com
FTSE Group is an independent company whose sole business is the creation and management of indexes and associated data services.

KLD.com
KLD Indexes constructs indexes for investors who integrate environmental, social, and governance factors into their investment decisions.

Lehman.com
Lehman Brothers is a leading provider of fixed-income benchmarks.

BOOKS ABOUT INDEX FUND INVESTING

Common Sense on Mutual Funds by John C. Bogle. An index fund icon shares his views in this must-read book for any index investor.

John Bogle on Investing: The First 50 Years by John C. Bogle. In-depth writings of Jack Bogle, including his Princeton thesis from the 1950s.

The Bogleheads' Guide to Investing by Taylor Larimore, Mel Lindauer, Michael LeBoeuf Written by individual investors for individual investors, this book is a wealth of knowledge from index funds to I-Bonds.

The Coffeehouse Investor by Bill Schultheis. An outstanding little book for those that want to get on with it and enjoy life.

Winning the Loser's Game by Charles Ellis. This classic book outlines how investors can increase returns and decrease risk by buying the market.

The Four Pillars of Investing by William J. Bernstein. An easy-to-read analysis of asset allocation and sensible advice for all investors.

The Only Investment Strategy You'll Ever Need by Larry Swedroe. Explains the difference between active and passive mutual funds and tells you how you can win the investment game through a long-term commitment to index funds.

A Random Walk Down Wall Street by Burton G. Malkiel. A comprehensive look at today's market and what is driving it.

Outpacing the Pros by David Blitzer. Learn about indexing from the S&P 500 committee chairman.

Mutual Funds: Profiting from an Investment Revolution by Scott Simon. An investment advisor shares his views on indexing and fiduciary responsibilities.

All About Asset Allocation by Richard A. Ferri, CFA. A plainly written discussion on designing the right asset allocation for your needs.

Active Index Investing edited by Steven Schoenfeld. A practical and detailed guide to the art and science of index-based investing.

ABOUT THE AUTHOR

Richard A. Ferri, CFA
Founder & CEO, Portfolio Solutions, LLC

Richard Ferri is the Founder and CEO of Portfolio Solutions, LLC, in Troy, Michigan, a fee-only investment firm with nearly $1 billion in separate accounts for high-net-worth individuals, families, nonprofit organizations, and corporate pension plans. The company specializes in a low-cost, tax-efficient, asset allocation investment approach to building wealth.

Ferri is also an adjunct professor of finance at Walsh College and has written extensively on low-cost investing. His four books are *Serious Money, Straight Talk about Investing for Retirement, All About Index Funds* (2nd Edition; McGraw-Hill), *Protecting Your Wealth in Good Times and Bad* (McGraw-Hill), and *All About Asset Allocation* (McGraw-Hill). A fifth book on exchange-traded funds (ETFs) will be published in late 2007.

Ferri earned a bachelor of science degree in business administration from the University of Rhode Island and a master of science degree in finance from Walsh College. He also holds the designation of Chartered Financial Analyst (CFA). Prior to joining the investment community in 1988, Ferri served as an officer and fighter pilot in the U.S. Marine Corps and is now retired from the Marine Corps Reserve.

12b-1 Fee   An annual fee charged by some mutual funds to pay for marketing and distribution activities. The fee is taken directly from fund assets, which reduces a shareholder's total return.

Active Management   An investment strategy that seeks to outperform the average returns of the financial markets. Active managers rely on research, market forecasts, and their own judgment and experience in selecting securities to buy and sell.

Alternative Minimum Tax (AMT)   A separate tax system designed to ensure that wealthy individuals and organizations pay at least a minimum amount of federal income taxes. Certain securities used to fund private, for-profit activities are subject to the AMT.

Annualize   To make a period of less than a year apply to a full year, usually for purposes of comparison. For instance, a portfolio turnover rate of 36 percent over a six-month period could be converted to an annualized rate of 72 percent.

Ask Price   The price at which a security is offered for sale. For a no-load mutual fund, the ask price is the same as the fund's net asset value per share. Also called offering price.

Automatic Reinvestment   An arrangement by which the dividends or other earnings from an investment are used to buy additional shares in the investment vehicle.

Average Coupon   The average interest rate (coupon rate) of all bonds in a portfolio.

Average Effective Maturity   A weighted average of the maturity dates for all securities in a money market or bond fund. (The maturity date is the date that a money market instrument or bond buyer will be repaid by the security's issuer.) The longer the average maturity, the more a fund's share price will move up or down in response to changes in interest rates.

Back-End Load   A sales fee charged by some mutual funds when an investor sells fund shares. Also called a contingent deferred sales charge.

Benchmark Index   An index that correlates with a fund, used to measure a fund manager's performance.

Beta   A measure of the magnitude of a portfolio's past share-price fluctuations in relation to the ups and downs of the overall market (or appropriate market index). The market (or index) is assigned a beta of 1.00, so a portfolio with a beta of 1.20 would have seen its share price rise or fall by 12 percent when the overall market rose or fell by 10 percent.

Bid-Ask Spread   The difference between what a buyer is willing to bid (pay) for a security and the seller's ask (offer) price.

Blue-Chip Stocks   Common stock of well-known companies with a history of growth and dividend payments.

Book Value   A company's assets minus any liabilities and intangible assets.

Broker/Broker-Dealer   An individual or firm that buys or sells mutual funds or other securities for the public.

Capital Gain/Loss   The difference between the sale price of an asset—such as a mutual fund, stock, or bond—and the original cost of the asset.

Capital Gains Distributions   Payments to mutual fund shareholders of gains realized during the year on securities that the fund has sold at a profit, minus any realized losses.

Cash Investments   Short-term debt instruments—such as commercial paper, banker's acceptances, and Treasury bills—that mature in less than one year. Also known as money market instruments or cash reserves.

Certified Financial Planner® (CFP®)   An investment professional who has passed exams administered by the CFP Board of Standards on subjects such as taxes, securities, insurance, and estate planning.

Certified Public Accountant (CPA)   An investment professional who is state licensed to practice public accounting.

Chartered Financial Analyst (CFA)   An investment professional who has met competence standards in economics, securities, portfolio management, and financial accounting as determined by the Institute of Chartered Financial Analysts.

Closed-End Fund   A mutual fund that has a fixed number of shares, usually listed on a major stock exchange.

Commodities   Unprocessed goods such as grains, metals, and minerals traded in large amounts on a commodities exchange.

Consumer Price Index (CPI)   A measure of the price change in consumer goods and services. The CPI is used to track the pace of inflation.

Cost Basis   The original cost of an investment. For tax purposes, the cost basis is subtracted from the sales price to determine any capital gain or loss.

Country Risk   The possibility that political events (a war, national elections), financial problems (rising inflation, government default), or natural disasters (an earthquake, a poor harvest) will weaken a country's economy and cause investments in that country to decline.

Coupon/Coupon Rate   The interest rate that a bond issuer promises to pay the bondholder until the bond matures.

Credit Rating   A published ranking, based on a careful financial analysis, of a creditor's ability to pay interest or principal owed on a debt.

Credit Risk   The possibility that a bond issuer will fail to repay interest and principal in a timely manner. Also called default risk.

Currency Risk   The possibility that returns could be reduced for Americans investing in foreign securities because of a rise in the value of the U.S. dollar against foreign currencies. Also called exchange rate risk.

Custodian   Either (1) a bank, agent, trust company, or other organization responsible for safeguarding financial assets or (2) the individual who oversees the mutual fund assets of a minor's custodial account.

Declaration Date   The date the board of directors of a company or mutual fund announces the amount and date of its next dividend payment.

Default   A failure to pay principal or interest when due.

Depreciation   A decrease in the value of an investment.

Derivative   A financial contract whose value is based on, or "derived" from, a traditional security (e.g., a stock or bond), an asset (e.g., a commodity), or a market index (e.g., the S&P 500 index).

Discount Broker   A brokerage that executes orders to buy and sell securities at commission rates lower than a full-service brokerage.

Distributions   Either (1) withdrawals made by the owner from an individual retirement account (IRA) or (2) payments of dividends and/or capital gains by a mutual fund.

Dividend Reinvestment Plan   The automatic reinvestment of shareholder dividends in more shares of the company's stock.

Dividend Yield   The annual rate of return on a share of stock, determined by dividing the annual dividend by its current share price. In a stock mutual fund, this figure represents the average dividend yield of the stocks held by the fund.

Dollar-Cost Averaging   Investing equal amounts of money at regular intervals on an ongoing basis. This technique ensures that an investor buys fewer shares when prices are high and more shares when prices are low.

Earnings per Share   A company's earnings divided by the number of common shares outstanding.

Efficient Market   The theory—disputed by some experts—that stock prices reflect all market information that is known by all investors. Also states that investors cannot beat the market because it is impossible to determine future stock prices.

Enhanced Index Fund   An index fund that is designed to generally track an index but also to outperform it through the use of leverage, futures, trading strategies, capital gains management, and other methods.

Equivalent Taxable Yield   The yield needed from a taxable bond to give the same after-tax yield as a tax-exempt issue.

Exchange Privilege   The shareholder's ability to move money from one mutual fund to another within the same fund family, often without an additional charge.

Exchange-Traded Fund   An exchange-traded fund is an index fund that trades on the stock market. Some common ETFs are the NASDAQ 100 Index Tracking Stock (QQQQ), which tracks the NASDAQ 100, and Standard & Poor's Depositary Receipts (SPY), which tracks the S&P 500.

Ex-Dividend Date   The date when a distribution of dividends and/or capital gains is deducted from a mutual fund's assets or set aside for payment to shareholders. On the ex-dividend date, the fund's share price drops by the amount of the distribution (plus or minus any market activity). Also known as the reinvestment date.

Expense Ratio   The percentage of a portfolio's average net assets used to pay its annual expenses. The expense ratio, which includes management fees, administrative fees, and any 12b-1 fees, directly reduces returns to investors.

Federal Reserve   The central bank that regulates the supply of money and credit throughout the United States. The Fed's seven-member board of governors, appointed by the president, has significant influence on U.S. monetary and economic policy.

Fee-Only Adviser   An arrangement in which a financial adviser charges an hourly rate, annual retainer, or an agreed upon percentage of assets under management for a financial services.

First In, First Out (FIFO)   A method for calculating taxable gain or loss when mutual fund shares are sold. The FIFO method assumes that the first shares sold were the first shares purchased.

Front-End Load   A sales commission charged at the time of purchase by some mutual funds and other investment vehicles.

Full Faith and Credit   A pledge to pay interest and principal on a bond issued by the government.

Fund Family   A group of mutual funds sponsored by the same organization, often offering exchange privileges between funds and combined account statements for multiple funds.

Fundamental Analysis   A method of examining a company's financial statements and operations as a means of forecasting stock price movements.

Futures/Futures Contracts   A contract to buy or sell specific amounts of a specific commodity (e.g., grain or foreign currency) for an agreed upon price at a certain time in the future.

Global Fund   A mutual fund that invests in stocks of companies in the United States and foreign countries.

Gross Domestic Product (GDP)   The value of all goods and services provided by U.S. labor in a given year. One of the primary measures of the U.S. economy, the GDP is issued quarterly by the U.S. Department of Commerce. Formerly known as the Gross National Product (GNP).

Hedge   A strategy in which one investment is used to offset the risk of another security.

High-Yield Fund   A mutual fund that invests primarily in bonds with a credit rating of BB or lower. Because of the speculative nature of high-yield bonds, high-yield funds are subject to greater share price volatility and greater credit risk than other types of bond funds.

Indexing   An investment strategy to match the average performance of a market or group of stocks. Usually this is accomplished by buying a small amount of each stock in a market.

Index Providers   Companies that construct and maintain stock and bond indexes. The main providers are Standard & Poor's, Dow Jones, Lehman Brothers, Morgan Stanley, Russell, and Wilshire.

Inflation Risk   The possibility that increases in the cost of living will reduce or eliminate the returns on a particular investment.

Interest Rate Risk   The possibility that a security or mutual fund will decline in value because of an increase in interest rates.

International Fund   A mutual fund that invests in securities traded in markets outside of the United States. Foreign markets present additional risks, including currency fluctuation and political instability. In the past, these risks have made prices of foreign stocks more volatile than those of U.S. stocks.

Inverse Index Fund   An index fund designed to go in the opposite direction of the stock or bond market.

Investment Adviser   A person or organization that makes the day-to-day decisions regarding a portfolio's investments. Also called a portfolio manager.

Investment Grade   A bond whose credit quality is considered to be among the highest by independent bond-rating agencies.

Junk Bond   A bond with a credit rating of BB or lower. Also known as high-yield bonds because of the rewards offered to those who are willing to take on the additional risks of a lower quality bond.

Large-Cap   A company whose stock market value is generally in excess of $10 billion, although the range varies according to the index provider.

Leveraged Index Fund   An index fund that is designed to move more than the market but in proportion to the market. A leveraged S&P 500 fund that has a 2-to-1 ratio will go up or down twice as much as the S&P 500 index.

Liquidity   The degree of a security's marketability; that is, how quickly the security can be sold at a fair price and converted to cash.

Load Fund   A mutual fund that levies a sales charge either when shares are bought (a front-end load) or sold (a back-end load).

Long-term Capital Gain   A profit on the sale of a security or mutual fund share that has been held for more than one year.

Management Fee   The amount a mutual fund pays to its investment adviser for the work of overseeing the fund's holdings. Also called an advisory fee.

Market Capitalization   A determination of a company's value, calculated by multiplying the total number of company stock shares outstanding by the price per share. Also called capitalization.

Maturity/Maturity Date   The date when the issuer of a money market instrument or bond agrees to repay the principal, or face value, to the buyer.

Median Market Cap   The midpoint of market capitalization (market price multiplied by the number of shares outstanding) of the stocks in a portfolio. Half the stocks in the portfolio will have higher market capitalizations, and half will have lower.

Mid-Cap   A company whose stock market value is generally between $2 billion and $10 billion, although the range varies according to the index provider.

Municipal Bond Fund   A mutual fund that invests in tax-exempt bonds issued by state, city, and/or local governments. The interest obtained from these bonds is passed through to shareholders and is generally free of federal (and sometimes state and local) income taxes.

National Association of Securities Dealers (NASD)   An organization of brokers and dealers designed to protect the investing public against fraudulent acts.

Net Asset Value (NAV)   The market value of a mutual fund's total assets, minus liabilities, divided by the number of shares outstanding. The value of a single share is called its share value or share price.

No-Load Fund   A mutual fund that charges no sales commission or load.

Nominal Return   The return on an investment before adjustment for inflation.

Open-End Fund   An investment entity that has the ability to issue or redeem the number of shares outstanding on a daily basis. Prices are quoted once per day, at the end of the day, at the net asset value (NAV) of the fund.

Operating Expenses   The amount paid for asset maintenance or the cost of doing business. Earnings are distributed after operating expenses are deducted.

Option   A contract in which a seller gives a buyer the right, but not the obligation, to buy or sell securities at a specified price on or before a given date.

Payable Date   The date when dividends or capital gains are paid to shareholders. For mutual funds, the payable date is usually within two to four days of the record date. The payable date also refers to the date on which a declared stock dividend or bond interest payment is scheduled to be paid.

Portfolio Transaction Costs   The expenses associated with buying and selling securities, including commissions, purchase and redemption fees, exchange fees, and other miscellaneous costs. In a mutual fund prospectus, these expenses would be listed separately from the fund's expense ratio. Does not include the bid-ask spread.

Premium   An amount that exceeds the face value or redemption value of a security or of a comparable security or group of investments. It may indicate that a security is favored highly by investors. Also refers to a fee for obtaining insurance coverage.

Price-to-Book (P/B) Ratio   The price per share of a stock divided by its book value (i.e., net worth) per share. For a portfolio, the ratio is the weighted average price-to-book ratio of the stocks it holds.

Price-to-Earnings (P/E) Ratio   The share price of a stock divided by its per-share earnings over the past year. For a portfolio, the weighted average P/E ratio of the stocks in the portfolio. P/E is a good indicator of market expectations about a company's prospects; the higher the P/E, the greater the expectations for a company's future growth in earnings.

Prospectus   A legal document that gives prospective investors information about a mutual fund, including discussions of its investment objectives and policies, risks, costs, and past performance. A prospectus must be provided to a potential investor before he or she can establish an account and must also be filed with the U.S. Securities and Exchange Commission.

Proxy   Written authorization by a shareholder giving someone else (e.g., fund or company management) authority to represent his or her vote at a shareholder meeting.

Quantitative Analysis   In securities, an assessment of specific measurable factors (e.g., cost of capital, value of assets) and projections of sales, costs, earnings, and profits. Combined with more subjective or qualitative considerations (e.g., management effectiveness), quantitative analysis can enhance investment decisions and portfolios.

Real Estate Investment Trust (REIT)   A company that manages a group of real estate investments and distributes to its shareholders at least 95 percent of its net earnings annually. REITs often specialize in a particular kind of property. They can, for example, invest in real estate such as office buildings, shopping centers, or hotels; purchase real estate (an equity REIT); and provide loans to building developers (a mortgage REIT).

Real Return   The actual return received on an investment after factoring in inflation. For example, if the nominal investment return for a particular period was 8 percent and inflation was 3 percent, the real return would be 5 percent (8 percent minus 3 percent).

Record Date   The date used to determine who is eligible to receive a companys or fund's next distribution of dividends or capital gains.

Redemption   The return of an investor's principal in a security. Bond redemption can occur at or before maturity; mutual fund shares are redeemed at net asset value when an investor's holdings are liquidated.

Redemption Fee   A fee charged by some mutual funds when an investor sells shares within a short period of time.

Registered Investment Adviser (RIA)   An investment professional who is registered—but not endorsed—with the U.S. Securities and Exchange Commission (SEC) or the state the RIA does business in. They recommend investment products and manage accounts.

Reinvestment   The use of investment income to buy additional securities. Many mutual fund companies and investment services offer the automatic reinvestment of dividends and capital gains distributions as an option to investors.

Return of Capital   A distribution that is not paid out of earnings and profits. It is a return of the investor's principal.

Risk Tolerance   An investor's ability or willingness to endure declines in the prices of investments while waiting for them to increase in value.

R-squared   A measure of how much of a portfolio's performance can be explained by the returns from the overall market (or a benchmark index). If a portfolio's total return precisely matched that of the overall market or benchmark, its R-squared would be 100. If a portfolio's return bore no relationship to the market's returns, its R-squared would be 0.

Sector Diversification   The percentage of a portfolio's stocks from companies in each of the major industry groups.

Sector Fund   A mutual fund that concentrates on a relatively narrow market sector. These funds can experience higher share-price volatility than some diversified funds because sector funds are subject to issues specific to a given sector.

Securities and Exchange Commission (SEC)   The agency of the federal government that regulates mutual funds, registered investment advisers, the stock and bond markets, and broker-dealers. The SEC was established by the Securities Exchange Act of 1934.

Sharpe ratio   A measure of risk-adjusted return. To calculate a Sharpe ratio, an asset's excess returns (its return in excess of the return generated by risk-free assets such as Treasury bills) are divided by the asset's standard deviation. Can be calculated versus a benchmark or an index.

Short Sale   Sale of a security or option contract not owned by the seller, usually to take advantage of an expected drop in the price of the security or option. In a typical short-sale transaction, a borrowed security or option is sold, and the borrower agrees to purchase replacement shares or options at the market price on or by a specified future date. Generally considered a risky investment strategy.

Short-term Capital Gain   A profit on the sale of a security or mutual fund share that has been held for one year or less. A short-term capital gain is taxed as ordinary income.

Small-Cap   A company whose stock market value is generally less than $2 billion, although the range varies according to the index provider.

Spread   For stocks and bonds, the difference between the bid price and the ask price.

Standard Deviation   A measure of the degree to which a fund's return varies from its previous returns or from the average of all similar funds. The larger the standard deviation, the greater the likelihood (and risk) that a security's performance will fluctuate from the average return.

Style Drift   When a fund moves away from its stated investment objective over time.

Swap Agreement   An arrangement between two parties to exchange one security for another, to change the mix of a portfolio or the maturities of the bonds it includes, or to alter another aspect of a portfolio or financial arrangement, such as interest rate payments or currencies.

Tax Deferral   Delaying the payment of income taxes on investment income. For example, owners of traditional IRAs do not pay income taxes on the interest, dividends, or capital gains accumulating in their retirement accounts until they begin making withdrawals.

Tax Free   An investment or account where the interest or gains are free from federal income taxes, even after withdrawals.

Tax Swapping   Creating a tax loss by the simultaneous sale of one index fund and the purchase of a similar fund.

Taxable Equivalent Yield   The return from a higher paying but taxable investment that would equal the return from a tax-free investment. It depends on the investor's tax bracket.

Tax-Exempt Bond   A bond, usually issued by municipal, county, or state governments, whose interest payments are not subject to federal, and in some cases state and local, income tax.

Total Return   A percentage change, over a specified period, in a mutual fund's net asset value, with the ending net asset value adjusted to account for the reinvestment of all distributions of dividends and capital gains.

Transaction Fee/Commission   A charge assessed by an intermediary, such as a broker-dealer or a bank, for assisting in the sale or purchase of a security.

Treasury Security   A negotiable debt obligation issued by the U.S. government for a specific amount and maturity. Income from Treasury securities is exempt from state and local tax but not from federal income tax. Treasury securities include Treasury bills (T-bills, one year or less), Treasury notes (T-notes, 1 to 10 years), and Treasury bonds (T-bonds, more than 10 years).

Turnover Rate   An indication of trading activity during the past year. Portfolios with high turnover rates incur higher transaction costs and are more likely to distribute capital gains (which are taxable to nonretirement accounts).

Unit Investment Trust (UIT)   An SEC-registered investment company that purchases a fixed, unmanaged portfolio of income-producing securities and then sells shares in the trust to investors, usually in units of at least $1,000. Usually sold by an intermediary such as a broker.

Unrealized Capital Gain/Loss   An increase (or decrease) in the value of a security that is not "real" because the security has not been sold. Once a security is sold by the portfolio manager, the capital gains/losses are "realized" by the fund, and any payment to the shareholder is taxable during the tax year in which the security was sold.

Volatility   The degree of fluctuation in the value of a security, mutual fund, or index. Volatility is often expressed as a mathematical measure such as a standard deviation or beta. The greater a fund's volatility, the wider the fluctuations between its high and low prices.

Wash-Sale Rule   The IRS regulation that prohibits a taxpayer from claiming a loss on the sale of an investment if that investment, or a substantially identical investment, is purchased within 30 days before or after the sale.

Yankee Bonds   Debt obligations, such as bonds or certificates of deposit bearing U.S. dollar denominations, issued in the United States by foreign banks and corporations.

Yield Curve   A line plotted on a graph that depicts the yields of bonds of varying maturities, from short-term to long-term. The line or "curve" shows the relationship between short-term and long-term interest rates.

Yield-to-Maturity   The rate of return an investor would receive if the securities held by a portfolio were held to their maturity dates.

INDEX

R
Radical funds, 159
Real estate
    in comparison to common stock, 134
Real estate investment trusts (REITs), 126
    design, 135
    index funds, 134–137
    low cost, 137
    tax benefits of, 134
Real rate of return, 188
Real returns, 221
Rebalancing, 237
Rebalancing accounts, 276–278
Redemption arbitrage mechanisms, 53
Regional index funds, 151–153
Regional markets index funds, 155
REIT. *See* Real estate investment trusts (REITs)
Resources, 291
Retirees
    index fund portfolios, 268, 269–271
Retirement
    amount of savings needed, 247
    inflation adjustments of, 251
    profit-sharing distribution
        during, 250
Retirement investments, 247
    aggressive allocation, 254–256
    five-step method of, 248
Return forms, 282
Returns
    procrastination of, 284
    scatterplot of, 30
Reuters/Jeffries CRB (RJ-CRB), 204
    index, 208
    inflation, 207
RICI. *See* Rogers International Commodity
    Index (RICI)
Risk
    avoidance, 245–246, 259
    tolerance, 245–246, 259
    understanding of, 244–245
RJ-CRB. *See* Reuters/Jeffries CRB (RJ-CRB)
Roaring Twenties, 40
Rogers International Commodity Index
    (RICI), 205
    rebalancing of, 205
Roll yield, 199
Roy, A.D., 42
Russell 1000 index, 101
Russell 2000 index, 101
    SmallCap, 48
Russell 3000 index, 99–100
Russell index funds, 100
    style, 102

top 50, 101
US equity, 98–102
Russell MicroCap index, 102
Russell MidCap indexes, 101–102
Russell US indexes
    adjustments of, 99
    determining style index membership
        with, 99
    exclusions of, 98–99
    maintenance of, 99
    membership of, 98
Rydex Funds
    contact information, 289

S
Sampling, 178
    definition of, 179
Samuelson, Paul, 42
Schultheis, Bill, 35
Schwab, Charles, 148
Schwab 1000 fund, 121
Schwab Funds
    contact information, 289
Schwab 1000 index, 121
Schwab Total International Index, 147
Scottrade, 281
SEC. *See* Securities and Exchange
    Commission (SEC)
Securities
    turnover of, 272
Securities and Exchange Commission
    (SEC)
    United States, 14, 27, 45
Securities transfer
    considerations of, 283
Security-based enhancements, 161
    strategies, 163
Share accounting
    actual cost method of, 79
Short-term bonds
    movement of inflation, 230
Siegel, Jeremy, 15
Silver
    ETFs of, 201–202
Socially screened index funds
    low-cost of, 139
Soft prices, 197–199
S & P. *See* Standard & Poor's (S & P) indexes
SPCI. *See* Standard & Poor's Commodity
    Index (SPCI)
SPDR. *See* Standard & Poor's Depositary
    Receipts (SPDRs)
Special funds
    types of, 159